westland ltd

Loya Agarwala began her career as a psychological school counsellor in 2004, working specifically with Indian students from Classes 7 to 12. Born and brought-up in the United Kingdom, her modern approach and fresh perspective on life has helped to bridge the gap between many parents and adolescents. An alumnus of Brunel University, West London, she graduated with honours and then went on to complete her Masters (Psychology) and Post-graduate Diploma (Counselling) in India. An avid writer too, she has written over a hundred articles in regional newspapers and national magazines on a variety of topics but her passion lies in the youth and issues affecting them. As a mother of two adolescents herself, her insight is not only based on theoretical and professional knowledge but personal experience as well. Loya is regularly invited to speak at educational institutions as a motivational speaker or to deliver academic lectures as a guest faculty. In her spare time, she freelances as a Personality Development Consultant focusing on Life Skills and has trained a myriad of professionals, undergraduates and even participants for beauty pageants who have gone on to participate at the national level.

Loya emigrated to India in 1992 and lives in Guwahati, Assam.

A School Counsellor's Diary

Loya Agarwala

Westland Ltd

westland ltd

61, Silverline Building, Alapakkam Main Road, Maduravoyal, Chennai 600 095
93, 1st Floor, Sham Lal Road, Daryaganj, New Delhi 110 002

First published in India by westland ltd, 2013

Copyright © Loya Agarwala 2013

10 9 8 7 6 5 4 3 2 1

ISBN: 978-93-83260-43-0

Typeset in: PrePSol Enterprises Pvt. Ltd.

*To my parents, Kamal and Dheera Hazarika,
for their infinite faith in everything I do
and have done*

A child needs your love most when
he deserves it least

— *Erma Bombeck*

A School Counsellor's Diary

PREFACE

In the very early stages of my career as a psychological school counsellor, I became aware of my unique perspective into two emotional worlds: that of the adolescent and of the parent. Slowly, through numerous one-to-one interactions, I began to piece together the causes and effects of weak links in this crucial bond and, rather selfishly, used the enlightenment that I'd gained to better my own life and role as a mother of two adolescents. A decade later, with my diary still bearing silent testament to the spectrum of problems that came to me in the counselling room, I feel that perhaps it is time to share my experiences with a wider audience.

Turning the pages and re-reading the few jottings I had made against the students' names was enough to trigger off a cascade of memories. I was taken back to those moments sitting across the table, listening to the plight of suffering directly from the mouth of the student once again. The catharsis was so vivid: I saw, heard and felt so many minute details again that my skin often erupted in goose pimples or my eyes tears filled with tears without my even realising it. In a way, the regression has been a deeply spiritual journey or a cleansing of my mind which, as the weeks progressed, led me to a sense of closure.

So, with this new realisation and propelled by some well-wishers, I felt a need to write this book. I believe that my perspective makes a refreshing change from generic parenting books which fail to address the unique predicament of Indian children or try to set down blueprints which are not always practical. In my experience, problems depend on many different aspects, which may all have a bearing on subsequent courses of action. The same problem may be handled in two different ways and both may yield successful outcomes. Similarly, what works for one adolescent or set of parents may not work for another. Trying to define a formula for every situation is hence neither practical nor useful.

Today, I am surer than ever that the best advice parents can receive on parenting is from those parents and adolescents who have trodden the same path and experienced the same problems. Whether or not they were successful in their outcome is incidental. What is paramount is that they handled the extraordinary challenges borne by the new generation of adolescents. It is from their stories that we can gain a deeper understanding into how these problems can be avoided or minimised.

So, it is through these individual interactions that I bring you my counselling experience. I have deliberately chosen common cases which may resonate with many parents; they may even see their own teenager, or a teenager they know, in them. I have tried to re-construct the conversations as authentically as possible to be true to what really happened because each one is with a *real* individual with a *real* problem. They are reproduced as first-person accounts, in just the way I remember them. I endeavour to show you the pain behind their problems, how it was manifested and from what it transpired, without using technical language. I am hopeful that, after reading each account, discerning parents will be inclined to introspect, identify their weaknesses, re-align their perspectives and make a change.

All the students' names have been changed and specific details in their accounts have been altered to protect their identities, although the gist of the issue being discussed remains intact. Any resemblance to real individuals or their stories is purely coincidental. At the end of each chapter, I have included a checklist of 'red flags' to watch out for and a series of tips on what you can do to proactively handle the issues, for quick reading. There are also some addresses of NGOs and websites that can help you at the end of the book.

It is because I consider myself to be a mother first and then a counsellor that I feel a certain simplicity has pervaded my words to allow me to connect to all parents and share what the students have taught me. After all, as parents, we share the collective goal of wanting the best for our children so that they can stand on their own feet, meet their potential, be responsible for their choices and make the best out of their chosen paths. I have faith that each student whose encounter I have reproduced will see the bigger picture of how we have been able to use our counselling sessions to indirectly help others. I know they will see how for every tear they have shed, they will spare the tears of another and for every emotional pain they felt, they will ease the suffering of another. Whoever has sat across my counselling table has undoubtedly contributed to bridging the gap between parents and their adolescent, and helped to bring my mission for change to reality.

These are their stories, reproduced for you, to ultimately make for a better tomorrow.

Loya Agarwala

Chapter 1: "You're Too Busy"

Modern parenting books have emphasised the words 'quality time' innumerable times, often sending parents into a tizzy about exactly what they imply. From the perspective of the counselling chair, I feel the term 'quality time' has been rather overrated and has needlessly sent many parents into soul-searching guilt trips. It's actually a rather simple concept and, as long as you keep two crucial factors in mind, it can be easily moulded to suit your lifestyle. Whatever time you are able to put aside for your child, it must keep you both *emotionally connected* and that too, *on a regular basis*. That's it. Period. Circumstances may physically distance us from our children but the all-important vital link is the one that links our hearts. I firmly believe that keeping a strong and regular emotional connection is the *real* key to solving the dilemma of giving quality time.

However, what is not so easy to understand is that the will to keep connected has to be nurtured from the moment your child is born. The cutting of the umbilical cord is only symbolic, for it is replaced by an emotional cord which all parents need to cultivate thoughout their lives. If parents can instill this in the child's early years, it can prevent the small problems of childhood from becoming the larger problems of adolescence. Parents can only find that exclusive space between themselves and their teen if they have kept it alive during the early years. If, for whatever reason, we no longer feel the desire to connect, we instantly de-link ourselves emotionally from our children and then open the gates for possible negative manifestations to invade in various forms. The first two case studies I explore in this chapter indicate contrasting ways in which this can manifest.

Many people think that having a parent staying at home is the perfect remedy for the child being deprived of parent-to-child time. However, I've discovered that this myth is utter rubbish, having seen several cases of maladjusted, emotionally-imbalanced adolescents, with mothers who are housewives. Take Vidya's mother, for example. She was a socialite, the wife of a senior-ranking service officer, and her world revolved around her public persona. Even though she always made it a point to be at home when her daughter got back from school, she was so obsessed with her own life that she neglected her own daughter's concerns. So whilst she was physically always present, she was also 'never really there'. Ultimately Vidya, who was an exceptionally beautiful girl herself, found the love and attention she so desperately craved in the arms of boyfriend after boyfriend, and all because she was spurned by a mother who was always there in body but rarely in mind.

Conversely, Ishaan's story will resonate with many parents who find it hard to squeeze out time from their busy schedules. Whilst most teens are quite forgiving, there may come a time when they may begin to slowly despise their parent who doesn't try to make time for them. Adolescents are not stupid and after a while of openly demanding you spend more time with them, will stop altogether. I have seen adolescents who soon turn away from their primary circle (family) to find love and acceptance from their secondary circle (peer group). Close-knit family units with open communication pathways are the best defences against negative peer influences on your teens. The effort of regularly bringing your family together may seem mundane and needless but it could well be the antidote to your teen straying into unhealthy practices.

Unfortunately for Ishaan, his parents continued to live their lives just as they did before he was born and often left him with domestic helpers whilst they went about their usual careers. Believing they could compensate for their lack of one-on-one time with him with materialistic commodities, they bought him expensive toys and the latest technical gadgets. However, when he entered adolescence, a chance visit to a friend's home catalysed a strong attitude change towards his parents. His pent-up frustration overflowed into uncharacteristic rebellious behaviour at school and he was sent to me by a vigilant teacher. After consultation with his mother, I discovered his lonely childhood manifesting in his present unruly behaviour. However, his parents were not so easily convinced, and the question remained: was it too late to make amends?

Many people believe that a child must have two parents to grow up as an independent, balanced and responsible person. Whilst it is true that in an ideal situation, two loving parents in a stable relationship are the best tools for a child to grow up in a balanced environment, this need not always be necessarily so. Sometimes, circumstances mean that children grow up with only one parent and, even though there's no denying that it's doubly difficult to bring up a child single-handedly, Kapil's story is one of the best examples of successful parenting I've come across. He grew up without any recollection of his father who died from a massive heart attack when Kapil was only three years old. His mother struggled to bring him up without a father figure through the tantrums of infancy and the turbulence of adolescence, along with numerous financial difficulties, the stigma of being a single mother, etc. In spite of struggling to make ends meet, she seemed to have got the concept of giving him quality time just right. Today he has completed his education and long flown the nest but his story is one I can never forget. It is a befitting final piece in the jigsaw of 'quality time'.

Vidya

Adolescence is such a beautiful phase of life for girls, in terms of physical attributes. To me it's like the blooming of buds which have remained closed during childhood only to open up into pretty flowers of different colours and varieties during adolescence. Still in Class 10, Vidya was already a stunning vision, indicative of the beautiful woman she was going to be. Flawless skin, straight silky hair and a child-like innocence made her quite a hit amongst the boys, especially those in the higher classes.

I was quite surprised when she came to me asking for an early-morning Friday appointment because she had never come for counselling before. She seemed to have everything every teenage girl wanted: intelligence, popularity and great looks. 'I just need your opinion on a decision I have to make, that's all,' she explained as I wrote her name in my appointment diary.

On Friday, as I walked up to my room, she was already waiting for me outside and I ushered her in. She smiled sweetly and a fleeting thought went through my head that it was very difficult not to like her. Her appearance was very kind on the eye. She wasted no time in presenting her dilemma to me: 'Ma'am, though I have had a boyfriend before, I've never had two boys like me at the same time...'
'Hmmm ... interesting ...' I smiled, with a twinkle in my eye.
'Yes. Two boys from Class 11 have asked me to be their girlfriend. I like them both but how can I find out which one of these two boys really loves me *for what I am?*'
It seemed she was afflicted with the curse of being a pretty girl. Having to choose who to give your heart to was not an easy decision for anyone, let alone for someone as young as her. I was intrigued to know why she felt she had to choose one of them at all.
'Oh, I just need someone to love and someone to love me back. There's nothing wrong with that, is there?'
'No, of course there isn't. I just wanted to know, that's all. Just out of interest.'

'I just feel I *want* a boyfriend. Simple.'

She was becoming a little defensive and I certainly didn't want her to think I was judging her. Counselling has taught me to never judge a student who has fearlessly expressed his or her thoughts to me. Even though I am not a robot who accepts and agrees with everything I am told, I need to keep a very open mind in order to establish trust, every time a student sits in front of me. From her eyes, I could tell she was getting a little irked and I gathered she might get irritated if I showed any questioning signs. So I made light of the situation. 'Oh, that's fine, if that's what you want. I was just thinking that you could always buy a teddy bear instead!'

We both laughed, thus diffusing the mounting tension. She seemed calmer instantly. 'Ma'am, I know what I'm doing. I started dating guys in Class 8 but I've never been in this kind of a situation before. They're both really nice guys and I want to love them both but I can't two-time. I just thought you might be able to tell me if there was a way I could tell which one liked me more. Like a test….'

'I wish there was a test-kit I could give you Vidya, but there isn't. I guess the only way you can tell is from within you, like a gut instinct…'

'I just want to know that they want me to be their girlfriend because of my personality and not my looks…'

'Hmmm … yes, you are a very beautiful girl Vidya…'

'Thanks ma'am. My friends tell me too. I think I get it from my mum. She's really stunning. I adore her. She's the most beautiful woman on our campus.'

'You live on a campus?'

'Yeah, we live in the police quarters.'

'What does your father do?'

'He's a Deputy Superintendent of Police and so there are regular social functions. Every time we go to a function, all the aunties tell her how stunningly she's dressed and how beautiful she's looking and lately they say I'm beginning to look like her, too.'

'How does that make you feel?'

'Very, very good. I really want to look like her….'Her eyes turned to the ground and she added: '… I just wish she paid me more attention.'

'Doesn't she pay you much attention?'

'Not really, we're not very close, you see. It's just that she's so obsessed with herself all the time that she hardly has time for me. She just seems so busy all the time, always doing her hair or filing her nails, glancing through magazines or chatting on the phone.'

'How about when you get home from school? Is she there?'

'Oh, she's always at home when I get back but she's usually getting her "beauty sleep" as she puts it.'

'What about in the evenings?'

'At least two or three times a week she goes over to the parlour to get some beauty treatment done to her like a facial or threading or waxing or massage. The list is endless!'

'So when does she come back?'

'Oh, she gets back after an hour or so, but as soon as it's eight o'clock, she's glued to the television because of all the serials she watches! I eat my dinner early along with my little brother because I have school the next day but she and my dad eat much later, so I don't really get to interact with either of them much.'

'So how about the mornings? Don't you get to spend some time with her then?'

'Well I never actually see her in the morning because she's always asleep. But it doesn't make a difference if she's asleep or awake because she's just not that bothered with my school life at all. She's just not very interested and doesn't ever ask me what homework I have to do or what happened in school.' I sighed. She seemed to be able to read my disappointment and tried to stop me from feeling it. 'But it doesn't matter ma'am, I have lots of friends and now I will have a new boyfriend again. If I know which one to choose! So, how will I decide, ma'am?'

There was no stopping Vidya. I knew that the sole reason that she wanted a boyfriend was to combat her loneliness and she was pretty determined on choosing one of the guys. There was no point in making her question her reasoning because she was not going to listen to me. It was better that I take her side. 'If you *have* to choose one of them and not the teddy bear, then choose whichever one makes you happier,' I told her.

She smiled, revealing a perfectly straight set of upper teeth. She looked upwards momentarily, obviously trying to think of which boy made her happier. I noticed she had perfectly threaded eyebrows too. 'Well, they both make me happy but one in particular makes me really laugh! Yes, Bingo! I know my answer! Thanks ma'am!' and before I knew it, the bell rang and she was gone.

Unfortunately that was the last time I saw her smiling face because the following week she was in my room again and cried most of the time. It had turned out that her mother had found out about her boyfriend through the mother of another girl in the school. Vidya's mother was livid and confiscated her mobile so that she couldn't contact him anymore. From being a person who hardly ever bothered about her daughter, she suddenly became like an MI5 spy and kept a close eye on her all the time. Perhaps she was spurred into action by the sudden shame of being told that her daughter had a boyfriend by the wife of her husband's subordinate! So Vidya's mother kept her under 24-hour surveillance. She even sent one of her husband's bodyguards to accompany her to the bus stop every morning. With no means of contacting her new boyfriend outside school, Vidya never missed a single day of school for it was the only way of meeting him. She became miserable because she couldn't text him at night or during the weekends. It seemed she had grown to love this boy very much.

'It was my only chance for someone to show me I was loved and shower me with affection and now even that's gone!'
'Don't your parents show you any physical affection?'
'Rarely. Mum only kisses me on my forehead when I do well in my exams or on my birthday. Dad never does. That's just the way we are so I don't mind but mum doesn't really compliment me when I do something good. That hurts more. I wish so much that she did. It would mean the world to me. I admire her so much. You know, when she is getting ready for a party and applying her makeup or putting on her jewellery, I pretend I am asleep but I am watching her every move from the corner of my eye.'
It was sad how Vidya's mother was like a porcelain statue, a mother in name but without the emotional touch. Daughters can be such a blessing and yet here was a situation where the mother's obsession towards herself was just too engrained and her failure to give regular time to her daughter every day had taken its toll, seriously affecting their relationship. This was why Vidya sought acceptance and love from others and, because she attracted attention from older boys, it was not surprising that she veered towards them.

I did get an opportunity to meet her mother one morning when she had come to pick up Vidya's report card. Her lipstick was the same shade as her sari and, with her huge sunglasses and flowing hair, she looked like a film star. She was extremely attractive, there was no denying that. Strangely, when I tried to talk to her it seemed that she was from another planet. I tried to make her understand but she simply didn't accept that she needed to give her daughter more time. 'But I'm a housewife! And I stay at home all day! I give her all the time she needs. It's her who stays in her room all day tapping away on her mobile phone or computer 24×7!' she complained.

It seemed her mother was too defensive at the moment to listen to me. I sensed that since Vidya was already grounded, I may actually end up making the situation worse for her. So, I refrained from saying too much, fearing that it may backfire on Vidya. Her mother stuck to her guns, resolutely refused to believe that she was to be blamed for Vidya's activities and in turn made me feel that I was siding with the enemy! Her manner was curt and rude, giving me no room to make her see her daughter's perspective.

Vidya continued to come for regular counselling every week and we slowly built up a warm and affectionate rapport throughout the time she studied in school. Unfortunately, the situation hadn't changed much at home and she continued to retreat and distance herself more and more from her mother. I had tried to bring together the stray ends but it seemed this relationship was broken beyond repair. However, she saw me as a mother figure and never failed to come over every now and again to share her diary jottings or a particular piece of gossip from her class or even or a silly snippet of information. In fact, we are still in touch today and we often talk about those days when she was changing her boyfriends almost monthly and both of us laugh heartily!

Sometimes I felt guilty for sharing a warm rapport with a teenage girl when she didn't share that with her own mother. Ideally it could and should be something that every daughter has with their mother. In Vidya's case, what should have been an enriching relationship with her mother had turned into a huge lifelong disappointment. Vidya simply yearned for her mother's personal one-to-one time. It wasn't much to ask and yet her mother's vanity blinded her from seeing that importance at all.

Vidya went on to study in Delhi after she finished Class 12 but kept in touch with me. She came over the other day and told me of her latest boyfriend who she feels is 'finally the one'! In her mid-twenties now, she's grown into a beautiful young lady and though she seems happy, she is still not close to her mother. Vidya showed me a recent photo of her mother. She had changed dramatically from the day she came to my office in her red sari. Her once-striking looks were gone but the bigger tragedy was that, over the years, she had slowly and totally lost her daughter too.

Ishaan

Ishaan first came to my counselling room when he was half way through Class 11. His circumstances for coming to see me were a little out-of-the-ordinary for he hadn't come to see me on his own accord as most students do; rather, he was sent to me by his class teacher for his aggressive outburst towards a male teacher during a science class. There are many students who are naturally boisterous but Ishaan's uncharacteristic behaviour – from someone who was mild in nature to someone who had suddenly turned volatile – was a cause for concern. In fact the teachers had noticed that soon after he'd joined Class 11, he slowly began to acquire an increasingly boorish attitude, ultimately culminating in this incident.

According to the class teacher, there was a heated exchange of words between Ishaan and the teacher, who was so taken aback by Ishaan's rudeness that he told him to leave the class. Apparently, Ishaan promptly got out of his seat and, with a smirk on his face, walked out of the classroom with his head held up high as if he had just been given some kind of an award. Ishaan had already been suspended from school for three days and was now back, but I wanted to hear the incident from his side too and try to find out what exactly accounted for his gradual behavioural change. So, it was a rather suspicious-looking Ishaan who came into my room that day. Already anticipating that I would scold him for his mis-behaviour, he walked with a defiant stance, as if he was walking about his own house. Tall and well-built, he was probably on the heavier side of average but his face, framed by his spiky gelled hair and long sideburns, still had the softness of a young boy. As he walked into my room and sat down on the chair, I noticed too that he wore extremely low-waisted school trousers and the knot of his tie was nowhere near the collar of his shirt but halfway down his chest. He was obviously pushing the school dress codes to the maximum allowable limits. The top two buttons of his shirt were open, revealing a gold chain with a pendant in the shape of the letter 'I'.

Introductions were pleasant enough, though he didn't smile once and kept his eyes suspiciously on me. I started by asking him a few questions but his curt monosyllabic answers told me that he was in my room as a formality and wanted to get our interaction over with as fast as possible.
'Are you happy in school, Ishaan?'
'Yes.'
'Did you study here before Class 11?
'No.'
'Have you made many friends here?'
'Yes.'
'Are you happy at home?'
'Yes.'

I'd run out of ice-breaking questions. There was a slight pause as I tried to think of what else to ask him. He really wasn't in any mood to talk. He wanted to give me a rosy picture, one in which everything was fine, and simply leave. It seemed we were not making much progress so I decided to ask about the specific incident. 'Actually Ishaan, your class teacher happened to mention something about some incident in the physics class. Could you tell me what happened?'

I'd obviously hit a raw nerve as I saw a sudden flash of anger in his eyes.

'What's the point in me telling you? You won't be on my side!'

With this instant injection of emotion, his earlier monosyllabic answers had started to form sentences. That was a good sign. He was slowly opening up.

'It's not about being on anyone's side, Ishaan. I'm not here to scold you, if that's what you're thinking. I simply want to know what happened, that's all. Your side of the incident is important for me to know and so that's why I'm giving you a chance to tell me. So what exactly did the physics teacher say to you that day?'

He was looking directly into my eyes now. He was listening intently. I felt an ever-so-slight relenting from him. He nodded slightly as if he understood that I was giving him an opportunity to show his perspective. 'Okay, I'll tell you. It was a normal class and since I was sitting near the back, I thought he wouldn't notice if talked to my friend. The short break was just over and I was still chewing the last pieces of supari (mouth freshener) I had brought with me.'

'Ok, I'm with you. What happened then?'

'First he told me to stop talking and then he asked me what I was chewing. I said it was supari and I think he got angry about that and told me that if I didn't concentrate, I'd end up running a paan shop. The whole class started laughing.'

'So, that was when you got angry, right?'

'Yeah, I got really angry, all of sudden. My head started throbbing and I felt really humiliated. I can't remember exactly what I shouted but think I told him that my dad could buy a hundred paan shops, more than he ever could.'

'Oh dear, Ishaan. Why did you say that? Can't you see you're being derogatory?'

'Yeah, maybe I am, but he started it. He had no right to insult me. Just because he's a teacher, he thinks he can get away with it, just because I'm a student.'

'Okay, okay …. and then he told you to go out of the classroom, right?'

'Yeah. And I did. I don't care.'

'Did you apologise to him afterwards?'

His eyes opened wide, eyebrows arched, seemingly shocked. 'No, why should I? He should say sorry to me first. I'm not a kid anymore. He can't embarrass me like that. What does he know about me? What right does he have to humiliate me in front of my friends?'

I kept silent but I could see his point of view. He had touched on a very important point. Many teachers are not aware of how personal comments affect an adolescent *especially* when it's in front of their peer group.

'I hate adults who insult me and order me about. Like teachers. Like parents…' His voice was slightly raised, his hands clenched but still on the table. I could sense the aggression within him.

'Do your parents boss you about too?'

'Yeah, a lot. I used to do whatever they said when I was a kid. Not anymore. They're starting to peeve me off nowadays too.'

'Why don't you want to listen to them anymore?'

'I don't know. They think they can tell me what to do and that I will *always* do what they tell me. But that's it. I'm fed up.'

There was something wrong. Something had caused this change, I was sure of it. That first session ended with him still being angry but I think he felt lighter because he'd told me his side of the incident without me judging him. I asked him to pay me a visit the following week. He was still slightly stand-offish the next week but seemed to be more willing to talk when I asked him questions about his parents and friends' circle. I realized that his parents were busy people who didn't give him much time but it was when he told me of a particular time when he'd gone over to his friend's house, that I felt I had found the catalyst to his behavioural change:

'A few months ago, I had gone over to a particular friend's house after school for the first time. His mum opened the front door and she asked him a few details about school. Then my friend introduced me and then we both went into his room. Later, when it was time for dinner, they called us and when I went to the table I saw that they had put an extra place setting for me and the entire family ate together.'

'So how did that make you feel?'

'At first, when his mum opened the door and greeted us, I couldn't help comparing it to my own situation. It dawned on me at that moment my mom's hardly ever at home when I get back from school. And then when we were sitting together at the table, there was a nice feeling like – I dunno - togetherness, I guess.'

'Perhaps they were only eating together because you were there?'

'No, my friend told me they always do.'
'And your family doesn't eat like that?'
'Bah, no!'
'But Ishaan, not all mothers can manage to be like that. Sometimes they work, sometimes they are busy elsewhere…'
'But my mother *never* bothers! If she's not at work, she's at some kitty party. If she's not at a party, she's shopping. My house doesn't feel "warm" like his house did, that's all. I can't explain it any more than that.'
'That doesn't make her a bad mum, Ishaan.'
'Maybe not, but the fact is that she doesn't have any time for me. She never has. So now I've decided to *make her* have time for me.'
'How have you done that?'
'Well if I don't do what she says or I don't answer her when she calls me, she gets annoyed and then she *has to* pay me some attention…'

This was how Ishaan's slow unravelling started. A mere peek into another's home and feelings of being together made him question his own circumstances and look at his situation from another perspective. Adolescence is often a time of greater introspective thinking, when the mind has greater capacities to think deeply and question the things that would have been accepted more easily when at a younger age. The differences in the home environment made Ishaan feel that somehow his parents had perhaps neglected him. Suddenly he felt angry. As he saw it, their neglect of him over many years was now going to cost them. It was 'pay-back time'.

'Lately I can't help this overbearing feeling that I don't matter to them. I never have.'
'Of course you matter! Surely a single visit to a friend's house can't make you label your parents like that?'
'No, but it made me look back into my childhood and look at many things differently. As a young child, I was so lonely and I didn't need to be. I spent a lot of time with my ayah or playing with the servants. As I grew up, because I didn't know any better, I accepted it was normal to be lonely. Soon, they bought me lots of computer games to pass the time.'
'Many children have to keep themselves busy if their parents are busy elsewhere.'
'Yeah I'm okay with that but there were times when my mom should have been there.'
'Like what?'
'Like the time when I was seven years old and had high fever. My mum gave me paracetamol, told the ayah to keep putting a cold towel on my head and

went off to work. She never even took the day off.' I felt a wave of sadness
come over him towards the little boy that he once was. He started to speak
again but his voice caught in his throat turning it raspy and broken. '...and
stupid me didn't mind she wasn't there with me because I "understood" that
her work was important to her. Today I have realised that my needs have
never been a priority. Why did *I* need to understand? *She*, sorry *they*, should
have understood. Why was I secondary?'
It was a difficult question for me. I didn't want to speak against them in fear
of turning him even more bitter towards them.
'Their priorities are different, Ishaan that's all.'
He managed a hugely sarcastic laugh. 'They're just damn selfish. Full stop.
I don't hate them and I don't feel sorry for them anymore. I just want to
teach them a lesson now.'
'So by not listening to them, you feel you are "teaching them a lesson"?'
'Yeah, kind of. I'm teaching everyone a lesson. Revenge is sweet, let me
tell you.'
He was smirking now, indifferent to authority. His pent-up anger was obviously reaching a peak and was being vented through his attitude, at school
and at home. If I didn't at least try to salvage the situation fast, it was just a
question of time till he would soon go from bad to worse. As yet, he hadn't
gone towards any negative activities. But that was just a tiny step away.

What he found even more difficult to accept, even more than the lack of
time, was that his parents had made him *feel* as if he wasn't important. His
frequent visits to his friend's house had started off a ticking time bomb,
slowly turning his earlier unconditional acceptance to a questioning anger.
He was intent on getting them to notice him some way or another and give
him the importance he felt he was due; perhaps neither he nor his parents
were quite aware of how deep his resentment was.

After the first two visits, Ishaan came the third time on his own accord and
that was when I felt it was time to talk to his mother if I wanted to make
headway and help the situation. She was unable to make it to school, so I
arranged to speak to her one evening on the telephone after work.

Parents are not usually happy when they learn that their child has confided
their feelings to another person who is no relation to them. It's often difficult for them to accept that their personal lives have been exposed to a
stranger. Ishaan's mother was not happy about my obvious intrusion into
their lives, but when she realised that Ishaan's first visit was instigated by
a teacher, she was somewhat relieved, knowing that her son didn't seek

me out to expose their home truths. Once she felt that my best interests were only with the welfare of her son, she took a deep breath and told me the circumstances of his birth: 'For many years after we got married, we had desperately wanted a child but I failed to conceive. Finally after ten years, we resorted to fertility treatments and a year later we were blessed with Ishaan. As we were relatively older parents and both already had busy careers, we didn't try for another child. Don't get me wrong, we were very happy he was in our life, but we were more set in our ways and lifestyle. So, as soon as Ishaan was a toddler I resumed my career as a practicing advocate and, since his father is a very successful businessman, he worked long hours too. Both of us are very ambitious, you see. I do admit that we didn't spend a lot of time with him on a daily basis but we were lucky we had excellent domestic help. He was always well cared for and had lots of toys to keep him busy and we had some great holidays.'

Ishaan's mother went on to candidly confess that she too had noticed a change in her son, ever since he joined this school. She put his behavioural changes down to having made new friends but she did not realise that the visits to his friend's home had initiated an attitude change towards. She admitted that he often went out with his new friends after school and only returned around 9 p.m. without ever ringing them or informing them of his whereabouts. She said that he often smelt of cigarette smoke and his father had complained of how he thought that the servant had been taking a tipple from the drinks cabinet because the levels of whisky were low; maybe things were starting to make sense after all.

My first priority was to make Ishaan's parents understand how his behaviour was linked to grievances about his past which were suddenly triggered after seeing how different his home environment was from his friend's. He felt they lacked concern for his needs; when it came to their work, he was always made to feel second-best, as if he was an obstacle in the way of them furthering their passions. Thus, slowly he began to feel sorry for himself in the different stages of his upbringing: the child-Ishaan, the pre-teen-Ishaan and now the adolescent-Ishaan and this was the cause behind his angry and defiant ways.

Comprehending the severity of the situation and more importantly what it could lead to, his mother took things seriously. Soon, both his parents made time to come and discuss the problem with me. Through several sessions of joint counselling, we were able to restore a sense of respect in Ishaan towards his parents once they realised that they were indirectly responsible for the downward spiral in his behaviour. Children aren't deliberately hurtful to their parents unless they feel an inherent injustice and they had to acknowledge that their long-term preoccupation with their own concerns had eventually taken its toll on Ishaan and it was time to shift the equilibrium. Luckily, they *understood, accepted, repented* and *resolved* to make a difference.

Ishaan's respect was somewhat restored when he saw that they were beginning to make changes. They regretted buying him materialistic commodities as a way of saying sorry for not being there. His mother made an effort to come home earlier from work and spend a little time discussing their respective days. She even brought work home where they studied together on the dining table. Both parents needed to open their channels of communication with Ishaan which were totally blocked! Simple niceties had to find their way back into conversations. Small words of appreciation, small anecdotes of what happened during the day, revelations of how they felt – even what they wanted to eat for dinner! It wasn't about the length of time that they spent together that mattered, but how connected they were with the day-to-day aspects of their days. Slowly Ishaan started to see a side to his parents he never knew and so, too, did his parents. They discovered their son again and included his choices, wants and desires in family decisions. They learnt to verbalise their appreciation, show their love and pride for him by making him feel that he was important. They spoke to him and asked him, instead of assuming. Slowly they were able to reconnect and discover a new identity that was hidden within their son, one that they had always taken for granted.

When I look back on Ishaan's case, I'm glad that we were able to salvage the situation in the nick of time. Left unmediated, there would have been a sure breakdown in respect, which would have ultimately ended in Ishaan becoming a delinquent. It had taken time, but his parents had pulled themselves back from losing him emotionally forever.

Kapil

The older teachers of the school had seen Kapil grow up in front of their eyes from kindergarten. They knew that he was always prone to sudden anger tantrums in class but now that he was in Class 8, teachers were less forgiving. Tall for his age and on the thinner side, he was otherwise a well-behaved boy. It was only when something upset him that he shouted out loud or worse threw a punch at the source of his anger, usually a classmate.

So this was why he found himself in my room, having been told to go and speak to 'the counsellor'.

It must be daunting for any child to go and speak to someone in authority about their apparent misbehaviour. Perhaps our children have been programmed to think that all adults follow the misbehaviour = punishment rule. Fortunately, counsellors are trained not to resort to that immediately, but to look deeper into *why* consistent mischievous behaviour is happening in the first place. As children respond to situations which upset them in an instinctive way, they may not necessarily know what exactly is disturbing them. Their behaviour is the most direct symptom of an underlying cause, often buried deeply in the psyche.

I'd watched Kapil slowly progressing from a young boy to an adolescent. Indeed, his voice was still changing to a deeper, croakier sound and a slight moustache of downy hair appeared on his upper lip. My familiarity with him meant that he was quick to confess the reason why he felt bad: every time he saw any of his friends with their dads, he was reminded of the absence of his own. He barely had any recollection of his father and there was no father figure in his family whom he could turn to. At only fourteen years of age, he was too young to accept that sometimes in life 'these things happen' and some children do grow up without a father.
'Why did God choose to take *my* papa away and not anybody else's? I hate Him! *Why me?*'
'Shshh … shshh Kapil,' I calmed him, 'There are many many children who are in a similar position to you and some even worse. Can you imagine that?'
He didn't answer but perhaps he was thinking. He was angry at his circumstances in life and was wallowing in self pity. It was an ever-present, underlying frustration that usually remained dormant but surfaced every time he got angry. Even seemingly small incidents, which didn't call for an excessive angry reaction in 'normal' children, were exaggerated in him due to these trapped feelings. These uncontrollable angry bursts were adversely affecting him and he was soon labelled a 'problem student' by the teachers.

It was because Kapil's problem affected him every single day of his young life that it became deeply ingrained. He felt the pinch of being without a father especially when other student's parents came to school for PT meetings and his mother came alone. His predicament caused him emotional pain because of its omnipresent nature. Self pity hung above his head like a cloud ready to pour down at the slightest provocation. Try as he might, he felt he was the forgotten one and that no one else in the world was as unfortunate as he was.

Kapil came to see me almost every week for a good few years – until he left school at the end of Class 12. It was not easy to change his self-pitying nature but slowly he began to understand that he wasn't so badly off after all and came to terms with his situation. He learnt to stop blaming others and started to be strong enough to cope with his slice of life. Kapil's eventual mental stability and acceptance had only come about through many years of counselling through the golden-triangle relationship: parent-counsellor-student. Though he didn't require in-depth heavy counselling sessions, gentle support and constant reassurances helped him along whenever he reached hiccups in his life. I was simply there to encourage him, explain why certain things happened and gently show him where he was going wrong. I had informed the teachers of his circumstances and they had cooperated by handling his tantrums differently.

Throughout this period, I was in regular touch with his mother. She too would ring me regularly whenever she had a particularly bad row with her son and would often put me on loudspeaker so that I could directly mediate. Eventually, we became friends and even met for lunch a few times.

Even though it has been almost ten years since we first met and Kapil is today a young man, I look back and salute her untiring efforts. She was not super human. She was simply an average woman whose life circumstances changed overnight. When her husband died, she was still only in her twenties. She had to contend with so many of her own demons and yet throughout his childhood, she was consciously aware that she had a responsibility towards another who, through no fault of his own, was suffering too. She never lost sight of what she believed was her biggest moral responsibility and even in her lowest phases of life and emotional upheaval, his wellbeing was always uppermost in her mind. Yes, they went through some extremely rough patches together but they resolved their differences and restored respect because, at the end of the day, they only had each other. This strong bond meant that they remained close to each other emotionally.

During a telephone conversation I had with her the other day, we were talking about Kapil's journey and she confessed that finally she can take a deep breath and look back at those dreaded adolescent years and feel good that her strength and patience paid off. Perhaps, there were some conscious decisions she made that were conducive to her mission of bringing up her son on her own: she chose not to remarry because she felt that her time would then be divided. She knew of instances where single parents brought up their children very successfully and gained the mental strength to do so. Though she tried her hand at business, it was a failing venture. So to keep the money rolling in, she opened her own nursery school and made sure that the timings coincided with when her son was at school, so that she would be at home for him when he returned from school.

Her close links to her son from childhood continued to his school and college days and today, even though he is working in a metropolis almost 2,000 kilometers away, he calls her regularly to enquire how she is and shares his worries and concerns with her. She is still playing the same role that she always had, that of nurturing of her son as her first and foremost priority. But today, it is a two-way road where he is old enough to understand, advise and look after her too. Empathy is a wonderful balm for the hurting soul and if you give it to your child in abundance when they need it most, I believe the tables will turn one day, when you too will be consoled in the same way you consoled, as in Kapil's story. Today I have learnt from them. I marvel at their happy symbiosis for I believe that what they share today is ultimately the culmination of every minute of quality time she invested in her son in his growing-up years. This close lifelong association where both parent and child continue to derive inspiration and warmth from each other is, to me, the pinnacle of successful parenting.

Checklist

When you can instinctively gauge a prolonged disengagement (physical or emotional) of your adolescent and feel that it is slowly becoming a way of life, it may be wise to introspect into your own shortcomings or ask them why they are distancing themselves. Remember teens may not disclose why they are upset; either they may not want to tell you or they themselves may not know why. It's imperative that you are able to trace the cause so that you can make a change or seek a mental health expert to help you.

Red Flags to watch out for

- Obsessed with lonely activities
- A general 'cut-off' disposition
- Irritated disposition when you try to talk
- Not initiating conversation or a desire to end conversations quickly
- Not interested in you or your activities
- Indifferent to whether you are present at home or not
- Putting their friends' needs ahead of family
- A feeling of being trapped in the home environment and preferring to 'hang out' with their peer group
- Over use of social networking sites or phones
- Reacting aggressively to disciplining attempts by you
- Expressing that they feel neglected during an angry outburst

What you can do

- ✓ Use time together to focus on closeness, love and belonging, and emotional and physical safety.
- ✓ If you sense a gradual distancing, start to slowly include one-on-one time but don't make it too obvious. The key here is that it must not be laid upon like a ceremony. Don't pre-arrange it like an appointment but treat it simply like an impromptu moment to connect. For example, the first day you might just share a small conversation over breakfast, the next day it may extend to a cup of tea and a two-minute chat. Building up the time frame is not as important as how that connection makes both of you – particularly your teen – *feel*.
- ✓ Make sure the conversation is pleasant and un-threatening and not too intrusive so that they don't cringe the next time you are together alone. Your teen must feel relaxed in your company.
- ✓ Once this keeps happening on a regular basis, you will slowly enable easier and easier communication.
- ✓ Even if you are not in town, make an effort to connect, even if it is just a bedtime phone call to say good night or a regular daily email. You don't need to have long meaningful chats. Just make the call simple and to the point but make sure it is regular. Whether you decide it's to be every alternate day or every 2-3 days, keep the connection consistent.
- ✓ Don't make lame excuses for not making contact. Adolescents can easily sense when you're feeling guilty and it may make them feel they are not worthy of your time.

- ✓ Set family time to keep communication pathways open. Whether it is a holiday, a weekend away or eating together, family moments act like glue in keeping you emotionally connected and creating memories.
- ✓ Keep emotionally connected by talking about happy times, sharing funny stories or anecdotes about your place of work, telling them about your childhood, sharing your worries and concerns (to some extent). A great game to play is 'Your Day-My Day' where both parent and teen can sum up in a nutshell the main events of their respective days.
- ✓ Laugh together! The more side-splitting it is, the better!
- ✓ Stay involved in your teen's school work. You don't have to check homework every day but ask about classes/projects. Keep communication pathways open with the class teacher.
- ✓ Respond promptly to their needs when they say they want to talk. Don't brush it away like a fly. If you are preoccupied at the time, set a mutual time later in the day (not next week) when you both are free.
- ✓ If you fail to keep a promise of taking them somewhere, apologise and make up for it by suggesting another outing. If you want to achieve trust in your teen's eyes, don't cancel the second chance they give you.
- ✓ Don't force your teen to talk when s/he doesn't want to. Instead make sure that you are open to them whenever *they* feel they want to. If a face-to-face chat is not forthcoming make sure that they are free to convey what they want to say through a letter, an email, an sms or through even an older adult who you can trust and with whom they are close.
- ✓ Keep vigilant about other adults that your teen may be latching onto for company in your absence. Not everyone has your child's best interests at heart.
- ✓ By the same token, notice the influence of your teen's peer group by the way they dress, behave, personal habits, language and how they treat others.
- ✓ Make it a point to always say goodbye when you're leaving the house and saying hello when you arrive. Insist that your teen does the same. Also, *always* say goodnight wherever you might be in the world.

Chapter 2: 'Don't Hurt Me!'

Listening to a student who is narrating painful memories is not easy. Not only is it an exhausting experience for the student, but I too am taken on their emotional journey. The empathy that emanates from intent listening is so powerful that it's impossible *not* to feel their pain as they recount their memories.

However, perhaps the most taxing sessions -- the ones where you *feel* your heart-strings move -- are those when a student relives incidents where they were deliberately, either emotionally or physically, hurt by an adult. In all fairness, I don't think there's a single parent in India who hasn't hit their child at least mildly, once. We have all done it and often don't think twice about it because children are forgiving by nature. Therefore, since there is minimal guilt, we brush our actions under the carpet. This leads our children to learn that hitting, beating, pushing, shoving or nasty name-calling are simply a way of life and are just 'the way things are'. As ten-year-old Nakul once told me after being swiped by his father the night before with the buckle-end of his belt, '*Maribo tu lagibo, nohole moi keneke dungor hom?* (*He has to hit me, or otherwise how am I going to grow up?*) Yes, in homes where physical punishment is regularly enforced, children easily accept it as something they have to endure, but neither they nor their parents may be aware of the deeper negative manifestations that it causes. Ironically, in the long run, it's the parents who lose out, for it slowly detaches their child psychologically from them.

There are those amongst us who don't care about the ramifications that physical abuse causes and yet there are some who feel remorseful if ever we inadvertently hit our child, promising ourselves that we will never repeat it. It's those parents that I appeal to: if you feel overwhelming guilt every time you abuse your child, be grateful that you still have the humane side of you intact. Now is the time to stop and take stock of the long-term effects. But first of all look after yourself: lingering feelings will eat away at your conscience, so help yourself by controlling yourself the next time you raise your hand. Kahlil Gibran once wrote: '*Your children are not your children....they come through you but not from you and though they are with you yet they belong not to you,*' and even though we may be nodding our heads as we read his words, we still unknowingly attempt to possess our children totally. Without realising it, we enforce our thoughts and actions and sometimes even show our power by physically hurting them.

Teens may react to physical abuse in different ways but ultimately it is something that lowers their dignity, especially when they reach the tail end of adolescence. If the child is already weak (either academically or in terms of low self-esteem) physical abuse does nothing more than turn them into even more submissive and broken human beings.

Ananta was a mild mannered, quiet girl who had a shameful secret: she was regularly beaten by her father, but it was especially severe when she performed badly in exams. She had never spoken to anyone about it but was propelled to come to my counselling room on the day her half-yearly exam results were declared because she was petrified of going home. She knew she would be mercilessly beaten by her father because she'd failed in two subjects. Poor Ananta, I can still see the fear in her eyes and her trembling hands as she told me intricate details of the 'beating routine'. Her story may make you cringe but I hope you will see how the effects of physical abuse go beyond the physical pain. They can affect so many other aspects of an adolescent's psyche.

Contrast this with Madhavan who was a robust and loud student. He was often caught fighting in class and was unafraid to verbally or physically abuse anyone who irked him, along with a barrage of swear words thrown in for good measure. The class teacher sent him to me because she was unable to handle him anymore. He was such a mischievous student that his behaviour was beginning to affect the whole class. As you will read, once we had had enough counselling sessions to enable a sense of trust to come between us, he started to give me an alarming picture of a tension-filled home life. His parents were hot-headed and were driven by impulsive bursts of anger, not only towards him but towards each other too. Soon, I was able to relate all this to his rebellious nature. The seeds of violence had been planted in his mind as a child and, having grown up in a hostile environment, he had learnt to fend for himself in the only way he knew.

Earlier generations have always believed that sparing the rod will spoil the child but, from my experience, I believe that it is counter-productive. The satisfaction that a parent gets by hitting their child is only short-lived but the adverse psychological effects on the child last a long time. The days of brandishing the cane or slipper and beating our children into submission have long gone. No child deserves to be hurt. Today our children are growing up in an environment that is starkly different from that of our and our parents' generation. And though certain values many not have changed, your teen knows that physical punishment is wrong and an infringement of their dignity. Many students continue to harbour deeply ingrained feelings of hurt and anger towards the abusing parent, even if they profess to have forgiven them. They may not show it outwardly but the memories will always be there. I have asked many students if they can recall particular negative incidents of abuse and am surprised to learn that their memory banks can recall incidents, frame by frame, like a movie clip. This is why I believe that we must be more aware of the long-lasting negative implications on the mental development of our teenagers on the threshold of adulthood. We must understand how our actions today can set the template of how our children treat their own children tomorrow; it's as significant as that.

As I sit in the counselling chair and look into the eyes of the student sitting in front of me, there's a fleeting moment where I see my own child in that child's eyes. As objective as my role is in this regard, there are no excuses to harm a child; no child is born bad or naughty or abusive. If they are, it's because the environment has conditioned them to be like that. You can see examples of this when you buy a puppy. Surround him with love and discipline and he will be well behaved, happy and rarely aggressive – *unless* you are aggressive with it first; it's the same with our children.

So, the next time your child verbally abuses you, lies to you, defies you or ignores you, before you react by raising your hand to hit them, ask yourself for a moment why this is happening at all. The reasons could be many, some even beyond your own reach nor even your fault, but the bottom line is that something somehow has de-linked the crucial functioning of a healthy parent-child relationship. Once you've given it fleeting consideration, then consider if your reaction will actually be fuelling your child's indifference.

There's no doubt that physical abuse is one of the most destructive forms of abuse affecting most teen psyches, but a form of abuse which is far more gut-wrenching is sexual abuse. It is far more common than you may think. It can occur in all populations, in both rural and urban areas, at all socio-economic and educational levels, and across all racial and cultural groups.

If abuse in general is about domination, then sexual abuse is one of the most complete forms of domination that an adult can have over a child. The premature catalysis of the child into the sexual world is an irreversible process. They become entrapped by the sexual abuse, as they are sworn to secrecy, often threatened by dire consequences. They are made to feel dirty or that they are responsible for it, such is the molester's game.

It's no wonder that it is very difficult for anyone, let alone adolescents, to admit that they have been a victim of sexual abuse. It's a dark and secret part of their lives locked away in the recesses of their mind. Students rarely come to me intending to reveal such ugly episodes of their life but as counselling sessions progress, I often get an inkling that something like this may be the root cause of their mental anguish. For example, when Ishi came to me and showed me the hairless patches on her scalp where her father had pulled out clumps of her hair in a fitful rage, the severity of the abuse and the father's total domination over her led me to ask her if he had done anything more than that. The look in her eyes was enough to tell me that he had. Though I haven't included her as one of the case studies, the horrific outcome of her story is beyond belief because her father began to rape her. This incestuous episode eventually ended with my intervention, but Ishi's case still makes me feel nauseous today. Ultimately all forms of abuse are a power game and are all closely linked. One can easily lead to another or they can co-exist simultaneously.

Girish's abuse began when he was in Class 8 but he only came to me when he was in Class 9. He had sunk into the world of sexual intimacy much before he was ready. He had suffered for a full year before he could summon the courage to talk to someone about it. What was even more appalling was that the perpetrator was a man he had trusted and respected. Contrast this with fourteen-year-old Nandana whose self-cutting could be related back, through regression therapy, to repeated incidents of sexual abuse by a young college-going aunt when she was a mere six-year-old. She kept the ugly truth within her for over eight years and like a maggot in an apple, her anguish continued to eat away at her psyche long after the incident was over.

Sexual abuse takes a multitude of hues and comes with no fixed agenda. It can happen to anyone, anywhere and at any age. Though consensual instances of sexual exploration between adolescent boys and girls, or between the same gender, are considered to be normal sexual development there is a definite difference between this and sexual molestation. *Whoever* the perpetrator may be, even if it is a same-age class friend, a sibling, or an admired student at school, when undesired sexual behaviour is forced by one person upon another, it is sexual abuse.

Bhavesh of Class 7 fell into the trap quite easily when he went to the toilet and was accosted by a senior boy who offered him five rupees if he undid his trousers in front of him. Thereafter, the senior boy sought him out every day, until a well-meaning friend of Bhavesh's came and told me about it. The senior boy was given a stern warning and was so scared by the prospect of being expelled from school that he immediately stopped his antics.

The line between sexual abuse and normal loving behaviour is a fine one and any behaviour by an adult, which stimulates either the child or the adult sexually, especially when the victim is younger than the age of consent constitutes *child* sexual abuse. It is imperative that a child can recognise that the loving Uncle they grew up with, in spite of being a good friend of Papa's, is touching him or her inappropriately. It is crucial that we teach them the difference between a 'good' touch and a 'bad' touch. Even non-tactile interactions, where the victim is exposed to pornography or the molester is *looking* at them in a suggestive way, is sexual abuse and will make a child feel uneasy. It is imperative therefore that our children can recognize warning signs that may not always be so apparent.

Stop to think for a moment if you have ever forced your child to 'Give Uncle a goodbye kissy' or 'Give a big huggy to Auntie' even if they were obviously uncomfortable about it? While it's true that not every relative is a potential abuser, if a child shows reluctance or displeasure to hug or kiss another adult, then you should never force them to do so. You must respect and defend your child's wishes before any other adult.

I hope that parents who read the following candid accounts will be able to understand how debilitating the effects of sexual abuse are, and how important it is to educate our children about the sick people in our society who get their perverted kicks from sexual gratification with children. Ideally, the most effective prevention takes place *before* there's a child victim to heal or an offender to punish. So, whether we have sons or daughters, we must do everything in our power to ensure that they have the *intelligence* to recognise sexual abuse, the *sense* to back away or the *courage* to speak out, if ever they encounter it.

Ananta

The knock on the door was tentative. 'Come in!' I called out. It opened slowly. In walked Ananta, a quiet thirteen-year-old in Class 7. I had seen her countless times but she rarely spoke up in class and was an introverted girl. When a student who is meek by nature is able to overcome the fear within her to approach an adult in order to discuss a private matter, you can imagine how desperate she must have been. She must have felt that I was her last chance.

Crisply dressed, with her hair neatly combed into two plaits hanging on either side of her neck, Ananta took a seat. From her quick jittery movements and fleeting glances around the walls, I could see she was obviously quite uncomfortable in a counselling room. I asked her a few introductory questions to make her feel at ease and then asked her what her problem was. She tried to answer but her top lip started to quiver and a cascade of tears dribbled down her cheeks even before she said a word.

Many students can zip up their feelings to the outside world but there is something about the four protective walls of a counselling room that enables them to let go without fear. I've seen it happen hundreds of times where my room acts like a hub of seclusion, a safe place to cry unabashedly. She took off her spectacles and wiped her eyes with her handkerchief and tried to start speaking again. I waited for her to compose herself and put my hand on her arm without saying a word. When the heart is talking, silence is often the best comforter. Ananta continued to dab her streaming eyes. When she calmed down, she had both hands on the table clutching at the folded up hankie, before taking a deep breath. She spoke with an obvious urgency and was to-the-point. 'Ma'am, I haven't done well in my exams and if I take my report card home today, my father will beat me.'
'Does he beat you often?'
'Yeah, he beats me regularly anyway but he beats me *really badly* if I don't do well in my exams. And I know it will happen again today.'
She swallowed hard to try to stop the sob stuck in her throat but the tears were too overwhelming and she started to cry again. Her head was down and her grey skirt had little darker splodges on it where her tears fell. She was terrified of what was in store for her. I kept quiet, giving her a chance to continue and sure enough, after wiping her nose, which had also started dribbling, she was quick to carry on. 'Ma'am, this is *exactly* what he'll do: when I'm studying at my desk in my bedroom tonight, he will come in and lock the door without turning his back to me so that I don't see the bamboo cane he'll be holding behind his back. As soon as I hear the key click as it turns in the door, I know the routine is beginning.'
'So, what'll happen then?'

'Then he'll come to me and start beating me mercilessly. Last time I screamed so much that the neighbours came out of their houses and shouted at him to stop. I don't know what happens to him. He just keeps on and on.'

I started to get worried. Physical abuse on this scale could lead to serious injury. 'Do you get very badly hurt?'

'Last time the backs of my legs and my arms had lots of red streaks on them and the pain continued for many days afterwards.'

I felt a stab of fury within me. 'What about your mother? Doesn't she stop him when he is beating you?'

'No, she doesn't. I think she thinks I deserve it. She encourages it because she says it will push me to study harder. There's no one I can turn to. That's why I've come to you.'

She spoke the last sentence quietly, almost like a plea for a last chance to save her. I had to act fast. If another beating was in store for her as she said, I had to protect her because she was placing her trust in me. I knew I couldn't just let her go home, because to her it would seem that I would not be doing anything. But at the same time, unless I dealt with this tactfully, my intervention could easily make things even worse for her. However, before anything else, my first concern was for her safety. I knew I had buy time to postpone the beating. Once I could do that, only then could I think about how to stop the beatings for good.

Thankfully, it didn't take long for me to devise a strategy: I decided that she shouldn't take her report card home at all. I told her to tell them that the class teacher had kept a few report cards back which were to be collected by the parents personally on Monday. 'Then, on Monday, I will talk to them about this, okay?'

She was not okay. Immediately her eyes widened and she looked as if she'd seen a ghost. The fear of her father was so evident. 'Please don't tell them I told you! He'll kill me!' Her voice was panic-stricken and desperate.

I kept calm and spoke reassuringly. 'I promise you, Ananta, that I will not tell them immediately. First I'll talk to them to see if they seem the type to understand. Then, *and only then*, will I tell them. BUT I won't do anything that will worsen the situation, for you. Please trust me, Ananta.'

She was quiet. I hoped she didn't regret coming to me.

'Ok, ma'am. I trust you. You know what he can do to me so I know you will try to save me.'

'I will handle it in the best way I can, I promise you that.'

Ananta left my room with a weak smile. She seemed relieved that she was spared her beating by a couple more days but was still scared that she would be punished for talking to me in the first place. She had taken a huge risk by telling me. I had to ultimately change her parents' mindsets so that they would stop hitting her at all.

When her father and mother arrived on the Monday to collect the report card, the class teacher told them that Ananta had come to see me. Obviously curious, they wanted to meet me. So there they were sitting in front of me, the father who beat his teenage daughter and the mother who enabled him, both as guilty as each other. I felt I should casually mention why she had come to see me and, as expected, her father's initial reaction was to become angry and defend his actions. 'Why should my daughter go to *you* to tell you of how *we* discipline her?' he asked, mounting anger evident in his voice.

'Because, Mr Barua, how you "discipline" her is affecting her negatively. It upsets her. So that's why she came to me,' I said calmly.

'We believe that's the only way to make her understand, Madam. Beating always works. Everyone does it.'

'Even if "everyone is doing it", not everyone is Ananta. It's time to stop, Mr Barua. She's growing up now and doesn't need to be beaten. Look at her! She's one of the best behaved girls of the class!'

'That's because we beat her!'

We were starting to go around in circles. He opened the report card and turned it around so that I could read it. 'Ananta will get a good dose tonight. Look! She's actually failed in these two subjects.'

'Please, Mr Barua, don't beat her about this. What good is it going to do?'

'She'll try harder next time.'

'No, no, you have got it terribly wrong. There are other ways of disciplining children and this is *not* one of them, especially for Ananta. Let me tell you that since she has spoken out to a third person about how much these beatings affect her, it's just a matter of time till her bitterness multiplies. Now that she is an adolescent, she will eventually distance herself and become indifferent to you both if you continue to do this, let me assure you!'

Her father listened in silence. Her mother looked at me questioningly and asked 'Why couldn't she tell *me*? Why did she have to tell someone else?'

'Perhaps it was because she felt that you agreed with the beatings. It seems you don't defend her and encourage your husband. I hope that now that you know how she feels, you might protect her from today onwards.'

'My wife doesn't need to "protect" her,' scoffed the father. 'She's my child too.'

'But *someone* needs to protect her from getting hurt…. and that's why she came to me.'

He was calmer all of a sudden. A moment passed between us where no one talked. It felt like an eternity.

'Madam, on the one hand I feel angry at you too for pointing your finger at me but if, as you say, it is beginning to affect her I guess there's no point in arguing with you…'
An instant smile came to my lips. 'You could try arguing with me, but I'd only keep saying the same thing! I'm not admonishing you for your behaviour, Mr Barua, but rather suggesting that you try another form of disciplining that won't be so harsh, that's all.'
It melted the developing iciness between us.
'If she's spoken out to someone else, it must be because she's desperate for help. I never thought she was so upset about it. It's how we've always disciplined her and her brother. I suppose my little girl has grown up now and, you're right, she doesn't need it anymore.'
We were making headway. The mother was merely a submissive woman who sided with everything he said. He looked briefly at her, at me and then at the tablecloth.
'I feel a sense of embarrassment by my actions,' he said meekly.

Shame and humiliation are wonderful motivators to make one stop doing something. Her father was feeling an acute sense of it now. When I reminded them that Ananta's polite and well-mannered behaviour was quite a paradox when one considers that she was actually being regularly beaten, her father kept his eyes down, guilt shadowing his face. Her mother had tears in her eyes. Was this the break I needed to change their ways? 'I know it's not easy to hear that your daughter has confessed ugly home truths to another person, but please don't be angry at her. She didn't want me to tell you because she was scared of what more you would do to her. But I took the risk because I knew you would understand. I knew you would be sensitive to the problem.'
They seemed slightly calmer once I told them I wasn't blaming them in any way and had faith in them.
'Okay, we won't tell her we met you otherwise she will think that you made us feel sorry for her for hitting her.'
'Well, aren't you? When you see the red marks on her skin the next day, don't you feel sorry?'

'I suppose I do …. it makes me feel a bit guilty afterwards for hurting her but I do it in the hope of her becoming better in her studies. She has to be the best she can be, otherwise how will she learn to cope in today's competitive world?'

This was exactly why so many parents hit their children. They feel they do it for their own good. Ananta's father felt that he was conditioning her to be tough and yet he didn't see how he was actually demoralising her more and more. Nevertheless, I breathed a small sigh of relief. I realised that her father did actually love her. In his warped mind, he felt he was actually goading her to ultimately become a better human being. As weird as it seemed, the beatings stemmed from a deep sense of love for her so that she would be pushed to excel in academics. What he didn't realise was that every time he did so, he was pushing her away from him and had he continued, she would have despised him more and more. Ultimately I believe Ananta would have totally broken off emotionally from both of them.

'There are other ways of disciplining her, like denying her a privilege or keeping her activities monitored until she proves herself.' They nodded.
'Actually, I don't think Ananta requires severe disciplining. She is a naturally obedient child. You are both very lucky.' Suddenly, I remembered Ananta's concern. 'I hope you will not beat her for telling me?'
'No, I won't,' said her father.
'I hope that's a gentleman's word because she's terrified of you getting her back for coming to me.' He nodded begrudgingly. 'And I hope that you won't harbour any grudge towards me for my intervention in your family matter but I was obliged to help; after all it was your daughter who came to me.'
'Perhaps, it was a blessing in disguise,' whispered the mother philosophically.
'Yes, tell me, how can a child live in such fear? Unless you stop physically hitting her, there may be far bigger consequences as she grows up.'
'Oh really? How so?' asked her father, suddenly seemingly interested.
'Increased aggression, antisocial behaviour, mental health problems, not to mention it being a violation of her human rights...'
'Pah!' sneered the father.
I continued undeterred. '... feelings of low self-esteem, powerlessness, fearful and unable to stretch herself in new fields and situations ... need I go on, Mr Barua?'
I heard him sigh. 'Okay, okay, I get what you are saying.'
'Please try to see that this is an opportunity for you to avoid all of that.'

They stood up. I wasn't sure if what I had said had made them see any sense. It seemed the father was still a little skeptical. 'Well, thank you for your little lecture, madam.' His voice was overflowing with sarcasm.
'Look, I'm sorry if I have upset you but as the school's counsellor, I have a right to say what I feel is best for your child. Even if you don't care a hoot

about what I say, I owe it to myself, the school and to your daughter to say what I feel is best for the situation. That is my job. If you don't agree with me, well that's your choice but I hope, for Ananta's sake *both* of you will see my perspective.'

A week went by without any contact. I hoped that 'no news was good news' and things were sorting themselves out. Indeed, one fine morning about ten days after I met the parents, a cheery Ananta popped her head into my room. The change was miraculous. Gone were the sunken eyes and sad disposition. Instead she was smiling and happy. I saw she wore braces, something I hadn't noticed the first time because she hardly smiled.

'Guess what ma'am! My father has stopped hitting me because he said that I am too old for it now! They both told me that I don't need disciplining with the cane anymore!'

'Oh thank goodness for that! At least you don't have to be scared to take home your report card anymore!'

'Yes, they looked at my card and said that I must study according to a fixed routine every day. They told me that I have to try harder next time. That's all! No canings!'

'Well be happy that you have parents who understand that hitting you is no longer the way forward. You are lucky, Ananta.'

'Thanks for your help ma'am. I know you must have told them but they haven't mentioned anything about meeting you.'

I kept silent. I didn't want to confirm anything but the relief in my smile was apparent, for not only were we able to save her predicament but somehow, perhaps, we were able to shift a mindset too.

Madhavan

There were many signs that told me that Madhavan was rebellious in his attitude, starting from the absence of a knock on my door when he first entered my room. He simply opened the door abruptly and, without any form of introduction, announced that his class teacher had sent him. He was a cute-looking rotund chap, with a mass of curly hair and as yet, no signs of reaching puberty. His face was round too and he looked like the rough-and-ready type who wasn't afraid of anything. The first counselling session was seemingly unproductive as I merely got an insight into his background but from his behaviour, he gave me many clues as to his temperament. Restless and fidgety, he shifted in his seat, sometimes doodling with my pen. He had a severe stammer and often got stuck mid-sentence.

His voice was loud and penetrating and at first glance, he appeared to be extremely uncouth. He told me that he was very happy both at home and at school though his friends often needed to be 'put back in place' every time they poked fun at him. In all honesty, Madhavan was the kind of boy who would not think twice about punching or verbally abusing anyone. He walked like a wrestler, as if he was ready at any point to throw the first punch. His outward bully-type appearance made him very disliked and unpopular in class, though the few friends he had stayed by him for his tough image.

It was in his third counselling session that he started to give me a real picture of his personal life. That particular week, his class teacher informed me that he had angrily thrown the board duster at a student. I decided to find out why.

'He made me angry and he was too far away to punch, so I threw the duster at him.'

'Why did he make you angry?'

'He called me a fat pig.'

'And so you threw the duster at him?'

'Yes.'

'But he got hurt, didn't he?'

'Serves him right. That'll teach him to stop calling me names.'

'Do you think it was right to throw the duster at him?'

'Yes, he deserved it. He was lucky I didn't throw the chair at him....'

Madhavan felt his behaviour was justified. There seemed to be a mix-up in his understanding of angry responses. He had responded to a spiteful remark with a revengeful act that was potentially far more dangerous. The crime didn't fit the punishment for his poor classmate. What should have been at most a war of words between classmates caused a flying missile to be hurled through the air and injure another. Why couldn't he see that the extent of his aggression was not justified? The answers came from his home life.

'Does your father throw things at you when he is angry, Madhavan?'

'Sometimes.'

'Can you remember the last time he did?'

'Last night.'

'What happened?'

'I was talking to my friend on the phone and he got angry because he wanted to use it and because I didn't put it down immediately, he punched the table lamp to the ground with his fist.'

'How often does he hit you?'

'Almost every day for some reason or another, even stupid reasons, like if I take too long in the bathroom.'

'What about your mother?'

'Yes, she hits me too but she's not as strong as he is and it doesn't hurt as much. And anyway, I'm older now so her slaps feel more like mosquito bites…'

'So aren't you scared?'

'Not anymore. I'm used to it. But I dare not answer back.'

'What will happen if you do?'

'I hate to even think about it. He would hurt me, maybe even knock me out.'

Madhavan was totally gripped by the fear of retaliation by his father. He accepted his parents' 'right' to hit him and stoically took it all. His stammering was an off-shoot of his pent-up fear. School was the only place where he could vent his anger freely without fear. That's why he went about throwing unjustified punches or using swear words quite liberally. His classroom was where he was king. At home he was like a mouse and made to feel that he was good at nothing and had much to achieve. Though it wouldn't seem so, Madhavan's self esteem was at an all-time low. His tough image camouflaged his low self confidence. He had learned how to fight for himself but in his heart he grew up feeling he deserved every criticism, every put-down and every beating.

Of course, I had to contact his parents but they were not very forthcoming at all. I didn't discuss the problem over the phone and just informed them that I would like to speak to them in person. They never turned up and Madhavan was very vocal in telling me that they would increase his beatings if I ever mentioned the issue to them. So unfortunately, with no cooperation coming from them, I had to respect Madhavan's wishes in this regard because their aggression towards him would increase. But I had another plan. I instructed the class teacher to tell his parents that Madhavan was an angry student and very reckless in his behaviour in class. I asked her to put forth the idea in their minds that young teens often mirror the actions they see at home and it's possible that his aggressive behaviour could stem from the home front. She was simply to suggest to them to be more aware of how they treated him.

With more counselling sessions, Madhavan's bad behaviour in school eased with time. The parents were aware that his behaviour in school gave clues about how they must be treating him, so they obviously were more careful.

At school too I informed his subject teachers to refrain from aggressive disciplining with him because he actually suffered from low self esteem, though no one would be able to believe it from the outside. I requested them to try positive disciplining methods where they use constructive forms of reprimand. For example, instead of shouting at him and saying: 'Don't do that!' or 'Stop talking!', I suggested they say 'Madhavan, I know you can keep quiet. Come on, show me, eh?' or 'Please Madhavan, I can trust you not to do that, can't I?' I also requested them to give him some responsibility as a class captain for a short while to prove himself.

With the situation handled on the school front, and somewhat reduced on the home front, his behaviour became less aggressive. Madhavan still came for counselling every week and would off-load all his problems to me and give me an update of his home situation. That in itself was enough to lighten the pile-up of emotional baggage he would have otherwise carried on his shoulders.

In due course, the effects of physical abuse which had once robbed him of his self-confidence and ability to make friends and trust others became less apparent. It took months of cooperation by the teachers to notice a palpable change in his behaviour. His earlier labels of being the 'class bully' and 'trouble-maker' were no longer applicable. However, although he became outwardly calmer at school, he was still prone to sudden emotional outbursts and physical assault on others which, unfortunately and inevitably, were off-shoots of the hostile and abusive environment in which he grew up as a child.

Girish

Girish was still only in Class 8 when his father had arranged for him to take tuitions with his old friend. They had studied together at university and his friend was still unmarried. He was a physics professor and was used to teaching much older students but he agreed to oversee Girish's studies simply because he was his friend's son. Once it was arranged, Girish would be dropped at his place twice a week after school for physics and maths tuition. Girish's father felt that his professor friend would be able to solve any confusions in these two subjects in which Girish was clearly struggling. Little did he know however, that his so-called friend was indeed going to tutor him – but in a subject matter that would ultimately cost his son his innocence.

It was unfortunate that Girish had come to see me much after his abuse was over. He was in Class 9 now and had come to confess to me that he found himself attracted to boys and simply wanted to know if it was normal. It was unusual for such a young boy to be so sure of his sexual orientation but his voice had already deepened and I noticed that he had already started shaving because he didn't have the downy moustache so typical of pubescent boys. There was a pungent body odour about him. His face was thin and lacked brightness, his cheekbones prominent and chin angular. Acne dotted his forehead and cheeks and he had greasy, limp hair. One of my first questions was when he became aware that he was attracted to boys. Initially he gave me vague answers like 'Oh, I just wondered' or 'I have read about it' but as the sessions progressed and he became more comfortable with me, he saw that I didn't judge people who were attracted to the same gender. So, one fine day he decided to tell me exactly what the precursor to it all actually was.

'What I'm about to tell you, I haven't told anyone. But I feel I can trust you.'

He examined my face to see if I understood the extent of what he was saying. I looked into his eyes and nodded. He started talking. 'I had already been going to my dad's friend's house for one-to-one tuitions for a month before the incident happened. It was summer and one particular evening, it was really warm. All of a sudden the electricity went. This usually happens anyway and because Uncle has an invertor, it's not a problem. However this particular evening he said that it was broken and since it was so muggy, Uncle suggested that I remove my T-shirt. I thought nothing of it. This happened a couple of times as the damn lights seemed to go whenever I had tuition. He never seemed to get his invertor fixed. Then one day he suggested that I remove my jeans too and sit in only my underpants. It sounds ridiculous I know, but at the time it seemed logical and because it was *really* hot, I did as he suggested.'

I sighed. I could already see the molester's game. This was how the seduction started. Obviously Girish was too naïve to recognize the signs. From there on it was going to be a step-by-step calculated sequence of events spreading over a few weeks and as Girish narrated them to me, I began to get a better insight into the perverted mind of the molester.
'From then on, he would deliberately touch my arm or stroke my thigh as he explained chapters.'
'Did you feel uncomfortable?'
'Of course I did ma'am, but it seemed to be an insignificant issue because he was doing it quite naturally as if it was no big deal. I never thought of telling my dad.'

'What happened after that?'

'A week before my exams, Uncle told my father that he wanted to teach me till late at night and then again in the morning so, to avoid bringing me to his place twice, he suggested that I stay over. Dad agreed and told me that he'd pick me up at lunchtime the following day.'

For some reason, as I was listening, I started to get a little tense. The events that were unfolding were starting to make my temples throb. The manipulative strategy of the seducer was so typical. Over a few weeks, he had slowly set the scene perfectly. He was trying to paint a picture that he was trying his best to help his son and because Girish's father was a friend who was not paying for the tuition, he was unable to refuse. So in good faith, he entrusted his son overnight with his friend.

'That night we did our usual tuition till quite late. He was a little more bolder this time when he touched me, skimming his hand over my private parts though it was very well disguised. He made me study till around 10.30 p.m. after which we ate dinner. Around 11 p.m. we studied a bit more till he sensed I was feeling sleepy. Then he told me to go to bed because I had to get up early to study again.'

The way Girish was describing the incident was like a thriller. His speech was automatic, his eyes were glazed, deep in thought, as he revealed what happened next. 'His house was small and he had given me a small room where there was a single bed. His bedroom was next to mine but there was simply a thin plyboard partition separating us. I tried to sleep but since it was a strange place, I failed to doze off quickly even though I kept my eyes closed. It must have been past midnight when he tiptoed into my bedroom and stood over my bed. I was sleeping on my back and, thinking I was fast asleep, he initially just touched me with one hand on my private parts but then he started to gently fondle me. I could sense he had his other hand down his own pyjamas, but I was too scared to open my eyes. So I continued to pretend I was asleep but I was very much awake and I was feeling very, very scared. My heart was beating so fast and hard that I could feel it pounding.'

I felt a wave of nausea come over me. I closed my eyes and could feel the thuds of my own heart. A slow anger enveloped me and instinctively my fists clenched. Girish, still absorbed in his catharsis, continued stoically. 'After about two or three minutes, I turned around onto my side and faced the wall. Now my back was turned to him so he had to take his hand away. He kept very quiet and stood still for a few moments. And then very slowly he left the room without making a sound. He didn't come back after that and must've slept in his own room.'

'What happened the next morning?'

'He was behaving pretty much normally, as if nothing happened. Of course, since he thought I was asleep, I didn't say anything either.'

'Did it ever happen again after that?'

'Not at night, because I never stayed at his place after that but I did continue tuition with him for a few more months. It had become our routine now. Without saying a word, he would stroke me under the table. I would continue looking at my books ignoring him but we both knew it was "our little game" and he knew I wouldn't tell anyone about it. And I didn't. I hated it but kept this ugly secret within me because I knew he would deny it and my father would think I was making things up. However, as luck would have it, my father found a home tutor a few months later after I complained that it was tiring for me to keep going to his place for tuition. So I didn't need to go to Uncle's place anymore and the abuse ended.'

'Did you see him again after that?'

'Yes I did on and off. He used to come over to our house as a guest sometimes.'

'How did you feel when he came over?'

'Scared. Petrified. He had a lot of power over me, even though he never directly talked to me about it. I hardly came out of my room when he was there but when my mum called me for dinner, I would sit at the table and never look into his eyes. I felt paralysed and became like a puppet in front of him. My hands would tremble and I could never eat.'

'Did he ever try anything like that again?'

'No, he didn't. The opportunity never arose again because I left his tuition but the memories are still there in my mind. It still scares me whenever I think about it.'

Even though I felt a sense of relief that it was all over, the man still had a hold over Girish in spite of not being in regular touch with him anymore. If he hadn't been his father's friend, perhaps the outcome would have been different; maybe he would have told someone and brought the abuse to light so that he could be brought to justice. But since his fear was fraught with the belief that he would be to blame, Girish kept quiet. He felt he couldn't risk telling anyone because he knew his abuser would make him out to be the guilty one.

With time and regular counselling, there were signs to suggest that Girish was healing. He was angry for a start. He accepted he wasn't to blame and began to feel rage towards his uncle. As his anger became more intense, he wanted to report this perverted man to the police and see him suffer but the only thing stopping him was that the man was still a good friend of his father's. Over many more months, the anger gradually subsided after he understood that hanging onto the anger meant that the abuser's hold on him was still in his system, affecting him. If he couldn't shake off the emotional remnants, he would not be able to move ahead. It was not easy for Girish and took a long time for him to move on but he learned to be indifferent, to be able to blot him out of his life, neither caring whether he was dead or alive. His early entry into a very adult world had left him with an early sexual awakening.

There are hundreds of young boys like Girish who are subjected to acts of molestation every day and are sworn to secrecy through emotional black-mail or threats to their family. My experience has told me that the only way to stop the abuser is to empower young boys and girls to judge *behaviour* as an indicator of potential abuse and not *appearance*. Abusers are not all wrinkled old uncles. They come in the most unlikely of avatars: seemingly nice aunties, domestic helpers, older cousins, loving family members ... but they all have one thing in common: the game of manipulative seduction, as they slowly invade those precious inches of personal space surrounding us, step-by-step, and in a way that becomes increasingly uncomfortable. If every victim could speak out and if every adult learns not to admonish them for what they say, perhaps we would be able to curb this evil. We owe it to them because no child should be a victim of perverted adults whose selfish momentary desires have the potential to mar lives forever.

Nandana

Nandana came to see me for a seemingly small problem: she simply wanted help to control her bad temper. But as it often happens, small problems are only the tip of a much larger underlying issue. Nandana was a plump girl but not obviously fat. Her hair was neatly tied back though she had wispy tendrils from either side. The sheen of clear lip gloss and a faint line of eyeliner were only adornments of the perfect skin of her face. However, the first obvious thing I noticed about her was her shirt: in spite of the heat of the monsoon, she was wearing a long-sleeved shirt. This was not the first time I had seen this amongst adolescent girls and I had an inkling that she was covering up her arms to hide the marks of self-cutting. Keeping my sus-picions at bay for the moment, I asked her what she did when she got angry. 'Sometimes I break things or throw things....'

'Do you hurt yourself?'

'What do you mean?'

'I mean like cut yourself. It's common amongst girls. I've come across many girls doing this.'

This seemed to put her at ease. 'Yes, I do it too. Sometimes.' She looked down when she said this, obviously feeling a little uneasy in admitting to it.

'When did you last hurt yourself?'

'Day before yesterday evening …. when I got scolded by my mum for getting 17 out of 25 for my maths test … so I cut my arm…'

'Nandana , let me see. Please unroll your sleeve.'

'No, I can't show you.'

Her eyes were downcast but I defended why I wanted to see her arm. 'I just want to see how bad it is, because it may be infected.'

That seemed to worry her. She hadn't thought about the medical aspect. She began to unroll her left sleeve and unveiled seven or eight horizontal angry red streaks along the underside of her forearm. One was still slightly oozing blood, probably having been cut a little too deeply. I didn't want to seem unduly dramatic. I pointed to the bleeding cut.

'See Nandana , that one is still bleeding. It's quite deep. What did you use?'

'For these, I used a razor blade because the pain is less with a razor blade but if I'm at school, I use a compass or even a sharp pencil…'

Without judgment or criticism showing on my face, I continued to ask her questions. 'Are there any scars of earlier cuts, Nandana ?'

Seeing I was behaving quite normally, she proceeded to show me several areas where she had cut herself – her thighs, upper arms – but she said she had some scars on her tummy too.

'You do realise that the implement you use can cause infection, don't you?'

'Never really thought about it.'

'Why do you do it, Nandana ?'

'I've been doing it for years. It's like a habit. Whenever my mom or my friends get on my nerves, I do it. It just makes me feel better.'

'Don't you feel sad to see your lovely smooth skin looking so scarred?'

'Not really. Sometimes I feel I deserve it and I like to punish myself. At least I have control over it. In fact, I cut whenever I feel angry or I feel I can't cope. It's nice watching the blood coming out of my skin as it slowly oozes out. It makes me feel calm, as if I am the one that is totally in control. It's a great relief.'

I sighed deeply. She was using self injury as a coping mechanism for some unseen deeper reason. Cutting is becoming increasingly common amongst adolescents, especially girls. Some girls carve out the names of the boys they

love or person they hate. Perversely, it has almost become a symbol of showing off, as if to say: *look at what I can do!* Cutting is not usually a sign of suicidal tendencies but more a cry for help, for understanding and helplessness.
It was possible that Nandana had some deep lingering feelings of anger,
sadness or frustration that she was unable to express openly. Maybe she was
unable to cope any more with building tension. I needed to find out.

So, over a few weeks, we began sessions of regression therapy where Nandana
simply talked about her life. Very often through this method, it is possible to
identify the origins of emotional issues pertaining to something more serious, as in Nandana 's case. I felt that there could be a particular incident or
incidents that remained hidden in her memory because on the surface, she
seemed to have a stable home and family life. Obviously there were no outward causes of frustration and her parents loved her a lot. Nandana told me
of her life as far back as she could remember. I listened and watched her as she
spoke, searching for any clue that could help me understand why she was regularly cutting herself. The biggest clue to her present behaviour came when
she recounted an incident of her life when she was only six years old which
she had never told anyone about. And as I listened, I realised that this was
the missing link that I was searching for. She spoke in short sentences with
a slight shortness of breath, as if she was getting flashbacks of memory. 'My
mother's sister – my masi – was still at college when she used to come and
stay with us sometimes …. she and I slept in the same bed …. and sometimes
she would ask me to pretend I was her baby and …. I can't say it ma'am….'
I understood. Without saying a word, I simply pretended to cradle an
infant and pointed to my chest. She nodded. 'Not only that ma'am … she
used to do other things too.'
'You mean like touching you, in your private areas?'
She nodded again. I kept silent now, waiting for her to continue. A few seconds passed in silence. She was obviously reliving those memories. A lump
came to her throat and she swallowed hard. 'Now I can see why she always
insisted we go to sleep immediately after eating our dinner. She was so loving
towards me that I never even thought what she was doing was doing. She
was my favourite masi but the other masis didn't do what she did to me. No
one knew what was happening when we were sleeping together. She told me
that I shouldn't tell my mother that I was pretending to be her baby because
my mother may feel bad that I consider her to be my mother and not my real
mother. So I kept quiet because I didn't want to hurt my mom or upset her. '
'When did you realise that what she was doing was not normal?'
'Well actually I didn't. I thought it was okay for her to touch me between
my legs and I had seen women breast-feeding, so even that didn't seem bad

to me. But I did wonder why she only touched me in those areas whilst my mother never did.'

'Did it happen every time she came?'

'Yes and because I didn't like to do it or be touched, I used to pretend I was unwell and insisted on sleeping with my mom instead of my masi but our house was small and we only had two bedrooms. She continued to do it every time she came over.'

'How long did it continue?'

'It lasted for over a year until she got married and left.'

'Did she ever try it again?'

'No, never again and she pretended as if nothing had ever happened. She used me and I never knew it was wrong. I was so young…'

At this point, she could no longer hold back the tears that had remained locked in her heart for over seven years. Her head was arched over and both her hands were covering her eyes. Her body convulsed in spasms of uncontained sorrow. My skin prickled. To this day I can still see the way she cried unabashedly for the little girl that she was then. In between sobs, she continued. 'I was so young….' she repeated.

'Sh … sh … it's okay … how were you to know?' I spoke calmly, trying to disguise the emotion in my voice. She took a tissue from the box I kept on my table and blew her nose, which was now pink. She had calmed down a little but little residual gasps of breath still made her breathing jerky.

'The funny thing was that I never, ever told my mum about it, even after my masi got married. Even though she was no longer around, I still felt emotionally blackmailed by her.' She slipped back into the memories, as if it was all making sense now. She nodded slowly as she spoke. 'You know she even joked with my mom that I had once told her a lie that my mother had hit me when she hadn't. I now realise that she was trying to put in a safety net for herself, just in case I ever did ever tell my mum because then she'd deny it, saying that I do lie, and she'd quote that incident. God, how I hate her!'

In a way I was happy that Nandana could now see the manipulation. It would help her to see that she was not the one who was at fault.

'Did the memories subside after she got married?'

'Yes, but I still had flashbacks every now and again. As I reached puberty, I began to realise what she had done and then initially I began to blame myself for it. I thought I was the guilty one. I thought I was a bad girl and not good enough and ugly and hopeless at everything.'

'So did you hurt yourself then?'

'No, not in terms of cutting myself but I would often hit my head against a wall or pull my hair whenever I got angry. But then I discovered that cutting myself was better.'

The saddest part of Nandana 's story is that, even after it was all over, she suffered totally alone. For her, she was made to feel 'special' before she could recognise that she was being abused by her trusted masi. It is unfortunate that Nandana couldn't do anything about the fact that she felt uncomfortable because she was trapped. If she had, perhaps this story would have had a very different outcome. It wouldn't have been here at all because it would have been handled in time before it snowballed into bigger proportion.

There followed many months of counselling for Nandana after that confession. She had extremely low self esteem and hated herself a lot. The urge to cut was triggered by strong feelings of shame, frustration or loss of control. Somehow it had become a habit where her brain had learned to connect the false sense of relief that she felt about these feelings with the act of cutting. So, every time she felt strong negative emotions, she was quick to resort to this form of self abuse. Counselling helped her to realise that she was not to be blamed for her abuse. There was nothing she had done to provoke abuse. She was not, and never was, the guilty one. She learned to love and respect herself again and slowly the cutting stopped as her self confidence and self respect grew. Nandana was able to get over such an ugly episode simply by facing her fears and changing her perspective. She successfully went on to pass Class 12 with flying colours and today she is a practising lawyer working for the family court where she often meets women and children victims of abuse. Having once been a victim herself, today she stands by and supports those who are abused. It seems Nandana has indeed come full circle.

Checklist

All adolescents are different in their short- and long-term responses. Many go on to live happy lives, others lead lives of escalating damage. Bear in mind that few adolescents are forthcoming about explaining signs of sexual abuse. Therefore non-verbal behavioural symptoms will often give a better indication that something significant and disturbing has happened to them.

Red flags to watch out for

Abuse cannot and should not be taken lightly. Due to its serious nature, this list is long! Any kind of abuse will have similar psychological manifestations, though they may vary in intensity. Initial signs may be vague and can be the result of a host of causes, some even indicative of normal adolescent behaviour! However *prolonged* bouts of sadness, tearfulness, lethargy, rage, fear, insecurity or social withdrawal are symptoms of deeper causes, not just of physical/sexual abuse. Similarly, the presence of a single mark does not necessarily prove physical abuse is taking place but when they occur repeatedly or in combination, or are extremely severe, immediate intervention must be sought to protect the well-being of the adolescent. If you have noticed recurring symptoms of this checklist and feel that sexual abuse could be happening, do not hesitate to seek immediate intervention by mental health experts. They are trained to handle these cases delicately. Some addresses and websites are given at the end of this book.

- Presence of unexplained burns, bites, bruises, broken bones, or black eyes which happen repeatedly or in combination
- Changes in sleeping patterns (oversleeping, insomnia or even nightmares) without any apparent reason
- Sudden changes in eating habits : refusing to eat, loss of or a drastically increased appetite, trouble swallowing
- Obvious discomfort when talking about a certain person or acts lovingly to the abuser to 'protect' their secret
- Leaves suggestive clues that seem likely to provoke a discussion about sexual issues
- Writes, draws, or dreams of sexually explicit or frightening images
- Talks about a new older friend and refuses to talk about a secret shared between them
- Suddenly has money or other gifts without reason
- Thinks of self or body as repulsive, dirty or bad
- Exhibits adult-like sexual behaviours, such as language and knowledge
- Self-injury (cutting, burning)
- Inadequate personal hygiene
- Drug and alcohol abuse
- Sexual promiscuity, especially in girls
- More seductive and sexualized manner of dress
- Conversely, less attractive dress sense: wearing baggy, unattractive clothing, avoiding cosmetics

- Because sexual abuse instills a sense of self-hatred, some victims think that their gender caused them to become a victim. So they may start to dress more like the opposite gender as a way of deflecting abuse
- Running away from home
- Suicide attempts
- Fear of physical intimacy or closeness, even with loving family members
- Heightened sense of vigilance, vulnerability and fearfulness, possibly combined with a new sensitivity, easily startled
- If someone seems 'too good to be true', ask more questions. Even a close friend or relative may not be a safe person to trust with your child.

What you can do

It's very easy to assume the worst but when it comes to accusing a person about any physical or sexual abuse they may have inflicted, you have to tread very carefully. It is always better to empower adolescents about abuse through a Early Safety Plan (see the end of this chapter for a sample) in which you give early awareness about sexual abuse, because once the abuse starts it becomes very difficult for the adolescent to untangle themselves from the complicated mesh of the abuser's tactics. If your teen tells you about being abused, count yourself lucky. Act on the information immediately. If they don't, you may have to wait and watch for a little while till you are sure it is happening and you have ticked off many symptoms on the checklist above.

If your teen confirms that s/he has been abused:

- ✓ Stay calm. It is crucial that you make the adolescent feel supported and relieved that they told you. You will not be able to provide support if you are overwhelmed with your own emotions.
- ✓ Keep your physical responses in check. Negative signs such as grimaces, frowns, raised eyebrows, tutting should be avoided as they may be interpreted (perhaps mistakenly) as blaming or shaming the teen.
- ✓ Reassure them that they are not to be blamed at all.
- ✓ Reassure them that they can trust you and you will not do anything that could backfire onto them like report or argue with the abuser, without informing them of your actions first.

✓ Acknowledge the courage they have mustered to be able to tell you. Commend their bravery and tell them not to be scared.

✓ Do not downplay the abuse in an attempt to make the adolescent feel better. For example don't say 'It wasn't that bad' or 'It happens all the time'

✓ Do not ask for specific details at this initial stage, unless s/he is willing to tell you on his or her own.

✓ Never force them to talk, or cross-examine them to get to the bottom of it all.

✓ Reassure them that you are grateful they have told you and you will now take charge of their well being.

✓ Seek professional advice on the best way to tackle the situation and work together.

The best predictor of recovery from child/teen sexual abuse is support, love and protection from their main caregiver and professionals specialising in sexual abuse victims.

The Early Safety Plan (ESP)

I am including this ESP for parents to start inculcating a relaxed and open atmosphere at home regarding sexual issues, where teens feel free and safe enough to share their concerns with you, if ever they feel intimidated. By living in an environment where they clearly know what is right or wrong behaviour, they are thus empowered to defend themselves if ever exposed to another person with ulterior sexual motives.

1. Make sure each family member knows what healthy sexual development in children is, and what sexual behaviours might be of concern.

2. Set clear family guidelines for personal privacy and behaviour. For example, as a child enters adolescence insist that other family members knock on the door before entering the room, instead of barging in. Start by respecting these boundary guidelines yourself. This will set the example.

3. When they are changing, look away. Allow teens to bathe themselves once they reach puberty.

4. Give adolescents their own room, or at least their own bed, when they feel ready for more privacy.
5. Pubescent teens should not sleep with members of the opposite gender even if they are family members (brothers/sisters father/daughter or mother/son) on a permanent basis.
6. Inform your teen that they do not have to hug or kiss someone hello or goodbye if they don't want to. They can shake hands instead. Don't ever force. Humorously tell the 'jilted' adult that your teen is finally growing up.
7. Identify one or more support person for each member of the family to talk to if there is a concern. Be sure that no one in your family is isolated.
8. Research shows that having someone to talk with and confide in plays a key role in how well an adolescent will bounce back from stressful events. Having a safe, responsible and consistent adult for a child or adolescent to turn to is critical.

The Heart-to-Heart – Suggestions on how to introduce the topic of sexual abuse

Once you have instilled a relaxed atmosphere at home, where boundaries and privacy have been respected, you will need to openly tell your child about the possibility of abuse occurring at home or outside. Though it may not quite be breakfast table conversation, don't make it a total taboo topic in your household either. Many Indian parents are uncomfortable with talking openly about the possibility of abuse but unless they open the doors to communication early, a prospective abuser can easily 'edge in' before them. Be as explicit and as honest as you need to be to get the point across.

- Start talking about the topic of sexual awareness as early as you feel your child will understand, but be age-specific in the language you use. Remember, the age of the victim is of no relevance to most sexual molesters. They are only on the lookout for easy chances.
- Don't delegate the responsibility of inculcating awareness in this regard to anyone else. It is the responsibility of at least one of the parents.
- For the nervous parent (and there are many!), start by talking about the right to privacy when someone is having a bath or changing and why we must respect each other. Elevate this topic to private areas of one's body where no one has the right to touch

or see any private parts without their consent. Don't make it seem seedy or crude but matter-of-fact and practical.

- Tell them they have a right over their body and can say no to anyone (even you) who touches them in a way that makes them feel uncomfortable. However there may be times when someone (like a doctor, for example) may need to look at them 'down there' but tell them they have the right to ask for you to be present too.
- Show them how a 'good touch' feels.
- *Don't* show them how a 'bad' touch feels. It will confuse them, especially younger children. Instead, use imagery techniques where you ask them to imagine how it would make them feel if someone touched them in a private region. If they instinctively feel a sense of knee-jerk disgust, tell them that that is what a 'bad touch' feels like.
- Make sure they are not scared of being forthright in their immediate reaction. Tell them that it's okay to feel disgusted or angry at the person and it's perfectly fine to express themselves through shouting, screaming or even crying *at the time*, should it ever happen. Tell them that it's a normal reaction to express anger.
- Though it sounds silly, practice a trial run by simply getting them to scream out loud. Practice shouting 'Don't touch me!' together (with younger children) or engage in a role-play situation with an older child, where the focus is on what the victim will say or do. Going through it like this gives them empowerment. Being afraid and remaining silent is the biggest curse to combatting this evil and incidentally the abuser's greatest victory.
- Assure them that you are simply enlightening them about this issue and not scaring them. Reassure them that there are more people who are good than evil in this world but it's wise to be prepared for anything untoward.
- Once they are aware, they must feel free to report any sexual advances made towards them to you or any activities that concern what you are telling them. Tell them that even if they feel they can't tell you, they can tell a trusted member of the family (mention their name).

If you consider yourself to be a traditional-thinking Indian parent and can get this far, you've done well. Only the most open of parents will be able to extend to other sexual topics such as masturbation, fantasies, homosexuality, contraception, teenage sex etc. Don't worry if you can't just yet. Most adolescents know a little about them anyway and will most probably cringe when you tell them!

Chapter 3: 'You're So Strict!'

Sometimes I wonder if we parents are *really* all from the same species: we may share the same mission of bringing up our children but the way we go about it differs so profoundly. Differences in cultural environment, family background, socioeconomic status, educational level and even religion play a part in this wide spectrum. To add another dimension, parents may have different approaches since they spring from individual belief systems, so there may be a conflict between their styles too!

Whatever the reasons are, it is a fact that how we bring up our children through the first three stages of growth -- namely childhood, adolescence and early adulthood -- directly impacts their wellbeing in three crucial domains: social competence, academic performance and psychosocial development. The parenting style – the extent to which parents influence, teach and control their children -- will determine how well-adjusted their child will become.

Let's take the simple example of giving a mobile phone to an early teen adolescent. Parents who absolutely refuse to give them a mobile, deeming it to be totally unnecessary, are said to be **authoritarian**. They are probably the most stringent of parents on the strictness spectrum and will turn a blind eye to their children's pleas and fail to explain any reasoning behind their rules, except for 'because I said so.' Expected to be obedient at all times, their children will be meticulously behaved and proficient but do not always fare highly in terms of internal happiness, social competence and self esteem. When they become older adolescents, however, they run the greatest risk of rebelling against such a controlling environment.

On the other hand, parents who give their children a patient hearing as to why they want that mobile and weigh the pros and cons before making a final decision are **authoritative**. If they do buy it, they may lay down rules regarding its usage and explain why they are being enforced. Psychologists believe that this parenting style is by far the healthiest because it establishes parental authority whilst *at the same time* takes into account their child's perspective. Authoritative parents tend to have less psychological control in the way they handle issues, resulting in happier, socially responsible and successful adolescents. Ultimately, effective parenting operates on the belief that both the teen and the parent have certain rights and that the needs of both are important. Effective parents set clear rules, explain why these rules are important and reason with their teen by considering their point of view even though they may not agree with them. In fact, those parents who profess to having had minimal friction during the adolescence phase have most probably respected their children's individuality and brought them up in an environment where they were assertive but not intrusive or restrictive.

Now take the parents who will listen and abide by every whimper-of-a-demand their adolescent makes. When it comes to the mobile, they will give in without even a question as to why they might need one, just as they had done to various demands when their teen was a child. We've all seen young children who don't even know how to read and write properly, clutching the latest mobiles in their hands. These are the children of **permissive** parents, who are on the lower end of the strictness spectrum. They are exceptionally lenient in their parenting style and have very few demands or expectations to make of their children, especially in terms of discipline. They don't like to upset their children, preferring to avoid confrontation, even failing to put their foot down on their children's tantrums and demands, however irrational. Those of us who have seen a child shout fiercely at a parent or, even worse, hit a parent should not blame the child; it's the parenting style that is the culprit here. Whatever the age of the child, permissive parents will buy that mobile phone without a second thought. They are nurturing and communicative and tend to see themselves as a friend to their children rather than the ones in charge. Children brought up this way have trouble managing their emotions and lack maturity and, since they are not used to adhering to rules set by adults, they often experience problematic behaviour with authority and tend to perform badly at school. However, rather surprisingly, because they have had so much indulgence, they often have higher levels of self esteem.

If the authoritarian parents were the ones at the top of the strictness spectrum, **uninvolved** parents are at the bottom. They won't care a hoot about the implications of why their child needs a mobile at all. They are so caught up in their own lives that they are detached from their children's. They may hand over the money or ask someone to get them the mobile but they will not follow up or monitor its usage. They have little communication and appear to be indifferent to their child's needs, often bordering on a rejecting or negligent attitude. Uninvolved parents might just as well be non-existent in an adolescent's life, for they are simply indifferent. They won't be bothered by the mobile phone issue at all, preferring to swat it away like a fly. Children of these parents grow up without parental guidance and influence and tend to lack self-control, have low self-esteem and are less competent than their peers in all domains.

So, with these four parenting styles, it's no wonder the disciplining dilemma has so many hues. There is no right or wrong way of going about it but, judging from the problems of adolescents, we can gauge a fair idea of what *not to do*.

Shankar's overbearing mother was an authoritarian parent of the highest order – to the extent that she eventually wore him down, both physically and mentally. His father, like a partner in crime, merely tagged along with his wife's idea of bringing him up. Shankar was over-pressured to study and followed such strict schedules that slowly he started to sink. They felt that academic achievement reflected successful parenting, as many still do, and so they pushed their son over his limits. Ultimately it was his mother's comment, spoken into his ear whilst he was studying late at night, that turned him into a 'study-holic,' who studied almost continuously, only sleeping for three hours a night. You will be shocked as you read the desperate measures that some parents go to in order to push their children beyond their capacities.

If Shankar meekly obeyed, Ambika violently rebelled. She and her little sister were part of a nuclear family in which their mother was a housewife and father a bank manager. Her mother ran the house like a ship, making strict rules and discipline, so it was inevitable that Ambika was fearful of her own mother from a young age. In fact her mother's dominance was so overpowering that as a child Ambika was incapable of making her own decisions. However, as she entered adolescence, all those years of oppression suddenly turned her into a rebel.

Finally, I have included Achintya's account of his sister's life who had one of the strictest fathers I have ever come across in my career. The relationship between his parents and sister had a great impact on the eventual outcome. I hope that parents with adolescent daughters who have brought them up in a rigid environment where they have been given no freedom whatsoever will take heed. For, as you will read, his sister paid the biggest price for her father's unbelievably stringent method of parenting.

Shankar

The board exams were not very far away. Class 12 students would soon be given a few months break in which to revise. Having been the school counsellor for a good few years, I had seen many batches of students climb up the ladder, class by class, until they reached Class 12. I had seen Shankar grow up from a cute baby-faced kid in Class 7 to a pubescent croaky-voiced teen in Class 10 and now to a young man in Class 12, but when he walked into my room that day, I was in for quite a shock. The radiance of youth was gone and instead here was a gaunt and thin person, almost skeletal, with dark eyes deeply sunken into the sockets.

'Shankar?!' I exclaimed 'I hardly recognised you!'

He hastily took a seat, but there was no smile on his face – just anguish.

'Yes ma'am, it's me. I need your help desperately. I don't know how I am going to cope!'

'Okay, fire away! Start at the very beginning, Shankar. I'm listening.'

Shankar took a deep breath and pitched forward slightly in his seat. He obviously had a lot to tell me.

'Well, my parents have always wanted me to be an engineer or doctor as most of my older cousin brothers are already in one or the other profession. So they are desperate that I become an engineer too. For that I have to score well in physics and maths. Now that there are only a few months left to go, I am studying all day. I only stop to eat....'

'Wait, wait ... what's your study schedule like?'

'I get up at 4 a.m. and study for about three hours before I go to school. Then I have a bath and breakfast and leave for school at 8 a.m. After school, I go straight for tuition till about 7 p.m., after which I come home and settle down again at 8 p.m. after tea. Mum calls me for dinner at about 10 p.m. and I study again from 10.30 p.m. till 1 a.m. Then I'm up again at 4 a.m.'

'How long have you been doing this routine?'

'For two months or so.'

I did a quick mental calculation.

'So, apart from the time you are in school, you are studying for almost ten hours a day, including tuition time....'

'Yes ma'am, but when I leave school in a couple of weeks, I'll be able to study for even more hours...'

Even more hours? No wonder this boy was beginning to look like a skeleton. He was pushing himself to his limit and there were still a few more months to go till the exams. I seriously began to think that he'd suffer a breakdown even before the boards.

'Wait a minute Shankar, this study schedule of yours is too intense. You are looking totally worn out. You're only human. You won't be able to keep this up. Your body will give up…'

'Ma'am, I have to do well. I just *have* to. My parents will be totally depressed if I don't make it to engineering college.'

'But you're only sleeping for *three* hours a night!'

'I'm getting used to it but I'm very tired all day. You see ma'am, if I don't get 90 per cent….'

Suddenly he stopped talking and looked down. I was quick to pick up on his abrupt mid-sentence halt. 'You were saying … if you don't get 90 per cent …. then what?' I asked, scrutinising him intently. He remained silent for a few moments and kept his eyes downcast. Since I knew Shankar from a young age, there was an emotional connection stemming from a familiarity he couldn't ignore.

'Look at me Shankar,' I said in a firm tone.

He slowly brought his eyes up to mine. I held his stare, without wavering. 'Now tell me, what will happen if you don't score 90 per cent? Has someone threatened you?'

He took a deep breath and leant in a little closer, as if he wanted to tell me a secret. 'If I don't get 90 per cent, my mother said that she'd commit suicide,' he said, his voice now barely a whisper. His eyes had welled up now and he was trying hard not to cry.

Inside my head, a hundred bells clanged. Being a mother myself, I immediately saw why he was working himself to the bone. It was because he loved his mother and her threat had fuelled this obsessive desire to excel. Losing a parent was every child's nightmare, but what mother would resort to emotional blackmail to push him to the brink of his capability?

I was silent for a few seconds, completely flummoxed as to what to say next. It was beyond belief that a mother could be so cruel. Though I kept calm, I remember feeling sparks of anger. I had to arrange an urgent meeting with his parents. The image of Shankar in front of me was pathetic. My heart softened. Poor kid. 'Mothers say that sometimes, Shankar, but they don't mean it. Try and forgive her.'

'How can I forgive her when she hasn't apologised? She hasn't told me that she didn't mean it. In fact, I know she meant it.'

'How do you know?'

'I know by gut instinct. It was the *way* she said it. It was late, maybe about 11 o'clock last night, whilst I was studying. She came into my room and quietly whispered it in my ear. Her tone was deadly serious.'

The depth of pain he felt was clear in the way he buried his face in his hands, with his shoulders hunched forwards, and wept.

There have been moments in my career which have remained transfixed in my mind. Moments I see again, even years afterwards, which still bring a lump to my throat. This was one of them. His utter desolation juxtaposed with his helplessness to avoid a situation that he never ever wanted to happen, still makes me feel so sad. I felt my stomach shrivel in disgust. What kind of a mother could burden her child with such a threat? I had to meet her.

'I'd like to meet your mother, Shankar, as soon as possible.'

'Okay ma'am,' he replied quietly. 'They'll be free tomorrow.'

I looked at him with the tenderness of a mother towards her son. 'I want you to come too, Shankar. We'll sort this out. Don't worry.'

Shankar didn't say anything. He seemed relieved. He wiped his eyes and managed a weak smile before he said a quiet goodbye.

The following day, Shankar and his parents came to school and turned up to my room. I asked Shankar to leave for a little while I talked to them alone first. After a few moments of pleasant superficial chat, we entered more personal territory and, rather strangely, the conversation veered towards another direction; it had nothing to do with Shankar at all! The issue was actually deeply ingrained and had festered even before his birth. Poor Shankar was merely a pawn in the game. His parents told me that theirs was a joint family where Shankar's cousins and uncles were intelligent and highly qualified, mostly being either doctors or engineers. The expectation that any child born to that family would follow suit existed even before the poor child was born. When Shankar was born, his mother wanted to keep up with this so-called 'tradition' and prove to her parents-in-laws and sisters-in-laws that he was going to be just as good and capable as any of the others. In fact, during the course of conversation, the mother confessed that she'd had some problems with her in-laws initially after marriage. So there were some deep-set underlying reasons for the totally irrational pressure on her son. With only a few months to go till the board exams, the mother's desperation was getting more and more frenzied. She was no longer the level-headed adult she once was and was resorting to drastic measures to push her son; indeed the threat of suicide had seemed like a great motivator.

'…but would you *really* do it?' I asked her.

An embarrassed smile came to her lips. 'Well no, I wouldn't, but I had to get him to push himself to his limits didn't I?'

The smirk on her face made me see red. She was playing with his life to prove a point to her family. She was so selfish that she failed to recognise how it might affect him.

'Don't you realise that what you said to your son was probably the most frightening thing he had ever heard in his life? Can you even imagine the trauma he has been going through since you said it?' My voice was raised, my eyes bored into her. I was angry and I couldn't help it. I continued. 'What's more, if Shankar continues studying in this intense manner, where he's hardly getting any sleep, he will burn out. It's just a matter of time till he breaks down from total mental and physical exhaustion, mark my words! He'll be in hospital even before the exams start!'

They were silent. I know I sounded harsh, but I said what I felt to be true. I wondered if she understood, so I thought of a housewife's analogy: 'He's like a pressure cooker. He'll burst if he carries on like this!' I added as a last nail in the coffin.

Shankar's father had been listening quietly all along. He was the more passive of the two and his presence served as a buffer for the conflicting opinions between me and his wife. 'So what do you suggest we do, Mrs Agarwala?' asked his father rather politely, possibly a little intimidated. I inhaled deeply, mentally counted to three, and exhaled slowly. I felt calmer instantly. 'I have a strategy in my mind but without your support, I will be unable to help Shankar.'

'No, no. Now that you have told us how serious this can become, we will support you,' affirmed the father.

I looked at the mother. She nodded.

'Well, first of all, I need you both to accept that you have indirectly put your son under undue pressure – both physically and mentally.'

They nodded in unison, but the mother was quick to add: 'But *we* haven't done it ourselves. He himself has chosen to study hard.'

She just wasn't getting the point. 'It's because of your expectations *and threats* that he's pushing himself to make it.'

'Okay, okay if that's how you see it.'

'Then secondly, I want you to remove him from the game of one-upmanship that exists in your family. Please tell your family that your son may actually be the first one who does something different from being an engineer or a doctor and you both are supportive of whatever he wishes to be. That will ease the pressure off him and you both - especially you,' I said looking directly at the mother. 'Thirdly I will be guiding Shankar to work out a sensible timetable where he studies *and* gets sufficient sleep. I hope you both will cooperate. In fact, I request your cooperation.'

They nodded instantly. 'We didn't realise the problem was so severe,' admitted the father.

My next request was directed at the mother. I was giving her a hard time, but her attitude would have eventually been the cause of her son's downfall. 'But before we even implement our strategy there's something more urgent I need you to do.'

Her eyebrows lifted in surprise. 'What is it?' she asked.

'I need you to tell Shankar that you will NOT be committing suicide. Please reassure him that you were not serious. I'll call him in now.' They looked at each other guiltily.

'Shankar!' I called out, 'You can come in now…'

He walked in, looking mildly shy. He was a young man now, his upper lip covered in a soft downy moustache, but he still had a childish manner. He sat down on the spare chair positioned at a right angle to mine. It must have been unusual for him to have his parents on his right and his counsellor on the left, but we represented the 'golden triangle' crucial to mediation in student counselling.

'*Baba, moi ene koisilu. (Son, I didn't mean what I said)*' said the mother smoothing down her son's hair with the palm of her hand.

He looked at her, his eyes widening. 'You promise, Ma?'

'Yes, I promise….and your Ma'am is the witness…' she smiled.

Tears welled up in their eyes. It was a poignant mother-son moment.

'And you'll never say anything like that again, right Ma?'

'No, I won't. I'm sorry,' she whispered.

The father looked on and swallowed. He didn't cry but I could tell he was moved. I broke the moment.

'So, now that that's cleared, Shankar I want you and I to work together to get a proper study schedule sorted out, one in which you get at least six to eight hours sleep per night. Please come to me tomorrow. I think today's session is heavy enough already!' We all laughed together. The mood lightened. They got up to leave – mother, father and son – in an obviously cheerier demeanour than when they entered.

With the three of us in regular touch and working together, there was a marked change in Shankar. His physical health improved drastically and his face lost his earlier pallor after his schedule was changed. Thankfully, his parents were cooperative and interactive; they called me from time to time to ask about his progress. By the time he appeared for his boards, he was as best prepared as he could be. Shankar eventually secured 83 per cent which was a very respectable score. Unfortunately he didn't make it to engineering college that year and decided to take a gap year. Luckily he got a seat at an engineering college the following year after appearing for their entrance exams. And, you'd be happy to hear that I spoke to the mother around that time; she was still very much alive and rejoicing in her son's imminent admission.

Ambika

Ambika had always been an obedient student. Impeccable in her manners and immaculately dressed, she was thought to be *the* model student. However, a strange metamorphosis had begun to take hold of her as she entered Class 8 and it was even more pronounced now that she was in Class 9: her behaviour had started to become more and more rowdy. She would talk and laugh in the library classes without a care in the world, something she wouldn't dare have done when she was younger. She started to wear kajal around her eyes and black nail polish. She had pierced her ears herself at least three times in each earlobe. Even her skirt was hitched higher up than her friends. She would deliberately scuff her shoes by walking through the dirt tracks and she wore her tie loosely hanging from the collar. Her hair, which had always been neatly combed and clipped back, now had a long fringe which hid half her face as she walked down the corridor with her head slightly cocked to the side. Everything about her spelled 'REBEL'. Her class teacher was mystified by this dramatic change and came to see me.

'I don't know what has happened to Ambika! The other day she even answered back rudely to the Geography teacher!'

'What do you know about her home life? Have there been any big changes?' I asked.

'No there haven't, as far I know, but maybe you can find out. Can I send her to you?'

When Ambika came to me, she took the opportunity to pop a piece of chewing gum into her mouth in the few minutes it took her to walk from her classroom to my room. By the time she had arrived, she had already taken it out of her mouth and, having found no place to throw it away, securely attached it under the chair on which she sat opposite me; I only discovered the chewed piece of gum much later.

When she sat down I saw a girl who was outwardly a total non-conformist. She didn't seem to care about anything or anyone. Her anti-authority attitude was very apparent. It wasn't long before she confessed that she didn't like being told what to do, especially by her mother.

'I hate rules. At home, mum makes stupid rules all the time and at school, some the rules are even more stupid! I've had enough! I'm sick of them!'

I was amused. A twinkle came to my eyes. 'Tell me about your home rules, Ambika.'

'I don't know why mom is so strict! When she was a little girl, she said she went to a convent so I think that's why she wants to run our home like a convent! She's a *total* control freak! We have timings for everything – from study times, dining times, bathroom times – even sleep times! She doesn't let me wear what I want or go out with my friends. I can't play my music player loudly, I can't put posters up in my room. I don't even have a mobile, for God's sake!'

'Hmm … so your mum is pretty much the ruler of the household, huh?

'More like the Hitler of the house! It's not much to ask. I just want to be free. I want to do things my way. Mom has had her way too long.'

'Have you told your father about your mother's behaviour?'

'Nah … no point … dad is totally henpecked by her…'

'So do you have big arguments with your mother about this?'

Her eyes rolled upwards as if what I was asking was a silly question. 'Yes, we have HUGE rows where there's lots of shouting and screaming. Sometimes I even throw things and slam the doors. One time last week I answered her back and so she slapped me but it didn't do any good. I still keep answering her back…'

She had a smug look on her face, as if the memory of her defiance was a small victory for her.

'Do you argue every day?'

'Yeah, practically every day. I'm just so sick of it, that I just don't care anymore.'

Sometimes when rules are so stringent, a sense of unfairness dominates many adolescents' thinking and they will cease to follow them. Whether they rebel sneakily underground or, like Ambika openly revolt, the fact is they are showing their intolerance to the idea of feeling obliged to follow rules, even though the rules per se may seem to be quite rational. Parents fall into the trap of thinking that their child will blindly follow their rules and do whatever they say, but that ideology doesn't necessarily exist anymore. Treating them like little children rather than budding adults simply alienates them and adds to their defiance.

Thankfully Ambika was not afraid to show that she was beyond angry. When emotions are blatant, the problems and the solutions are easier to spot and investigate. Understated unexpressed emotions, that hide the real wrath of bitterness, camouflage the depth of the problem.

'Okay Ambika, I can see you're pretty peeved off. What would make you happier?'

'I just want mom to lay off a bit and let me make my own rules for a change. I know I'd do okay.'

'Yes but surely some of her rules are okay?'

'It's not that. My point is why does *she* have to make all the rules that are to do with me?'

Being a mother myself, it was my instinct to say '*because she's your mum*' – but better judgment prevailed! In fairness to her, she did have a point but she had become so adamant that she wasn't willing to listen to anyone who opposed her opinion. The real root of the problem lay in her mother's inability to loosen her hold on her daughter. So I decided that I had to talk to her mother. Was she really such a dragon? I wondered.

'Ok, so can I talk to you mum on the phone tonight?'

'Yeah, if you think she'll chill a bit. But I doubt it, she's a hard woman. I'm beginning to hate calling her my mother....'

On the surface it may have seemed that Ambika's case could be solved by simply allowing her to make some of her own rules but actually the issue was deeper: this had turned into a full-on power battle between her and her mother and, because neither was willing to give in, they were always at loggerheads. To be fair to her mother, it can't have been easy for her to accept that she was losing control of Ambika, especially when everything had been fine for so many years. It was a vicious circle: the more frustrated the mother, the greater her impulsive anger towards her daughter and the greater her daughter's rebellion.

When I spoke to Ambika's mother on the phone, the first impression I got was that she was very forthright so I knew where Ambika was coming from when she said she was like Hitler. She dominated the conversation from the very beginning, hardly allowing me space to get my words in; she must have been extremely domineering by nature. She bluntly told me that being her mother *she* knew what was right for Ambika and that all she needed were some good tight slaps to straighten her out! There was no point in trying to convince her with any alternative way of thinking. She was behaving like an adult replica of her own daughter! I decided this issue was better discussed face-to-face and asked her to come to school.

What surprised me when she came was that she was a small woman, hardly the big feisty woman I was expecting! After a few minutes of conversation, I felt she began to trust that I genuinely wanted things to work out between her and her daughter. She started to let go of her tough attitude and began to talk to me with some softness. Surprisingly, I could empathise with her angle on the whole issue too. It turned out that Ambika's mother was a housewife and her whole identity was defined by how she was bringing up her daughters. Since she was a stay-at-home mum, the only place where she was in control was in the home. This was her domain and everything ran according to her wishes and quite smoothly too.

'This is how I've managed the house for so many years. It's always been fine – but I just can't understand what's got into Ambika. She was never like this before!'

'Maybe, she's just growing up, maybe she needs less rules....'

Sensing that I was speaking on Ambika's behalf, her eyes grew bigger in surprise as if I'd said something absurd. 'We've all grown up Mrs Agarwala – as if Ambika is the only one!'

'Yes, I agree – but things have changed a bit since you and I were children, haven't they?'

'Whatever, Ambika should understand that she's still a child and that I know what's best for her!'

We seemed to be hitting a wall. Ambika's mother had gone back to her overpowering self. Now that I tried to show her Ambika's perspective, she was not easy to talk to. Her headstrong disposition gave me the clues to the crux of the problem. She had very staunch ideas of discipline and only saw the world in black and white. I felt that that was the first obstacle we needed to overcome, so that she could see the shades of grey present in the situation. There had to be a redefinition of barriers so that they could amicably decide upon and set new ones. Unless a third non-biased person entered the equation, it was destined to become a downward spiral. Ambika's rebellious streak sprung from this rigid world of rules and, unless I tried to mediate quickly, Ambika's defiance would go on increasing.

'Look, the thing is this: these issues between you and Ambika won't disappear unless you *both* listen to each other's wants. There's no point you forcing her do what you want by threatening her or hitting her. It just won't work. And from the reports I am getting from the teachers, your once well-behaved girl is now becoming more and more uncontrollable in school too!'

The mother quieted down a little when she realised that the school had also noticed Ambika's behavioural changes. 'Yes, I can see what you are saying but are you expecting me to bow down to my daughter? There's *no way* I'm going to do that!'

'It's not about bowing down to anyone. It's not about pride. It's about respecting her wishes and making compromises. It's not about winning or losing. It's simply about living peacefully!' I laughed. That seemed to relax her.

'I try so hard. What else do I have in my life except my family? I am willing to listen to her – but only if she stops being so rude to me!'

'She's rude because she feels you treat her like a kid. She's actually much more mature than you think.'

Maybe it takes someone else to make us realise that our children have grown up and moved into another phase of development. In our earnest struggle to discipline our children, we may fail to appreciate the invisible boundary line between childhood and adolescence because it varies from child to child. I believe we can sense it by our interactions with our teen, a certain psychological and emotional maturity which wasn't there before. If we are not tuned to this change, we fail to allow leeway for the mental changes that an adolescent goes through and, as a result, often continue to treat them in the same way. This is not to say they no longer need guidance, it just has to be handled in a more adult manner, with discussion, negotiation, and understanding of the conflicting needs of maturing teens.

'So, let's talk together – all three of us – and try to make some changes. Hopefully, there'll be some peace in your household!'

There followed a long session of heated discussions between them where I sat and acted as the mediator. The first thing I wanted to do was instill a sense of mutual respect. For that, the mother had to give Ambika trust. She needed to understand that left to her own devices, Ambika may not be such a bad controller of her own life after all. I tried to tell her mother that while she may feel that anything Ambika does is her business, to help her become a young adult, she must grant her some privacy. We were able to piece together a rough outline of Do's and Don'ts which both reluctantly agreed to follow as a trial run for a week. At the end of the session, a game plan was devised which both promised to adhere to because they both wanted to overcome this hitch in the daughter-mother relationship.

A week went by and though it took time for them to put it all into practice, they slowly gave each other more space and respect. Their problems were gradually becoming easier to handle and the atmosphere at home became more harmonious. Once Ambika's mother started to talk to her nicely, asked her opinions on things and accepted that her daughter was a new individual with her own wants, needs, tastes and preferences, the entire situation changed for the better.

Achintya

I knew Achintya had a serious problem as soon as I saw his face. He was unshaven and looked as if he hadn't slept for days. He'd been absent for at least a week and only came into school in order to speak to me, on doctor's advice. He was already taking sleeping tablets and tranquilisers to help calm his frayed nerves but his doctor suggested he also seek counselling to cope with his emotional turmoil. Since he was in Class 12 and was familiar with me as the school counsellor, he came to my room in the hope I would be able to ease his mind. Indeed, Achintya had a very sad story to tell and though it didn't concern him directly, it affected him deeply and I knew it would put a scar on his life. I can still recall the conversation quite clearly because of its pathetic nature and I distinctly remember how I couldn't stop my own tears from flowing just as he finished telling me. By the end, there were no questions for me to ask. In fact I don't remember speaking much at all but I do remember listening intently. The cause behind the unfortunate outcome was so clear that once he'd finished telling me, I had no comments to make. I was lost for words. I simple had a heaviness in my heart that stayed with me for the rest of the day.

'Ma'am, my big sis Subhadra was only six years older to me but she always treated me like a baby brother. She was beautiful and slim with long hair down to her waist. Didi always did thoughtful things like bringing me a chocolate bar whenever she came back from college. She was very protective of me especially when our mum scolded me. I grew to depend on Didi for advice and support through my own niggly problems at school and she always listened and advised me on what to do. She was like a mother figure to me.'
He spoke slowly but articulately and, every now and again, stopped to take a breath and recollect his thoughts as the memories came flooding back.

'But ma'am, Didi had problems of her own. Our father was very strict and ruled the house with an iron hand. Strangely, he was not so strict with me and I was allowed out on my own to go to the shops, tuitions or the bus stop but Didi never did. She was always accompanied by my mother wherever she went. Every evening over dinner Dad would ask Mum about Didi's behaviour and Mum would duly and meekly report the day's events from the morning to the evening. Mum was so terrified of Dad that she could never speak out against something he said or even express her opinion about what she thought. Dad was simply the overall master of the house and what he said or did, was final. None of us ever opposed him. I know for sure that Didi disliked him and hated that she was constantly supervised. She had no freedom or privacy. Things that most teens her age took for granted like speaking to her friends on the phone or even having her own bedroom were a far-off dream. She often told me about it but there was nothing I could do to help her. I suppose many parents worry about the welfare of their daughters more than their sons but my parents were so strict with Didi that they dictated what she should wear, who she could speak to, where she could go, what foods were good for her, what she could watch on TV, even what time she should sleep. Didi had no identity because she never expressed herself. It was if she had totally lost herself in the swamp of their rules.'

The circumstances were being more and more defined. I was getting a picture of the home environment in my mind. It was turning out to be like a prison where Subhadra, like an inmate, had no liberties of her own.

'Often Didi would get slapped by Dad for something she wore and she slowly learned not to disobey him because whenever she did, she suffered for it. So she never wore western clothes like jeans and T-shirts anymore nor even sleeveless kameezes that showed off her bare arms. She never wore anything tight that revealed the shape of her figure and always covered herself up with her dupatta whenever she went out with Mum. She knew what was expected of her but, even so, sometimes she slipped up. I remember once when we were having dinner, Mum mentioned that Didi hugged her friends goodbye. One of them was a boy and this sent Dad into a rage. His eyes bulged out of their sockets as he slapped her hard across the face with the hand he was eating with. I can still hear the resounding sound and can still see Didi's instant recoil as silent tears rolled down her cheek, smeared with grease and a few rice grains from his palm as he struck her. But it didn't stop there, ma'am. He then flung her plate off the table in a single swipe, the clang of the steel plate against the floor tiles making me cringe as her food was now a mess on the floor. He then grabbed her hair with his greasy hand, twisted his clenched fist so that he had a better grip of the clump of hair and spoke to her menacingly. With pursed lips he told her that if she ever dared to speak to, let alone touch, another boy again, he would kill her.'

He paused for a moment and then spoke quietly. The memories were talking now.

'That night Didi remained numb. She didn't even talk to me. She quietly went to sleep next to my mum, as she always did. From my mum's eyes and composure I could tell she totally agreed with my dad and must've felt that Didi deserved the treatment, so there were no comforting words or kindness from her.'

Achintya coughed slightly and cleared his throat. He took a sip of water from the glass on the table. It was as if by telling me all this, he was seeing it all again from another angle. This time, because he was relating what happened to someone else, he realised things he didn't notice before.

'Ever since that incident ma'am, Didi kind of closed up. It was like a turning point. Dad had hit her countless times before so it wasn't the physical violence that changed her. We realised why much later. Unbeknown to us at the time, that boy she had hugged was actually her boyfriend and somehow after that day, she was never the same again. She would talk only when she had to and did everything she was told without question. She never smiled, never laughed and what was worse was that she stopped confiding in me. Yes ma'am, from this point onwards, there was a change in Didi…'

'When was this, Achintya?'

'About two years ago. She was in her second year at college. What I don't understand is how, in spite of all these restrictions surrounding her, she managed to be involved in a relationship with a guy. I guess love somehow wedged itself between them and connected them. She continued to be emotionally cut off from us all for at least a year after that. Once she graduated, she got a job and started working and then, one evening, as we were seated at the dining table, Didi dropped the bombshell.'

I was riveted. Even though Achintya and I were in a counselling session, I was so rapt by the way he was talking that, for most of the time, I kept quiet. He spoke with so much clarity and ease that the sequence of events unfolded effortlessly in front of my eyes. What's more, he spoke with feeling and quiet reflection. It wasn't as if he was just telling me a story. By introspecting and analyzing the entire saga in this way, it was somehow slotting itself neatly into his mind so that it made sense.

'In spite of being petrified of my dad, I don't know how she managed to say what she did. She announced that she had a boyfriend and wanted to marry him. I stopped eating because I felt a flurry of nerves well up in my stomach. I knew my dad would probably kill her tonight itself. But you know what, he didn't. Just as I was shocked by Didi's s confession, I was equally shocked by my dad's reaction. He shouted at her and insulted her character and then told her he was disowning her. He wanted her out of his house by morning. He said he didn't want to see her face again. Mum just sat there wide-eyed because we all understood the implications of what was happening: Didi was going to leave us and, most frighteningly, sever all links with us. Didi stood up and stoically walked out of the room. I had never seen her behave like that. You could hear a pin drop in the house, it was so silent. She went to the bedroom, packed a few things and, after half an hour or so, she opened the front door carrying a single cloth bag in her hand. There was an autorickshaw already waiting outside. Without saying a word to anyone she walked quietly went out and closed the door behind her. I remember running out of my bedroom, out of the house and down the front path as fast as I could to say goodbye....'

Achintya stopped at this point, too overcome to continue. He looked down and pressed on his closed eyelids with his fingers. The memory of his sister leaving the home forever was too painful to express vocally. We remained in silence for at least a minute while he collected his thoughts and was able to continue.

'I remember seeing her eyes, ma'am. They were glistening with tears but she was strong. There was a resilience about her which I'd never seen before. She must've just had enough. She told me not to worry about her, that she'd be fine, that she'd be in touch with me. She told me to be good and to study hard. The autorickshaw started its droning engine and sped away. That was the last I saw of her. Coming back into the house felt like I was walking into a ghost house. My mum was in bed crying silently under the covers. My father was locked in his bedroom. I think none of us could fathom the enormity of what had happened that evening and how significant an event it was in the journey of our respective lives.'

'We didn't hear from Didi for the next few days but she called my mum to tell her she was fine. A week later she came to school and met me at the gates when school was over. She was wearing a sari and I couldn't believe it was her because she had never worn a sari in the daytime before. I had always seen her dressed like that for weddings. The moment I saw her, I knew there had been a dramatic change in her life: she was wearing sindoor in the parting of her hair; she had got married. She told me that there were hardly any people at their temple wedding, just a few close friends and a couple of relatives from the groom's side. It was no big deal, she said, and she wanted me to tell Mum and Dad that she was now a married woman and would never trouble them anymore.'

'I remember walking home that day with a heavy heart. All those times I had thought we would have a grand wedding for her and this is what really happened. Such were the ironies of life! When I told my parents, the only thing my father said to my mum is to think that she was dead, that she no longer existed and to focus only on their one child from now on: me. So, in a matter of two weeks, our family of four became one of three. No longer was she talked about or referred to anymore, at least not in front of my dad.'

'What about your mum?'

'Mum was in a no-win situation. She was forbidden to contact Didi and if Dad ever found out she did, he would have thrown her out. So she had no choice really. She kept the peace at home by keeping quiet, though I often saw her crying for no reason.'

It was indeed a tragic story. Subhadra had been cut off from her family for following her heart. Even though she had led a life of total subjugation, finally when her own wants became stronger than her need to obey, she didn't listen to her authoritarian father. He too reacted fiercely by ostracizing her from their lives, leaving a gaping hole in Achintya and his mum's heart.

'But ma'am, that's not all. There's worse news. About ten days ago, we got a call from the police station asking us to identify a suicide victim. They had found out her home address and details from her identity card. Fearing the worst, my parents were too shell-shocked to go, so they sent me. When I arrived at the hospital, I was taken to the morgue and as they lifted off the sheet....'

He couldn't go on. Gasps of loud sobs pulsed through his body.

'DIDI!!! DIDI!!!' he screamed into the air with glazed eyes, 'WHY??? WHY??'

I was quiet. I didn't know what to say. I swallowed involuntarily.

'She had strangled herself. People in the locality had told me she was often heard crying after her husband beat her at night. But ma'am while I feel bad enough for that, what makes me feel so utterly grief-stricken is that she couldn't even turn to us in her hour of need. My dad's strictness and attitude had taken its toll on her. She knew she couldn't come home and so no one saved her. This is what I can't forgive my dad for. It's all his fault. Even I couldn't do anything! If my parents had brought her up with some freedom of her own and given her the security to know that she could always turn to them if she needed them, I know Didi would still be alive today. They kicked her out and slammed the door on her. What hope did she have?'

'I'm so so sorry Achintya,' was all I could say. I wiped a tear.

He looked at me. Seeing me overcome, he sighed. 'Well ma'am, you know it has helped me a lot by telling you all this. Thank you so much. It feels as if I've unburdened myself. I think I'll need a few more of these sessions, ma'am. They're helping to cleanse my mind and sort my thoughts out.'

'Sure Achintya, please do come again next week.'

Indeed he did, and for a few more weeks at that. Achintya recovered from this huge ordeal by coming to terms with what happened. No longer a young child now, he slowly started talking about Subhadra at home and slowly through many months, his dad began to acknowledge that perhaps he had been too stringent with his deceased daughter during her childhood and adolescence. During another counselling session a month later, Achintya told me:

'You know ma'am, one day I'm sure I will be a father to a daughter but I will never ever treat her the way my dad treated my Didi. I know I can't do anything about Didi's death now but I promise that her death will never go in vain because nothing like that will ever happen in my family again.'

Raising children who are self-reliant, cooperative, and considerate is a challenging process. We all toe a fine line in knowing how much or how little to discipline our teens and it's not always easy to know if we are doing the right thing every time. Someone once likened strictness in parenting to flying a kite: if you hold the string too tightly, it may cause it to snap; too loose and it might get out of control. Indeed, the right amount of tautness in holding the string is analogous to the right amount of discipline in handling your teen. Your firmness of hold will depend on *your* children, in the environment of *your* own home but even so, as you have read, some parents let go too soon or hold on too tightly for too long, thus losing control of their child either way. Let's take heed of their stories so that we can glean deeper insight into how to adjust our own sails to the winds of our parenting journey.

Checklist

Somewhere during early adolescence, our emphasis must slowly switch from protecting to preparing, from lecture to discussion, and from dependence to independence. This is the crux of disciplining during adolescence. However, watch out for signs that suggest your adolescent is internally angry because anger is the first emotional response to feeling a sense of injustice. Introspect within yourself to see if their feelings are justified.

Red Flags to watch out for

- Shouting or screaming at you quite often, even in front of others
- Thinking nothing of physically hitting you during an angry outburst
- Doing the opposite of what you say
- Refusing outright to do something important for you, even if they can
- Defying your rules with a daring look in their eyes
- Conversely, meekly abiding by everything you say in an automated, unhappy way
- Dressing in ways that they know irk you with a smirk on their face
- Using language, especially slang and swear words, that they know you don't like/use
- Lying easily
- Making up elaborate far-fetched stories
- Showing no regard for things that are personal and special to you (either living or inanimate)
- Indulging in anti-social habits and not caring that you know
- No regard for the home or treating it like a hotel

- Taking you for granted:
  - Invading your privacy, for example, looking into your purse/bag/cupboard without asking you first
  - Blaming you for when something goes wrong, even if it's not your fault
  - Demanding more money than they need for vague reasons
  - Making you feel that, as a parent, you owe them what they want
  - Making you feel guilty for not giving them what they want
  - Not showing remorse about hurting your sentiments
  - Not offering to assist you when you are working and they are lounging around doing nothing
  - Going out without telling you
  - Showing no gratitude/appreciation for kindly acts that you have done for them

What you can do

The checklist above consists of signs that suggest that there is a serious breakdown in respect in the adolescent-parent bond. Thankfully, this is not irreversible and can be rectified through mutual understanding, once you are both on the same level. Just remember that unless there are boundaries, consequences, discipline, consistency and rewards which are agreeable to teens and parents, there will be more friction than you desire!

✓ Start to shift your style from the lecture method to the discussion method in enforcing rules. Once your child becomes a teen, be a 'guide' not an 'enforcer'. For example, tell them *why* they have to study as opposed to just telling them they *have* to.
✓ Give more age appropriate independence and assertiveness.
✓ Don't stare over their shoulder during study time or have exam schedules planned out for them. Give them the opportunity to create their own rules and open your flexible mind to try and accept it within reason. This teaches them responsibility towards themselves.
✓ Consistency and predictability are the cornerstones of discipline and praise is the most powerful reinforcement for learning. So:
  - Decide on rules and consequences in advance. For example, lay down various penalties for breaking rules such as confiscation, grounding from going out, reduced pocket money, less internet use, suspension or delay of a privilege or outing, etc.

- offer positive reinforcement and support when your child follows the rules.

✓ Positive disciplining implies logical consequences for misbehaviour. If, for example, your teen argues with you about the use of the remote control and will not compromise, turn off the television. If your teen breaks something in anger, have them pick up the pieces and replace it with their own pocket money or withdraw a privilege. Next time they can control their anger, remember to praise them for being more in control.

✓ When you enforce disciplinary measures, don't disengage from your adolescent emotionally. This communicates that you'll be 'with' them as long as they don't do anything wrong.

✓ Make sure your teen doesn't think that you only love them when they're 'right' and won't when they are 'wrong'. Let them know that you love them when they are wrong too. This is especially important with regards to doing badly in exams.

✓ Don't yell for small infractions because your teen will become immune to over-blown reactions and will fail to take it seriously when you really do mean it. It's better to intercept the moment by walking away before you over-react and come back when you're calmer.

✓ Never set disciplinary consequences out of anger. Calm down first.

✓ Don't openly ignore your teen after an altercation. Keeping quiet and ignoring are two different things! The latter will only stir them to anger which they might act on by finding attention elsewhere. If you have to, do it for yourself to reach a sense of normality, not because you want to teach them a lesson. It should not last more than one minute of every year of their life. So 15 minutes time-out for you, for your 15-year-old teen.

✓ If your teen shouts at you in public, resist the urge to shout back because s/he might embarrass you further. Rather, it's better to do one of three things till you have a proper conversation: ignore till you are alone with your teen, walk away or politely ask him/her to stop being rude. Whatever you decide, remember you are stopping the situation from getting worse.

✓ Try and find out the inner cause of why they reacted like that but tell them that whatever the reason, it doesn't excuse their public rudeness.

✓ Don't frown upon their gestures or activities in public. This shows you rule over them and that's the best way to lose their respect.

✓ Listen wisely when they speak out. For example, if they say: 'You are *always* right,' they actually mean 'I am the one who is always wrong.' See it from their perspective.

✓ Use good manners to each other at home.

✓ Nobody's perfect. Notice when you take out your bad day on your teen. Take some time out and inform your family not to disturb you for a while. This will send the message that frustrations can be handled through positive behaviour.

✓ Admit it when you're wrong. When you do, you diffuse the reason to argue, bury the wrongdoing and move on to solve the real issue. Stubbornly fighting on wastes time and breath.

✓ When you show that admitting to being wrong doesn't make you small or makes you lose your dignity, your teen will be able to do the same in due course.

✓ Be friendly but don't try to be your teen's friend. Do not abdicate your authority over your teen. Direction, guidance, limits and structure (which are necessary to keep teens on track) can only be established through clear parental boundaries.

✓ Many parents view the good deeds they do for their kids as simply part of the job. Insist on your teen showing appreciation for what you do for them. For example, every so often when you've gone out of way, tell them: 'I'd really like to hear a 'thank you', please?' Make sure you're *not* taken for granted.

✓ Youths desire relationships with calm, confident, and competent adults from whom they can gain acceptance, understanding, guidance, and a sense of commonality.

✓ When you buy anything for your teen, tell them how hard you worked to earn the money to buy it. Never let them feel that life is so easy and can be led without hard work and being lazy.

✓ Give unconditional love regardless of what they do. Make it very clear that it's their behaviour you may disapprove of but never compromise on love.

✓ Allow your teen to solve their own problems, feelings and behaviours because they need to learn how to fix them themselves. Be informed about the problem and its progress but don't own it. Advise at your discretion but allow your teen to make the final choice.

✓ Don't be afraid of seeing your teen go through pain. We are sometimes too quick to rescue our teen from their discomfort, thus keeping them from learning from their mistakes or choices. Watch from afar but only intervene if you see things spiralling downhill.

✓ Insist on your teen doing home chores, even if it's just making their bed or keeping their desk tidy.
✓ If you've tried everything you can and you feel that all else has failed and your teen doesn't seem fazed by all of the above, get help. Turn to a professional counsellor or psychologist to help mediation between you and your teen.
✓ Be patient. You will get to the other side of this word, adolescence!

Chapter 4: 'I Am Different'

For parents and teenagers alike, adolescence is an awakening, to say the least. Marked by myriad changes ranging from the physical -- shorter skirts, ripped jeans, body piercings, tattoos, spiky/long hair, makeup, dietary changes, using slang, drinking or smoking; to the emotional -- unpredictable anger outbursts, crying for no reason or being irrationally argumentative; to the simply annoying -- locked bedroom doors, hours in the bathroom, loud music, late night mobile conversations and indiscriminate time on Facebook. It's no wonder that of all the developmental stages of humans, this one is probably the most turbulent!

This stage has received much bad press and unfortunately there is no 'Code of Conduct' for a smooth transition since all parents will differ on what they consider to be 'tolerable rules'. There is an element of subjectivity as to how much parents are willing to open the 'flood gates' of their moral mindset, but if it's any consolation, most of the trends shown by teens are transient and will pass in their own time.

In our earnest desire to do the best for our child and blot out all negative habits, we come down hard on anything we consider to be wrong. However, parents should try to assess whether the antics displayed by their teen are *temporary and harmless* OR *life-changing and potentially dangerous*. If teens want more privacy in the form of their own room, texting, e-mails, and phone calls or they streak their hair, paint their fingernails black or wear funky clothes, think twice before you object. By the sheer nature of this stage, teens want to be more independent and express themselves by shocking their parents and it's a lot better to let them do something relatively *harmless and transient* than *dangerous and long term* such as smoking, taking drugs, drinking alcohol or making permanent changes – such as tattoos and piercings -- to their appearance.

That's not to say, however, that we turn a blind eye totally. We have to use our parental instincts to gauge the warning signs of something that could grow into a bigger problem. For example, if your teen is suddenly sleeping late, missing classes, not being open about introducing new friends, we may consider it to be 'normal teen behaviour' and wait until the situation is urgent, but burying our heads in the sand to avoid confrontation and overlooking more displays of our teen's belligerent, hostile attitude may be the wrong thing to do. If you notice warning signs, then you should invade your child's privacy until you get to the heart of the problem.

Sometimes however the changes that occur during adolescence are of indelible significance. Often a strong indicator of the type of person the teen is growing into, the changes I am referring to are of a more permanent nature. During adolescence, when the mind is capable of deeper introspective thinking, many teens get strong feelings of their own identity, which can include sexual orientation, religious inclinations, unusual goals and ambitions. However, if these yearnings do not conform to the norm, they are not always easily accepted by Indian parents. While teenagers in the West are mostly encouraged to express their individuality, many of their Indian counterparts remain cloistered, harbouring their secret desires and wishes deep in their heart, afraid that they will be ridiculed by their parents and labelled the 'black sheep' of the family. But then parents are often at the mercy of their family or society and, if they have children who stray away from what is considered to be 'normal', they will be frowned upon or pitied. With this double-edged sword, teens are not left with much choice. They only have two choices: either to openly rebel or bottle up their inner desires and pretend that all is fine. If it's the latter, moral fear keeps teens silent and they will inevitably end up leading double lives. This is bound to cause a wedge of emotional and psychological distance between them and their parents with an eventual breakdown in their relationship. It's ironic that freedom of expression is one of life's greatest liberties and yet it's very difficult for many Indian adolescents to truly rejoice in it.

The following case studies are all related to each other in that each student has, in some way, aspired to follow their heart, though this has not always been easy. I have chosen cases with differing circumstances and eventual outcomes though there is a consistent thread of an inner desire to be or do something different. But along with their sprouting individuality, you will notice that in each of them, there is an earnest longing for mere acceptance by the people they value most -- their parents – though it is not always met with understanding and approval. Some parents are so obsessed with what they consider to be right or wrong that they fail to understand at all. Not allowing teens to express themselves within reasonable limits will in turn bring more unrest. It's a simple concept but I have seen that this is where many parents go wrong. Smart parents will surely find some middle ground to build peace within their home.

At this point, I feel I have to diverge and tell you the true story of Tony Bosner, a father, who was also a teacher by profession. His work ethic was so engrained that he felt he was failing himself and other people if he relaxed his regimen of discipline. So when it came to the adolescence of his own son Neil, there was inevitable friction, disagreements and rows. Bosner said that his son Neil was neither rebellious nor anarchic but he still felt compelled to show contempt towards him for the rock magazines he read, the music he listened to and most importantly Neil's failure to comply with his idealised vision of a son. He said that there were periods when he didn't speak to him because of it. The saddest part of this story is that Neil was diagnosed with cancer when he was 35 and subsequently died. Today, when Bosner looks back at those adolescent years, he confesses he has some deep regrets about the way he treated his son. 'I did not give him the space to evolve; the space to become himself. I constantly strove to be principled, the father I thought I should be, trying to mould Neil into what I thought was right. How I regret it all now.'

Kedar's mother got the right idea when she listened to her son. She had been increasingly concerned about his erratic behaviour, where he would often turn violent without any reason. It took much soul searching for Kedar to find a life philosophy which finally answered the questions of his restless mind -- the root cause for his unpredictable behaviour. Though she was not very highly educated, his mother came to understand that he had found peace in the unusual faith of wicca, otherwise known as witchcraft to you or me. So passionate was he to follow the teachings that he became a witch. Most parents would reel in horror at their son becoming like Harry Potter but the surprisingly flexible response of Kedar's parents was key to them all finding some solace in a situation which, handled differently, could have led to much commotion.

I've always supported the view that if parents are willing to have an open mind without judging too quickly, very often they will find that they can see their children's perspective. Issues should be discussed in confidence between spouses – and no one else – on how you should handle the issue before putting across your perspective to your teen. Many parents hold family meetings and discussions with other family friends before even telling their adolescent and then they wonder why their teen is aggressive! If there's something that enrages them, it's when everyone else knows before they know. Teens will have much more respect for parents who carefully and confidentially explain their reasoning than those who have discussed the issues with the world and are hell bent on forcing their own way down their throats. Issues do not have to end in verbal or physical clashes. Whether parents reach a conclusion of acceptance, mutual compromise or carefully-explained rejection, it's how they put it across, not necessarily what they say. Stick to the rules of discretion, appreciation and respect and you may be pleasantly surprised.

Contrast this with Shivraj's father whose vehement objection to his son wanting to be a chef was tinged with deep shame. His sexist father was so afflicted by the stereotypical images we hold of certain jobs that he insisted his son consider an alternative career. Shivraj, on the other hand, was adamant about what he wanted to do and so they ended up at loggerheads. Eventually the father's unrelenting attitude sent Shivraj spiralling into a disappointment so bitter that it almost took a turn for the worse.

Whilst career or ambition choices are easier to accept, homosexuality still poses quite a challenge to the Indian psyche. Social acceptance is still in its infancy and even though legislation for gays has become much more positive in the last few years, it is still unpalatable to many – especially when it is *your* child or a member of *your* family. Tarita was always a tomboy and her acute reaction to a classmate's rejection was so intense that it seemed she had developed extremely strong feelings for her. Unfortunately she didn't understand why she felt so emotional and it was only a couple of years later that her reactions made sense to her. Yes, Tarita eventually realised that she was a lesbian but couldn't openly express her individuality and remained closeted, fearing that she would be ostracised from her family if they ever found out. Her story is only one of the many that I encounter regularly, but if truth be told, very rarely do gay people at the student level dare to be bold enough to 'come out'. However, in the counselling room, many students are coming forward to confess their sexuality but, until the general public can accept it as a part of life, those still underground will continue to remain in fear of society's wrath.

Kedar

There was something about Kedar that stuck out from the average student: he was extremely well read and knowledgeable, much more than his peer group. Though he looked young with his curly crop of black hair, his mental age was much older than his mere sixteen years and as a result, our conversations often veered on the philosophical. He was the quintessential thinker and when he first came to me, he wanted to know how to handle the chaos of thoughts that plagued his mind; he had even begun to get headaches. Thus began weekly 'loading off' sessions where he openly discussed his ideas and thoughts as well as shared his diary which I had asked him to maintain. As our sessions progressed, his headaches slowly ceased as he began to find outlets for his mind's energies but I understood that Kedar was naturally a deep-thinking person; he was often immersed in introspective thinking, pondering on the greater truths of life. He was constantly searching for a path of life which would give him answers to all those questions that tickled his mind.

His dabbling had led him to find his calling in the pagan religion of wicca, which involves the ritual practice of magic. For him it held all the answers he desired to know, thus bringing about a sense of peace within him. His excitement was palpable when he came and told me of what he was doing when practicing his new teachings. He seemed like a changed person, complete with a new name which he used when he practiced his new way of life.

Many wiccans believe magic to be a force of nature which makes use of the five senses we possess. As such they believe that spells can bring about real changes in the physical world. When Kedar first told me about the spells, I confess I wasn't too comfortable in hearing the details. I recall times when he told me how the previous night, he had pricked his own fingertips to extract droplets of blood which he mixed with certain herbs and leaves in order to fulfil the requirements of a particular spell successfully. He even carried a wooden wand in his pocket, special crystals and his spell book at all times. For someone who knew nothing of his new faith, he would appear to be a little eccentric and his antics peculiar but I knew that if I showed any obvious signs of disapproval towards his activities, he probably would have stopped coming to my counselling room. Any disgust emanating from my face towards his practices would have caused him to close up. By maintaining a degree of interest, I was able to keep an eye on his activities and his overall state of mind, since he was keen to tell me what he was doing and inevitably came every week.

I have to maintain a very fine balance between my personal opinion and an objective viewpoint and I am very aware of my reaction whenever a student confesses a deep secret to me. I know they put their heart on the line and it takes a lot of courage for them to open up to a secret confession. As a counsellor, it is paramount for me to keep the connection going and appear to be non-judgmental in spite of what I might be feeling inside. However, that is not to say that I wouldn't state my disapproval if I thought a student was indulging in something potentially destructive or ethically wrong. Thankfully, Kedar practiced white magic and did not resort to the gory ways of black magic where he was bringing doom to others. However, I was aware that if word got round and fell on the wrong ears, he could easily be misunderstood and become a target for discrimination, so it was imperative that his new inclinations were kept under wraps.

Another reason why I didn't show any displeasure was because there was an obvious change in Kedar's disposition. His persistent frowning face with the creased forehead disappeared. He smiled and there was a sense of calm about him now; he was not the agitated, fretful Kedar of earlier. He always seemed to walk with a spring in his step and seemed content in life.

Counselling aims to bring a sense of peace through either resolution or closure and I felt that Kedar would have been far unhappier without this new-found spiritual guidance that he had discovered. I felt it was not harming him and as such knew not to take it too seriously because it was a good outlet for his ticking mind. Ironically, he was performing better in class tests too. Nevertheless I felt that, just as I was monitoring what he was doing, he also needed a confidante in his home environment because there was a very fine line between what he was doing now and its progression to a more sinister level.

Whenever I counsel students who are engaging in activities that could have negative repercussions on them, my first question is always to ask if their parents are aware of what they are doing. Very often parents are in the dark about their teen's activities but flexible parents with open mindsets will be the most understanding in situations such as these. If the parents can accept and respect the importance of their child's activities to their mental wellbeing and can gauge whether it is or it isn't potentially detrimental, then teens will be more willing to share the truth with them. It's because teens fear disapproval that they keep their activities secret. When Kedar told me that they didn't know about his new lifestyle, I suggested he tell them but his initial response was to be aghast. He just didn't want his parents to know. I explained that if they could empathise with his need to pour his spiritual awareness into wicca and they understood its teachings, they might accept it and he wouldn't have to conduct his spells undercover anymore. He wasn't keen his father be told but he said that his mother might be more understanding. That particular counselling session ended with Kedar being quite apprehensive and nervous but he promised that he'd tell his mother as soon as he could muster the courage.

The following week, it was my turn to be in for a shock. Kedar came to see me with the biggest smile on his face. Just as he promised, he *did* tell his mother and, amazingly, she was absolutely fine with it. Apparently, he very tactfully unfolded his new beliefs in wicca by explaining the concept of living in harmony with nature in ecological balance. He slowly revealed that he engaged in practices known as spell casting where he could channelise his thoughts, willpower, feelings and physical exertions to a higher divine energy. The best part was that his mother seemed to understand the force behind what he was saying. She said that many tribes believe in the concept of channelising these energies, which were just like those of nature -- air, water, fire and earth. Most importantly she knew that in wicca, Kedar had finally found the answers to his questions on life. She realised that he was happy and, what's more, she told her husband about their son's new life's interest. Being a busy businessman, he simply told her that as long as Kedar was happy, wasn't harmed by the practice in any way and wasn't declining in his studies, he wasn't too bothered about these 'teenage phases'! The mother was so supportive that she even helped him construct an altar in his room where he could pray. His happiness was more important to her than anything. We know only too well that internal happiness leads to optimal performance in others aspects of life too. Indeed, with her support, he continued to do well in academics and his pastimes.

Ultimately Kedar went abroad to pursue further studies and I lost touch with them thereafter but whenever I think of them, I feel happy that here was a son and mother duo who put respect towards each other above all else. I guess in a way that is what love is: allowing someone you love the freedom to express, simply because it makes them happy.

Shivraj

Parents have always aspired to push their children academically so that they can be successful in life. It's a sad reality that society considers these two factors to be proportional and measures the worth and success of a student by a percentage and mark sheets. However, it was Howard Gardner who first put across the idea of multiple intelligences; that intelligence is not merely reflected by academic brilliance but by competencies in many other areas of subjective intelligence which cannot be measured quantitatively by IQ and such other tests. It's worth bearing this in mind when we label children as incompetent and failures just because they may be academically weak.

Shivraj was an under-average student in Class 9. His parents were at their wits' end whenever they came to school about what to do with their 'donkey-brained' son. They had tried to push him up by giving him maximum tuition after school hours but try as he might, Shivraj was just not improving. When the mother came to me to discuss what to do, I was keen to investigate any possible reasons as to why he was always a slow learner. I found out that her son was born very prematurely and concluded that this *could* be one of the reasons for his apparent slower pace than his peer group.

Amazingly, Shivraj managed to scrape through the board exams and took to studying humanities in Class 11. It turned out that though he was academically weak, he showed great flair in other areas, especially cooking. I found this out when one day he had come to see me regarding study schedules but our conversation veered to his favourite topic: cooking! As a child he had often watched his mother cook in the kitchen as she prepared supper whilst he sat in hunger waiting for the food to be ready. Shivraj's eyes positively lit up when he talked of how she used to prepare certain dishes. We started discussing recipe ideas and what new dish he would try out. Sure enough the following week, he would come to my counselling room just to tell me how they turned out and how they tasted! Soon, inspired by celebrity Indian male chefs like Sanjiv Kapoor, he started to think of cooking as a career. Every week he would speak with such enthusiasm on topics like his favourite chicken recipes, fish recipes and how passionate he was about becoming a chef. He would tell me how he had researched it on the internet and how intended to go about it. His excitement was so palpable when he spoke that it was almost as if he finally began to see a glimmer of hope that, in spite of knowing he was an academic failure, he would eventually find success in this domain. Unsurprisingly, with a mission in sight, he started performing better in the pre-board exams. It was a conspicuous, tangible metamorphosis.

However, not everyone was happy with his newfound path in his life. It was met with increasingly disapproval from his parents, to the extent that they had lately resorted to taunting him, as he revealed to me: 'Last week they told the cook at home to take the evening off and that I'll be cooking dinner instead of him. This morning, before I left for school, my father asked me why I was bothering to go at all, if I only wanted to cook. When we go out to restaurants, they even look at the cook and laugh, saying that while some of my friends will be engineers and doctors, I will be wearing a long white hat and cooking. They take it as a big joke.'

The influence of his parents on his disposition was so alarming that his whole composure changed. No longer was he the smart confident boy who once talked about his passion with so much vibrancy that flecks of saliva would fly from his mouth. Where had that boy gone? I wondered. Slowly Shivraj stopped coming to see me as frequently as he once did. He still came once in a while and I felt sorry to hear the heartfelt woes of a boy whose ambition was being squashed under his father's feet like a smoked cigarette butt. Shivraj became increasingly depressed and withdrawn. The sparkle had faded. The enthusiasm was gone, as if it had been squeezed out from him by his parents. Seeing him deteriorate like that, I had a word with the Principal and asked that his parents be called into school.

Unfortunately, his mother couldn't make it but his father came to see me. He was a bespectacled, well-dressed man and, from the way he combed the strands of hair across the top of his bald head to make it appear as if he had hair, I realised that was quite conscious of not 'appearing' bald. As soon as he started talking, I could sense he was an 'old-school' boy, someone who believed that the only credible career options around were doctors, accountants, engineers and IT consultants. He was apparently so appalled that his son had ambitions to be a cook that it had become an issue of pride.
'Initially I dismissed the idea thinking it was just a fleeting phase but when I saw him scour books and the internet, it began to dawn on me that he could be serious. Look, I'm a successful businessman and my entire image will go down in front of society. People look up to me to set an example. How can hold my head up high?'
I remained silent. Perhaps I had a smile on my face. He must've thought that my silence meant that I opposed him. Suddenly he pointed a finger at me. 'When he told you, Mrs Agarwala, why didn't you deter him? Whoever has heard of a man being a cook?! Doesn't it sound ludicrous? Why didn't you try to put him off?'
He was getting angry at me for not reacting to Shivraj's unusual career option. I had to defend myself. Shivraj's face flitted through my mind and all I could remember was the excitement radiating from his face. I took a deep breath.
'He was so passionate about it. He felt he could finally do you proud, that he could be something in life after all. Initially, I too thought it was just a passing phase but when I saw how much he wanted to train as a chef, I didn't stop him. Why should I stop him?'
'Oh c'mon!! Chef, cook, bawarchi – it's all the same damn thing! He wants to mix vegetables and curries for the rest of his life and you just sat there and listened. What if he was *your* son?'

He was accusing me now and I began to feel twinges of anger too. 'Look Mr Sharma, *even* if Shivraj was my son, I would have done exactly the same thing. I would have helped him to find a good institute, found out what the cut-off percentages were and aided him with the admission process.' I glared at him.

'Oh come on, of course you'd say that! He's not your son, after all!' he laughed sarcastically.

'NO, I wouldn't. I'm not a hypocrite. And I don't like your accusatory tone, Mr Sharma.'

'Why didn't you think of how we would feel?' his father asked me again. His hair had flown away from his head due to the fan above him, now revealing a shiny pate.

'As far as I was concerned, I thought you would support his decision because it made him happy. His excitement was so obvious!'

'Have you thought of what will become of him? He'll be nowhere in life.'

'That's your fixed mindset, Mr Sharma. Chefs don't go hungry nowadays. It pays well to be a properly trained chef. The food and beverage industry is a respectable career path to be in.'

His father was looking at me with a blank expression. It was as if he could only hear me but not *listen* to me. Suddenly his eyes widened as he remembered something and the colour drained from his face. He brought both his hands up to his face and covered his eyes. 'How will I be able to show my face to my family? My father, my brothers?' he said in despair. 'What hope do I have of turning him into a respectable man now? He's our only son and he's wants to do a woman's job for a living! Oh my God! I would rather die!! It was a lightbulb moment. His cry of anguish had inadvertently revealed exactly why he didn't want his son to enter this profession: it was because he was ashamed of how he'd be thought of by his family. Suddenly his earlier angry tone melted into self pity. 'You know all of his life, we have tried everything to push him up in academics. I have given him the best tutors, all the books he needs, even his own room – so that he could become something in life. We've tried our best and we do not deserve this! We don't want him to be something as shameful as a ranhoni (cook)!' he blurted in disgust. The conversation was now verging on the emotional. He twisted his palms together. I couldn't believe it but his eyes were glistening with tears. Obviously this was a big deal. Seeing a grown man so upset, I decided there was no point trying to convince him otherwise at this time. I decided to be practical and take it step by step. We could handle the finer points of this later.

'Mr Sharma, please don't get so upset. For the moment, let's just concentrate on the boards. Let's get him to prepare for them in peace. We'll talk about this again after the exams are over. My request to you and your wife is not to discourage him whilst he's preparing for his exams because he'll spiral downwards. Ever since he saw direction in his dreams, things had fallen in place. He was more focused in his studies and did remarkably well in the last exams. It's was the only motivation he had and now, ever since you have deterred him, his world has caved in.'

The session ended with the father's long face still very evident but he nodded and stood up. This counselling session was obviously taxing for him.

Shivraj did in fact come to see me the following week. He seemed calm but it wasn't because anything between him and his parents was resolved; on the contrary, things were getting worse. He had become stubborn but also increasingly unhappy. Whatever inclination he had to do well in his exams had dissolved with his parent's ongoing refusal to accept his chosen career. The more they ridiculed him, the greater was Shivraj's resolve to be a chef. In an extreme step, he had finally decided what he was going to do and his revelation was unnerving: 'Ma'am, if my parents aren't going to support me, then I'll deliberately perform badly in the exams. That way neither of us get our own way.' There was an icy anger in his voice.

'Shivraj, this isn't about *them*. It's not their life. If you deliberately do badly, *you* will suffer, not them. You can't do that!'

'Ma'am, I have researched so much into this. I just can't seem to convince them.'

He seemed determined but he was practical too. 'I had even thought of ignoring their wishes and taking off on my own but I need my dad's help financially. He has to support me. So I'm in a no-win situation. Please help me to convince them, ma'am.'

'Okay, I'll call them again. Maybe they'll soften this time. For now though Shivraj, please reassure me that you will sit those exams and do the best you can. I will inform them of what you have said. Maybe it will make them accept.'

Shivraj was silent. Then: 'You're my only hope, ma'am.'

'Leave it with me, I'll handle it. For now Shivraj, focus on those exams. You can do it. You can do well. Don't throw your chance away. *Please* promise me.'

'Okay ma'am, I'll try my best. You've helped me so much. I won't let you down.' He bobbed his head with a slight decisive nod.

When I phoned his parents later that day, they were shocked to hear that he was prepared to go ahead on his own and even more flabbergasted that he would deliberately do badly to prevent them from getting their way. Their adamant ways were going to backfire unless they backed down. I suggested that they pay heed to my suggestion and support him until his boards were over, at least. I told them that this was the only thing I requested of them so that he could study in peace without any mental aggravation.

Thankfully they reluctantly agreed and did indeed keep to their word paving the way for Shivraj to appear for his exams in peace. It worked. They gave him space and stopped harping on the same tune and it achieved results. Shivraj did well in his exams, securing 78 per cent, which was excellent for a boy who had never achieved anything more than 60 per cent before.

Unfortunately Shivraj's story didn't end in exactly the way he had wanted it to, though it wasn't entirely negative either. During our last meeting just before he left for Bangalore, he told me that he had decided to first pursue a degree course in Hotel Management before specialising to become a chef. In spite of doing well, he felt that he should not join a Food Institute directly to train as a chef even though it would have been a quicker route. At least this way, his parents were spared the humiliation of saying that he was studying to be a chef. He just hoped that by that time he had graduated, his parents would refrain from deterring him but, even if they did, he would still go ahead with his dream.

Shivraj's story is not the only unusual career choice I have had coming from my students. Racing car drivers, astronauts and artists are just some of the unusual choices and I never discourage any one of them. Through my work, I know only too well that ambitions that are forced to be locked up within don't die away but end up lying dormant. They remain alive deep in the psyche, causing twinges of regret even after many decades.

I firmly believe that the roots of amicable resolution lie in the way parents have brought up their children during the childhood period. A certain amount of flexibility is necessary for the parent-child relationship to withstand the shocks and knocks of growing up which can be achieved only when they have been brought up with copious quantities of open communication, trust and compromise. Those parents with young children are luckier because they can start to build the self confidence and self worth of their child early. It is imperative that there is no pressure on them to be what their parents want them to be in life. This way they will feel assured that they have some say in their dreams and aspirations.

Tarita

With the western world already accepting same-sex civil partnerships and the rearing of adoptive children by gays and lesbians, we still have a long way to go here in India. And though we have officially loosened legislation on homosexuality, many would tell you that we are still our own enemies. Yes, it's us, the people, who scorn other people who are different and taboos are still very prevalent, in spite of the attempts towards acceptance.

The counselling room is a safe place for revelations. The number of students who are coming forward to express their sexual orientation has increased over the years. Today, there are many students who willingly come to talk to me about their sexual feelings towards others of their gender; perhaps speaking to someone who won't be shocked and who won't judge them is a huge comfort. It's sad that they have no choice but to remain tightly closeted from the outside world, so much so that even their parents wouldn't have a clue if they were gay or not. And if any student dared to be bold enough to tell their parents, far from being commended for their honesty, they will be made to feel shame, considered to be outcasts and will lose the support of their families. So the message that filters through is: if you dare to be different, watch out, we may well disown you.

Tarita was in Class 10 when she first came to see me because her friend had suddenly stopped talking to her. It's quite a common situation and nothing out of the ordinary but for some reason it upset her immensely because she was very dependent on the friendship. Tarita was so depressed that it was as if her heart was totally broken. Unable to cope with the loss, she had sliced herself countless times on the inside of her arms because she felt she had no control of the situation. When I listened to the way Tarita talked about her friend, she sounded like she was talking about a boy she was had been romantically attached to, pointing me in the direction of her possible lesbian tendencies.

To understand why Tarita's behaviour was so extreme, I needed to find out more about her background. She was someone who had joined school in Class 8 but she had grown up in a village over 300 kilometers away. Her parents wanted her to study in an English-medium school in the city and so admitted her just as she was entering adolescence. With such differences in mindset and having always attended an all-girls vernacular medium school,

Tarita found it difficult to make friends. Even though she stayed in the nearby school hostel and had ample opportunities to make friendships, she felt very misunderstood and so spent much of her time alone. Having grown up amidst nature, she loved the outdoors and so chose to play basketball at school. After school, twice a week, she attended the practice sessions and that was how she first met her friend. By day her friend had lots of other friends but during the practice sessions, there were fewer students and her and Tarita were often in the same team. Slowly a friendship flourished and Tarita found herself looking forward to the basketball practice sessions. She was so happy that she had finally found a special friend. She wasn't lonely anymore.

Strangely, her friend was only friendly with her during the after-school basketball sessions; otherwise she was distant with her during the day when they were in class. This dual-faced behaviour on the part of her friend seemed as if she didn't want to be associated with her publicly. Nevertheless because the friend was so nice to her, Tarita didn't mind that she ignored her during school hours; she was simply grateful that someone had deemed her worthy enough for friendship, something she hadn't been able to find ever since she started school. Once she had started coaching classes in basketball she grew quite attached to her friend. She would call her almost every night to say goodnight. It's very possible that her friend could have felt uncomfortable with Tarita's nightly phone calls and 'clingy' disposition. One fine day she simply stopped picking up her calls.

Tarita was the only daughter amongst four sons, so she grew up under a strong male influence. She behaved like her brothers too, wore their old hand-me-downs, and for a long time believed she was just one of them. They too treated her like one of them, so she was a total tomboy and refused to think of herself as a girl. She often thought that God had made her the wrong gender as she had the mind of a boy but the body of a girl. She hated the fact that she was a girl and always wore loose-fitting clothes that hid her femininity. After fate brought her to the city, she had to wear the school skirt which she detested. As soon as school was over, she would change into her brother's jeans and shirts which she had in plentiful supply. She cut her hair short and she even walked with the stance of a boy; unless you saw the telltale curves of her breasts and slim hips through her clothes, it was very difficult to tell she was female.

Devoid of any traces of make-up so familiar with teenage girls, Tarita had a face which could be mistaken to be of a young male. Her eyebrows were

untidy and she had a lot of hair on her arms and upper lip. Her voice was the only confirming indicator of her femininity though everything about her was unisexual. With her face still moist from tears, she told me of the moment she realised her friend was deliberately avoiding her: 'When I called her last week, her phone was engaged for a long while and when I did finally get through, the phone kept ringing. And then when I called again ten minutes later it was engaged again. I had a feeling that she deliberately didn't take the call because it was my number. So after a while I called again but from my hostel mate's phone and she picked it up. When I asked her why she didn't pick up my call, she mumbled something but I knew it was because she wanted to avoid me.'
'How was she the next day in school?'
'She totally ignored me and she even stopped basketball coaching.' Her voice was thick as she swallowed deeply, trying to get the words out. The tears had started flowing again.

Already I was aware that the acute feelings of rejection by her friend were similar to that of a break up between a boyfriend and girlfriend and though I was almost sure that she was sexually attracted to her, I kept my thoughts to myself. I strongly doubted that Tarita realised that her feelings were of lesbian inclination towards her friend.
'So I got so angry and upset that I used a compass on my arms,' she said without a hint of shame. She examined my face to see if I found this incredible and proceeded to roll up her sleeves. Sure enough there were at least ten red streaks across the top part of her forearm. She obviously felt that she was to blame for the break up. She couldn't continue because more sobs muffled her words. After a while, she composed herself and then, avoiding looking at me, she sat staring into space and continued talking. 'Ma'am, I dream about her every night ever since she broke up our friendship. I am so scared she'll become close to someone else. I loved her so much and I thought she loved me. She would tell me that she was close to me and I would have done anything for her....'

I sighed. I knew never to underestimate the feelings of rejection that an adolescent feels. For them the feelings are so raw and often overpowering. It's easy to belittle them if we do not understand the depth of pain they are going through. The session ended with me telling her to immerse herself in activities which distracted her mind whenever she thought of her friend. I didn't tell her what I thought of her sexual orientation as she needed to recover from this rejection first. I urged her to try and make new friends and to focus on her studies. She needed to keep her dignity by not pining for someone else who didn't want her friendship anymore. She needed to channel those hurt feeling by turning them into something positive, not by hurting herself.

'Look Tarita, if you want me to help you, you have to help me first.'

She looked surprised. 'How do you mean?'

'The thing is that I won't be able to help you unless you stop hurting yourself. That has to stop first.' I looked piercingly at her.

'I can't help it ma'am,' she said.

'I know, but it's all in the mind Tarita.' I tried to think. 'Okay Tarita, let's try this: whenever you feel the urge to cut, will you call me instead of picking up a razor blade?'

I knew that by asking her to contact me, I was intercepting the build-up of the need to cut herself and buying time for it to subside. She thought for moment before nodding. 'Hmm….I'll try to ma'am. If I remember…'

'If I'm trying to help you, you will surely try to help me, Tarita. I trust you, I know you won't let me down.'

She smiled weakly. She seemed to understand what I was saying.

The following week she was back again and this time there were no new cut marks on her arms. She had texted me during the week and our spate of messages had diverted her mind and caused the need to cut to diminish. I saw a sense of resilience in her eyes this time, which wasn't there the previous week. She was healing. Surprisingly, she had started writing sad poetry and brought it to show me; I was happy that she had found a healthier outlet for her pain than self injury.

Slowly time healed Tarita's heartache and she stopped coming once she had overcome this period of rejection. I didn't see her again for over a year until she came again out of the blue. She looked happier and more relaxed so I could feel that there was nothing major to worry about. But I must admit that I had to stifle my smile when she sat down and asked me: 'Is it unnatural to have strong feelings of attraction towards another girl?'

'No,' I told her and there began our first conversation in which she understood that same gender love is real, normal and common amongst many women of society.

Finally, Tarita had discovered the truth about her own sexuality, something that was apparent to me the first time I met her. It turned out that she had developed strong feelings towards another girl in her tutor group who reciprocated her feelings. Tarita positively radiated in the first flushes of mutual love. By the time she left my room, I was relieved that any doubts she had about her love being ugly and distasteful had evaporated.

I am still in touch with Tarita today, even after all these years. She went to Kolkata to study commerce and even though we don't discuss it anymore, it makes me happy that she found solace and acceptance in the dilemma of her sexuality by speaking to me about it all those years ago.

Checklist

Expressing one's individuality is an essential part of personal growth and if one's right to the freedom of expression is stifled, anger and its associated symptoms will be the first to manifest. Pay particular attention to these signs that suggest your teen wants to be different, but in a way that may not be healthy.

Red Flags to watch out for

- Irreversible changes to physical self like tattoos, piercings without asking you
- Obsession with physical features they cannot change. For example, nose shape, ears, lips, skin colour, stature
- Under-eating (especially in girls) or making themselves vomit so that they look like a supermodel and don't put on weight. Anorexia/bulimia nervosa start like this.
- Obsessively going to the gym to gain the perfect body
- Excessive intake of body enhancers to gain more muscle
- Use of dubious creams, lotions, pills to acquire a fitter body especially if they contain hormonal ingredients
- Fostering friendships with a peer group who encourage potentially destructive expressions to look cool
- Going to extreme lengths, for example stealing, to acquire things to appear hip and trendy: latest mobile, branded clothes, jewellery, latest gadgets
- Over-indulging of anti-social habits like smoking or drinking.
- Self injury
- Depressive and prolonged signs of moodiness, low self esteem, isolation, irritability

- Anything that the teen is so obsessed with that it affects normal day to day life/activities
- Talking about death/killing, exhibiting sadistic tendencies, setting things on fire, hurting animals

What you can do

✓ Differentiate between unusual habits and abnormal mental functioning. For example, if your teen is waking up every night to venture outside, check that s/he is not sleep walking! Ask questions and refer to a medical expert if necessary.

✓ Determine if your teen is experiencing teenage individuality for real or simply adapting to a trend or category that they believe they could be best suited to.

✓ Learn to be selective in choosing your battles. For example, let go of a messy room, crazy clothes at weekends, non-permanent hair dying or tattoos, spiky gelled hair, music, posters, compared to something that could do them harm like smoking, drinking, going out late at night, joy-riding etc.

✓ Have the foresight to protect your teens from the harmful effects of their behaviour that they can't see.

✓ Gently steer them away from activities/actions that are potentially harmful by suggesting alternative forms of expression such as poetry, art, writing a song, playing an instrument in a band, sport.

✓ Compromise, compromise, compromise!! Stretch your tolerance level as far as you are comfortable with taking it. Tell your teen that they too have to come halfway. That is the only way to pass through this stage with minimal conflict.

Chapter 5: 'Please Stop Fighting!'

At the outset, I'd like to clear a myth and say that there's nothing wrong in having the odd argument in front of your children. As long as parents share an otherwise loving and respectful relationship and conflicts are amicably and quickly resolved, children are remarkably resilient to the once-in-a-while quarrels that any relationship undergoes. In fact, a healthy relationship between parents – complete with ups and downs *followed by* returns-to-normality -- shows them a living example of how relationships work.

However, when there is ongoing, unresolved conflict which consistently flares up in the form of hostile interaction between parents, it becomes psychologically destructive on the adolescent in the long run. Hostility doesn't only mean open aggression. It can encompass any negative vibe between parents that puts 'an edge' in the atmosphere. Persistent put-downs, name-calling, harsh criticism, blaming, ignoring, mocking, sarcastic remarks, threats of harm and intimidation or even stony silences can also be categorised as 'hostility' because they all have one thing in common: they illustrate that things between parents are not quite right. This vibe can be instantly picked up by children. Ask any new mother and she will tell you that even newborns can sense tension in the air, causing them to sleep erratically, have fitful crying episodes or feeding problems. So, if tiny babies are so sensitive, it's no surprise that long-term conflict manifests itself in a host of behavioural problems in children and adolescents.

From the counselling perspective, having sat with numerous victims of parental conflict, I have come to a conclusion that no child is totally immune to it. Though it may affect them on different levels, it will inevitably place some degree of emotional strain and psychological distress which may even become incorporated into the child's personality development in due course. I had once conducted a survey, a standardised test called the Life Events Study of Indian Children (LESIC), to measure the stress level of two hundred students and found for myself that there is indeed a direct link between stress and academic/social performance. My findings justified what everybody already knows, that the higher the stress, the greater the emotional damage leading to problems in different areas of the adolescent's life. The test comprised 50 life events which were listed in order of increasing stress level. The last event on the list was 'Death of a parent' and considered to be the most traumatic event in the life of any child. Listed at 48 and 49 were 'Divorce of parents' and 'Separation of parents' respectively. Interestingly, separation was considered to be more stressful than divorce because the uncertainty factor as to whether the parents will be together again induces stress. In divorce, however, there is closure in that divorced parents rarely get together again and so the overall stress is relatively less. In any case, with both these events listed so high in the order, no one should undermine the enormous stress they bring upon children.

And that's not all. If parental conflict is the big bad wolf of the child's growing phase, what's worse is that it affects them even more adversely in adolescence due to the already-present vulnerabilities that adolescence brings. Though the extent may vary according to the individual's emotional intelligence levels, it can have a profound impact on social behaviour. It can fuel a teen's anger to the point where they feel flooded by a rage too powerful to keep under control. Add to this other elements like confusion, insecurity and the hormonal changes of adolescence and you've got yourself a potentially destructive cocktail; believe me, no teenager can totally shrug off the traumatic effects of their parent's troubled marriage and, though many of them may not openly express it, it lurks deep within their minds.

But perhaps the biggest irony of parental warfare is how two people who once would have run into a burning building to save their child's life, become indifferent to how their conflict is tearing their child's heart and spirit apart. They become so focused on themselves that their child's needs are irretrievably compromised. They lose sight of doing what is right for their child's future development, which goes against everything parenting represents. So what is the answer, then? How can parents protect their children from the effects of their own bickering?

Well, I believe the first thing is that we must accept that we cannot stop conflict. In whatever degree, it is a natural part of any marriage and so suppressing it or living under pretence are not healthy solutions either. It's impossible to stop having differences and expressing what we feel inside is important to keep communication pathways open. However, it's the *face* that that expression takes that determines its impact on children. Bitter, unresolved episodes leave the worst scars. Parents who are sensitive enough to acknowledge this should make a monumental effort to intercept an escalating aggressive episode before it reaches the peak of hostility. Interception buys time to resolve it in an alternative, less destructive way. If parents have the will to pause and change state during an altercation, they have the power to reduce or even eliminate its detrimental effects. It's certainly not easy, but in the long run I believe it's the only way for parents to honour their mission to safeguard their children's welfare -- even when their darkest feelings dim their awareness.

When conflict has so many negative manifestations on the psyche of the child, perhaps it's a blessing in disguise that many of the offshoots are displayed as behavioural or discipline problems at school and it's no surprise that many of these affected adolescents end up in the counselling room. Rather unusually, many of them are not aware that their behaviour has a direct connection to their unhappy home situations.

One of the most serious repercussions of parental conflict that I have seen happened to Mahesh, a student of Class 10. I want to tell you his story to show you how far-reaching the effects of parental conflict are and how it can totally destroy a child's future. Though his parents ultimately divorced, the damage was already done much before that, even before he became an adolescent. He was brought up in an environment where his parents thought nothing of hurling abusive language at him or each other, even extending to physical punches. This inevitably caused Mahesh to view himself and his social world in an overly negative and hostile way too. The repeated exposure to the violent relationship between his parents sensitized him to abuse and made him even more aggressive. Soon, he fell into a delinquent peer group and engaged in anti-social activities. To an outsider, it may seem that Mahesh was the 'tough guy' but in reality, he was the victim.

But, as I've already reiterated, conflict need not always be violent for it to cast its long shadows either; prolonged tension is another key factor that adds to the emotional baggage that a child carries. Chandika's parents were persistent squabblers and though they didn't have violent outbursts, there was always a persistent tone of unrest in her home. It is a myth to think that children get 'used to' unrest -- just as she entered adolescence, the simmering negativity eventually took its toll on Chandika.

Behula's story lends an even more surprisingly angle to the turns that parental discord can take. She was only five years old when her parents underwent an extremely turbulent patch in their marriage, after which they divorced, so you might be forgiven for thinking that she wouldn't really have been all that affected by the conflict. However, for her, the memories of her parents fighting whilst she trembled like a frightened mouse as she watched from the keyhole came back to torment her when she entered her teens in the form of terrifying flashbacks. She began to experience nightmares in which she lived through that period again. Often waking up swathed in sweat, the memories were like a horror movie springing up from the depths of her mind to haunt her despite it being so many years later.

Finally, I recount the case of Bhargav, a boy in Class 8 who lived in a huge joint family. Whilst there are many advantages of family members living together under one roof, there can also lurk much hostility between feuding members which can adversely affect the younger members.

Mahesh

It's such a shame that so many children carry the emotional baggage of parental discord so silently on their shoulders. As is often the case, it is something that children instinctively don't like to talk about, especially to another adult *whilst it is ongoing*. Children are perpetually optimistic and they wait for 'one more day' praying that the arguments will cease and normality will be restored. And so it was with Mahesh. I only got to hear about his turbulent childhood after he'd been caught with drugs in school when he was a student in Class 10.

But Mahesh wasn't always a 'bad' boy. There was a time, during middle school, when he was an excellent student and actively took part in extracurricular activities, especially debating. Fluent in English and extremely articulate, he regularly took part in ex-tempore speaking, storywriting and poetry competitions and often got awards and prizes. And because he was always taller than his class friends and had a good posture, one's eye was naturally drawn to him. However, the signs of deterioration crept into the situation so slowly that it was hardly noticeable. When I looked back to his academic and attendance records, both showed a steady decline over many months.

At the tail end of Class 10, Mahesh was almost seventeen years old when he was sent to me by the Principal due to a general decline in his attitude and lack of focus in studies juxtaposed with unruly and angry behaviour. The natural air of charisma that existed about him had melted away. He looked tired, as if he'd just run a marathon and judging from the story of his life, he had indeed been through much more emotional turmoil than an average adolescent his age. His home situation had robbed him of a rosy future and instead pushed him into a world of delinquency. With the right guidance, he had the potential to go far in life. Unfortunately, he was already part of a notorious gang, engaging in habits that were potentially life-threatening. The drift into this peer group happened because of the desperately unhappy environment at home. His parents were so obsessed with their own squabbles that he became a mere fly on the wall and his needs were totally neglected. So, when his parents had deprived him of love and attention, he naturally sought refuge in the company of his peer group. I suppose this story would have been less severe if his peer group were positive influences on him where the focus was on education and good clean fun. Unfortunately for Mahesh, they were already into what every parent fears: alcohol, cigarettes, sex and drugs. And so, during the space of only a few months, Mahesh underwent such a drastic transformation from that mild-mannered well-spoken boy with oodles of potential to someone who only dreamt of where he could get his next fix. This metamorphosis from one extreme to another only emphasizes how great his personal turmoil must have been, leaving him incapable of backing away from indulging in activities that he knew were wrong.

If there was to be any hope for Mahesh, we had to act fast, as he only had a few more months to go before he appeared for his boards, but he was completely disinterested. He looked haggard and worn out. The state of his shirt told me he simply didn't care: it was smudged with grime in places and there were a couple of buttons missing. Through the gaps of the missing buttons I noticed a faint dark blue outline of a tattoo and the glisten of a silver chain hanging from his neck. His eyelids drooped a little and there were a couple of pimples around his lips – a classic sign of drug taking. He looked generally shabby -- rough and unshaven – and his countenance was indifferent. He still spoke well but his voice was dull and lacked emotion. As he told me of his former life, I could tell from his tone that he pined for some normality to return once more.

'I am an only child and had such a happy life when I was in middle school. But it all started to go wrong when mom and dad started to have big quarrels. Major ones. It was difficult for me to know exactly what the arguments were about but all I remember is that they were so angry at each other that my dad threw things around the house and even at my mom, which scared me a lot.'

'Do you remember why they started arguing?'

'Errr yes … I think it all started when my dad's business was going downhill and so my mum had to start working to meet our financial needs and, because there was no one at home after school, I went to my grandmother's place straight from school and my dad picked me up after he came back from work. I was only in Class 6 then.'

'Did you enjoy it at your grandmothers?'

'No. She would complain a lot and say that it wasn't her duty to look after me. She was an old lady anyway and she would often get angry if I made her house untidy. It was like staying in a glass palace. Normally she was nice but when I became troublesome she would start shouting at me and blame my mother for leaving me with her.'

'So, how did that make you feel?'

He sighed. A trickle of emotion was evident through his voice as he croaked: 'Unwanted.' He paused for a few seconds, coughed to clear the tightening of his throat, before resuming. 'I just felt like I was a burden to everyone. As if I got in everyone's way. No one showed me any warmth or importance.'

He was wallowing in self pity but I didn't want him to indulge in it. I brought the conversation back on track. 'So tell me Mahesh, what was the atmosphere at home like after your dad picked you up and brought you back?'

'I just remember an overwhelming feeling of gloom at home. It was like walking into a dark cloud. When I got to Class 7, I insisted on my own room which then became my refuge.'

'What about their fights? Did they decline?'

'No. They got bigger and more violent as I got older. Sometimes there was so much shouting and screaming that, even though I stayed in my room, I could hear it. They insulted each other using terrible language so I used to cover my head with my pillow to shut it out. If they weren't arguing, they completely ignored each other for days on end and so the atmosphere at home was generally awful. That's what I remember the most. I never had those happy days back again.'

Time and again, a sense of self pity overcame him but I had to keep igniting the memories so as to get a holistic picture of his life.

'Do you remember any particularly bad fights?'

He looked upwards, thought for a few moments as if he was looking back into the pages of his mind, and nodded. 'Yes, actually I do. I remember once when my dad started accusing my mum of having an affair with her colleague at work. He had once dropped her at home after work and my dad was watching from the window. So, as soon as she came into the house, my dad started abusing her and she started crying. I was eating bhujia at that time in front of the television and when I saw her crying, I went to her and tried to comfort her. She was tired. She had just come home from work and she didn't need that. But my dad didn't care. He slapped her on the face so hard that she recoiled and I also went flying. As she lifted her head, I saw a trickle of blood running out of her nose. I can never forget that.'

From the hardened exterior, I saw a softening in his eyes. They were welling up. The memories of his mother getting hurt were too painful. I knew not to ask him anything and kept silent but he was determined to keep telling me more.

'By the time I got into Class 8, my father stopped picking me up from my grandmother's place. I didn't always come home and often stayed there overnight or even for a couple of nights on the trot. Even so, I would be always be terrified that my mum was being hurt and when I told my grandmother she told me that it was my fault they were arguing in the first place. I began to believe that I was to be blamed for their fights.'

Even though Mahesh told me the details of his parental conflict and how he felt, he didn't tell me about how he drifted into his peer group and found an outlet for his feeling of helplessness. When I discussed his behaviour with the teacher who taught him in Class 8, she recalled that he wasn't an attentive child and would forget to do his homework on many occasions. He was often absent and whenever he did come to school he was scruffily turned out: unpolished shoes, un-ironed shirt, un-combed hair. The period of discord at home coincided with problems at school, so things were beginning to fall into place. In fact, there was a slow decline in all aspects of school life at the same time he was going through the mental upsets at home.

I decided that I should gently broach the topic of the antisocial habits he indulged in. 'So, Mahesh, since you didn't go home for days on end, what did you do in your spare time?'

'I stayed more and more at my grandmother's place and my cousin would often come round to see her. Even though he was five years older than me, we got on well and I grew forward to seeing him. In the meantime, my parents filed for divorce but since I was hardly going home, I don't know too many details.'

'Didn't you go home at all?'

'I did but I didn't like it there. I preferred to stay at my grandmother's place because she minded her own business and watched tv all the time, especially in the evenings. She didn't interact with me so I was free to do whatever I wanted. So I often went out with my cousin who came round a few times a week.'

'Was he into any bad habits, you know, like smoking or drinking?'

'Yes, I knew he smoked and drank because of the crowd he hung with. Actually, he was part of a gang and they were all into drugs too, but I only smoked cigarettes at that time.'

'So, did you slowly start after that?'

'Couldn't help it. It was quite a natural progression really. First I started smoking and then drank the odd beer. Soon, I moved onto harder stuff. But the drug thing started because my cousin was a supplier of cannabis so he always had a joint in his pocket. I puffed now and then but liked the effect so much that I soon got addicted. It made me forget all my sadnesses. I know I shouldn't be telling you all this but I don't think it's a big deal anymore. I have been smoking drugs for over a year now and it helps me to get away from the troubles in my life. It makes me feel good and happy.'

'Are you injecting drugs?'

'No, not yet but when I stop getting the buzz from the joints, I know I'll need to inject eventually. But it doesn't matter, I know where to get hardcore drugs if I want them.' He was adamant about the journey and willing to go to the extreme to get his kicks.

'How do you pay for these habits?'

'My mother gives me pocket money from the alimony she got from my father but I take extra money from my grandmother's purse if I run out. Perhaps I shouldn't be telling you this but my gang is into pick-pocketing, shop-lifting or simply stealing personal stuff like mobiles. We even break into cars to take out music systems which we sell and share the profits.'

My eyes must have instinctively widened in shock. His moral conscience was nowhere to be found. He spoke as if indulging in immoral acts was a normal, everyday activity. Seeing my surprise, he was fueled to tell me more. 'We even made Rs 10 lakhs once by sending a terrorist note to a business man....'

We were traversing off course into an area which was criminal. My heart was pounding. I felt increasingly uncomfortable. Their activities could get them arrested and jailed. This was really serious but I had to keep my focus on Mahesh. He had trusted me in revealing so much. I changed the topic.

'So how do you foresee your own life, say in the next five years or so?'

He shrugged his shoulders.

'I don't live for the future. I live in the moment. I don't know what will happen.'

The discord at home had taken away ambition, hope and aspiration. It had pushed him into the wrong peer group, which was now his way of life. Mahesh was on the road to becoming a full-fledged delinquent. In a few weeks he would be finishing school to revise for his exams, but from what I could gather, exams were the last things on his mind and stopping the habit was the last thing he wanted to do.

I was ready to help him, but without a desire to come out of it, it was going to be next to impossible. He needed some focus to pull him out but his outlook was bleak. Happiness is a subjective word and for him, in spite of his drug-stricken world, he was happier than he'd ever been because he found people who accepted him and made him feel wanted.

I was limited in my capacity to help him as a school counsellor especially since he'd be leaving school soon but when I asked him if he'd be back to study for Classes 11 and 12, he simply said: 'Let's see.' I quickly wrote out the number of a friend of mine who ran a drug rehab centre and handed it to him. I told him to contact him any time he felt he needed help to get out of the addiction. He took it but I later found the chit of paper screwed up into a ball under the chair he'd been sitting on in my room. I made a silent pledge to myself that, if he ever came back, I would pull him out of the depths of his strayed path.

Mahesh did appear for his Class 10 board exams but unfortunately he failed in every subject except English. I don't know whether he re-appeared for them the following year as I couldn't locate him after that. Even though Mahesh's story happened a good few years ago, I still can't help feeling as if I failed him. As a counsellor I have always believed in reformation, but because he left and never contacted me again, he slipped through my fingers; I couldn't help him. Ultimately he was simply an innocent victim whose life took a turn for the worse. Through no fault of his own, the stress of his home situation and total neglect by his parents and family had pushed him onto a tightrope way of life where just one wrong move meant that he could topple forever. To this day, I wonder about Mahesh, where he is and what he is doing. I wonder if he had sunk deeper into the world of drugs or whether he managed to pull himself out and become a success. I pray it's the latter.

Chandika

We are inclined to think that educated parents would know better, but the truth is that in spite of being aware of the effects of family discord, it's still difficult to think about how children are affected during a heated argument.

Chandika's father was a bank manager and was posted about a hundred kilometres away from the city. During school holidays, Chandika, her younger sister and mother would go and stay with him but when they had school, he usually came home most weekends to be with them. With the four of them together at the weekends, what should have been fun reunions were marred by endless niggly squabbling between her mother and father. Usually they tried to confine their altercations behind closed doors, but sometimes this was just not possible. Chandika started to dread her father's return on a Friday evening not because she didn't love him but because within hours of his arrival, the tension would mount and both parents would ignore each other or speak in monosyllables at best. Ironically, whilst her mother was a cheerful woman all week, she turned into an angry, sarcastic woman as soon as her husband returned home.

Though Chandika was only in Class 7, she was a mature child and her intuition into gauging this persistent tension was very high. As a result, she tended to needlessly worry about things she knew she could do nothing about. Luckily, she knew she could seek help at school and sought refuge in the counselling room by telling me of her worries. Pig-tailed and chubby-cheeked, she spoke animatedly, as if she was just waiting to gush out her concerns. What perplexed her was that why two people who obviously disliked each other should have got married in the first place. Her eyes looked at me questioningly. I tried my best to explain in simple terms: 'Well, sometimes you only find out your differences after you get married and the adjustment takes time.'

'Yeah, that happens when parents arrange marriages for their children. I once I heard my mum blaming her parents for arranging her marriage with Papa. Arranged marriages suck! I would never have one!'

'Oh really?' I was quite surprised. It was unusual for a mother to tell her daughter that she regretted marrying her father.

'Yes, she tells me everything! She thinks of me as a friend. She tells me what annoys her about Papa. When he's away, she'll complain about him all the time. She says that he's a selfish man or he's untidy or he's rude or ... anything!'

'How does it make you feel when she speaks badly about him?'

'Obviously I don't like it. After all, I love him. He's good to me and makes me feel special whenever he comes home and he always brings gifts and sweets for me and my sister. I don't think he deserves all that bad talk that Mum says about him. I wish she didn't.'

Though the mother may not have realised it, by openly criticising him in his absence, she was indirectly trying to make Chandika disrespect her own father and take her side.

'Does your mother nag him often?'

'Yes, as soon as Papa arrives home, it starts. I don't know why. Then they start arguing which always starts with small issues. Like, for example,

if there's too much salt in the curry, Papa will mention it and then she gets angry. Or if she tells Papa that the money he left her the earlier week ran out, then he gets angry at her. So it's like a tennis match! Our home is never happy!'
'It sounds like you're a piggy in the middle!'
We both laughed but then her eyes became serious again.
'That's why I get so upset. I love them both very much but when they are together, they just don't get on. Lately I've noticed that my mum tries to use me to make him do what *she* wants, because she knows he won't refuse me.'
'What do you mean?'
'Well, last week when we were having dinner, Papa said he wasn't hungry and so he didn't come to the dining table. Then my mum told him that I wanted him to be there. She said that I was crying, which of course I wasn't, and because he thought that I was upset, he immediately came to the dining table.'

The signs were not good. On top of all the discord, Chandika was also being used as emotional bait too. I was beginning to get a holistic view of the problem and although there weren't any outward, full- blown and violent scenes, the constant negativity between them was eventually beginning to erode the psyche of the daughters. Thankfully Chandika was freely sharing her anxiety with me and it was essential that she came for counselling every week, so as to off-load her pent-up worries. I also made a mental note to meet the mother as soon as possible. So, I went to the staff room during lunchtime and asked Chandika's class teacher about her.
'Chandika is absent at least one day every week.'
'Why is she absent so often?'
'Mostly for some minor health issue or another but the other day, after four days absence, she brought a doctor's note certifying that she was on medication for a gastric ulcer! Can you believe it? She's so young and yet she's got an ulcer.'

Things were all clicking into place. I was beginning to feel like Sherlock Holmes solving a mystery. It seemed Chandika was under obvious continual stress with the home situation and this had manifested as physiological problems too. It's a fact that lingering bitterness between parents stresses children far more than one or two separate major incidents. Marked by a slow release of stress hormones, it has significant impact on children's emotional, behavioural, interpersonal, and even physiological functioning, causing headaches, stomach aches, ulcers etc. It was highly likely that this was why Chandika was suffering too.

Ideally I needed to speak to both the parents in person but with her father being a 'weekend dad', I knew I would only be able to speak with the mother for now. When I spoke to her, she professed that she had no idea how her petty arguments with her spouse were affecting her daughters. Luckily, she was an empathic lady and willing to listen to what I had to say though she didn't understand immediately how their 'mild' altercations were impacting Chandika in such a profound way. Many parents don't see the damage of long term bitterness because of its milder nature and, in Chandika's case, because her father was away most of the week, her parents' disputes mostly remained unresolved and stretched over the entire week. So, it was high time to make a change. I told the mother that when her husband came home next for the weekend, there were a few issues she needed to discuss with him. Firstly, they both should acknowledge that there is a persistent thread of unrest between them whenever they meet. Secondly, she must be able to convince him that Chandika's emotional and physiological problems were symptoms of this negativity existing in their relationship. Thirdly, once they accepted responsibility, they must resolve any underlying issues amicably and immediately so as to keep a healthier atmosphere in the home. Unless both of them ironed out the creases in their relationship, things would not get better. I also advised that they might need a mediator to provide a third perspective, and to seek marriage counselling. In the immediate future though, for the sake of their daughters, I suggested that she should try and keep the atmosphere as tension-free as possible. She should try to stop herself from arguing on minor issues such as too-much-salt-in-the-curry or tea-too-cold which were relatively insignificant. She promised she would try her hardest to refrain from reacting, now that she understood that something as significant as her daughter's health problem was actually a symptom of their bickering.

Chandika continued to come to me once a week after that and, every week, a slow transformation in her demeanour became more and more apparent. Her attendance improved. She became calmer and less anxious. She confessed that the arguments at home had declined significantly especially after her parents had gone to see 'an uncle' once a fortnight who was trying to help them with their problems. Although there were still some minor squabbles, it was nothing like it had once been. I smiled, aware that her mother had taken a proactive role in the situation after our conversation and had initiated the discussion with her husband. I was happy that they were meeting a marriage counsellor too. While it brings me immense gratification when parents understand and accept responsibility for their actions, it becomes even more so when they are able to become better parents as a result.

There is a special reason why I wanted to recall and include Chandika's story here. For me, it represents the essence of adolescent counselling. The successful outcome was bought on by two critical factors: firstly because Chandika was open enough to share her unhappiness in the first place and secondly because her mother was accommodating enough to accept that she and her husband were at fault and needed to make a change. My role in being able to empathically listen, piece together all the symptoms and convey a route for restoration of normality was simply enacted by providing a third perspective. Through this three-way system, we were able to restore peace to the affected areas of their lives. Indeed, Chandika's quality of life improved markedly: her ulcer healed totally, petty health issues ceased, she could concentrate in school and, as a result, improved academically too. Soon after the annual exams, she came bounding to my room one morning. Looking refreshed and happy, she told me that she had come first in class in the exams!

I wish all problems had as happy an ending as Chandika's but it just goes to show that if parents acknowledge that their personal issues do inevitably overflow into their children, they can be the driving force to put an end to it altogether as well.

Behula

Behula's parents had divorced when she was only in nursery school and her mother was given full custody of her. Her father had visitation rights but the courts deemed him unfit to look after her. He was an alcoholic and an adulterer and the judge decided his lifestyle was not suitable for a young girl. After the divorce, Behula's life returned to a state of stability. She seemed to be a normal and happy girl as she went up through the middle school years. Indeed, from her countenance, it would appear that she had moved on past those fearful memories of her childhood but when she entered adolescence, she became extremely troubled by that tumultuous period preceding her parents' divorce, even though it was now a decade since it happened.

For some reason the demons of memory were awakened and she began to be haunted by the fights, the violence and the abuse in her dreams. She was becoming extremely traumatised by the nightmares and turned up to see me, hoping that I would be able to help her. She was a thin girl anyway but looked even more gaunt because she hadn't been sleeping well for the last couple of weeks.

'Ma'am, the dreams are so realistic, it's frightening!'

'Can you describe one to me?'

Without another word, she closed her eyes and breathed in deeply. She looked as if she'd slipped into a trance. Without opening her eyes, she started to speak as if she was watching it happening in front of her again. 'My dad is throwing a glass at my mum. It misses and smashes against the wall sending flying pieces of glass everywhere. Once splinter hits my mum's cheek, cutting it instantly. She is screaming at my father but he doesn't care. I am hiding under the dining table now, though I was sitting on the chair having dinner just a few moments ago. He picks up a plate from the dining table throws it, food and all, at the wall again. It smashes instantly leaving a dirty smudge of curry on the wall. My mum rushes to my hiding place under the dining table and crouches over me, trying to protect herself and me from any more flying food or crashing plates as my dad continues his unabated rage.'

I was taken aback. The images conjured up in my mind formed a terrifying sequence. She was clearly able to recall every sound, sight and feeling. 'Do you feel the fear again?' She nodded. Trails of tears were seeping out of her closed eyes. I touched her palms. They were cold, clammy and quivering ever so slightly. We sat in silence for a while whilst I tried to put myself in the shoes of the five-year-old girl that she used to be. 'Are you always able to remember the fights with so much clarity?'

She sniffed and dabbed her eyes. When she had calmed down, she continued:

'Actually, for a long time I couldn't actually remember the details of the fights. I suppose my mind had shut it all out for so long. But lately it feels like I'm going back in time and going through it all again….'

'So, is it like you are watching a film of yourself?'

'No, ma'am. I'm not watching myself. I AM myself. It's like a time machine. It all seems so real again. I can even feel myself shaking and when I wake up, I am sweating.'

'Is that the only incident that you recall in your dreams?'

'No, ma'am. I see others too. Like different episodes. Some are recurring.'

'Which type are the recurring ones?'

'The more horrific ones are recurring. One time I remember I had temperature and my father was trying to feed me a teaspoon of medicine but I didn't want to take it because it tasted so bitter. So I kept my mouth shut and ran away to the corner of the room. That was when he got angry. He threw the bottle at me. It landed so hard against my temple that it broke, whilst I fell onto the floor. My head started bleeding.' She bent forward and parted the hair on the top of her head near the hairline and sure enough a silvery jagged scar proved what she was saying. 'All my hair was covered in sticky pink medicine which poured down my face. It was streaked with the blood trickling from my head. I was so petrified that I screamed and my mother, who was in the kitchen, came out and saw blood dripping down my face. She probably didn't realise that it was blood *and* medicine. She let out an ear-piercing scream and immediately charged at my dad with the kitchen knife she was holding in her hand. He grabbed her wrist and pulled away the knife. Then he started slapping her as she continued to scream … Oh my God ma'am….'

She couldn't continue anymore as her voice was overcome with heavy sobbing. I closed my eyes. I felt a wave of nausea come over me. I could hardly imagine the extent of trauma she was going through. There are times when I am taken to the depths of raw emotion during a session, when I feel the pain too. Tears came unabated to my eyes just thinking about that little girl growing up witnessing the terrible abuse her father was causing, not only to her mother but to her too.

'It's my mother's scream that I hear over and over again in my dreams. I can't go on like this anymore!' She broke down now, her chest heaving up and down as she tried to breathe in between her sobs.

I was worried. I knew that counselling alone wouldn't help her. The intensity and frequency of the nightmares were typical of Post Traumatic Stress Disorder (PTSD), a severe anxiety disorder, and I suspected this was a case of delayed-onset PTSD. So I decided to inform her mother and refer her to a renowned psychiatrist immediately. She agreed to take her as soon as possible. Behula was prescribed medication for her recurring anxiety attacks and even though she was being treated medically, she continued to come to me for regular counselling sessions every week, as advised by the psychiatrist.

Over the next few weeks, Behula continued to tell me more incidents where her mother was always being severely abused by her father and she herself was like a frightened helpless mouse either witnessing it all by peeping through a slightly ajar bedroom door or was in bed clutching her teddy bear for comfort. All these separate incidents had manifested in her mind during this period. With nowhere to go for so long, the flashback memories were being relived through her nightmares causing a catharsis so strong that it was as if she was physically going through it all over again.

Slowly, with psychiatric help and counselling, her symptoms subsided. Nevertheless, she never totally overcame the hold of the past. No amount of medication or number of counselling sessions could ever completely take away the depths of trauma and fear she faced during that unfortunate period in her life. It's a shame that her parents never had the foresight to see how their severe altercations would be holding their daughter to emotional ransom for the rest of her life.

Bhargav

Joint families are still prevalent in Indian society and are often thought to be conducive for growing children due to the numerous interactions with different members of the family and the huge support factor. However, when there are undercurrents of tension between the adults, they can spill over into the lives of the children and disrupt the sense of stability they need to thrive. To have to come home from school and face an environment where there is an atmosphere of verbal hostility or silent tension between family members can be debilitating for the psyche of a growing child, especially if it is long term and unresolved.

Bhargav was a bubbly chubby boy of Class 8 who had grown up in a big joint Marwari family. He was very fair and round-faced and two little dimples showed up on his cheeks whenever he smiled. Strangely, even though he was already fourteen, he still had yet to develop any signs of puberty; he still looked baby-like. There were twelve members of his family, all living under the same roof: his father's older brother and wife with their two older children, his father's younger brother and wife and their two younger children and of course, Bhargav, his younger brother and his parents. He told me of very happy times during his childhood where there was always a very congenial and friendly atmosphere. They went on holidays together and there was great camaraderie between all the aunts and life was perfect. But then all that changed drastically.

'When I was in Class 5, my grandfather passed away, but what was worse was that, a year later, my grandmother passed away too. It was a big shock to our family to lose both of them in such a short while. I remember I was so upset because I was very close to her and she loved me very much. We all were much sadder about Naniji's loss because with her death, we lost the head of our family.'
'How did your family cope with her loss?'
'Oh my God, it was difficult and it took many months but slowly we all got back to normal. I began to notice that my younger chachi used to answer back to my mum, which she never used to do when Naniji was alive.'
'Did you notice any other changes?'

'Not really obvious ones but gradual ones. I remember some nights when I pretended to be sleeping, my mother would often cry to my father, saying that the other two sisters-in-law would pass cutting remarks to her that because she and Papa had a love marriage and not an arranged marriage like them, it showed that her family background is lower class. They used to say that that was why she didn't know how to conduct herself or bring up her children. My mother was very upset but my father refused to interfere in women's issues.'

'Were they ever rude to you?'

'Yes, my chachis became ruder to me especially if I did something wrong. My older chachima even hit me once because I ate a besan ka ladoo she had just made without asking her.'

'Why didn't you tell your mother?'

'I did but since my chachima is the older daughter-in-law and she is in charge of the kitchen, no one dared to speak up to her.'

Bhargav had touched upon a very pertinent point. There does indeed exist a strong hierarchy in joint family set-ups with the older members harbouring a sense of power over those on the lower rungs of the system. While all this is respected as being a traditional norm, it's not always easy to accept when the older members are unjust in their behaviour. In Bhargav's household, they had suffered a double loss and the family struggled to accept new heads of the household especially since both members of the last surviving generation were lost within a year of each other. It seemed that the oldest daughter-in-law took the lead in running the home, but this can't have been easy for her, or for everyone else.

'Bari chachima is so dominating, ma'am! She snaps at my mum for even the smallest things. Once I heard a loud crash of a steel plate falling to the ground in the kitchen followed by a big shout from my chachima. I thought she was shouting at the servant, so I went to see. But instead I saw her scolding my mother who was standing there with her head down listening to the angry gaali she was giving her. My father heard too but even he didn't say anything.'

'So how is the atmosphere now?'

'Bad, really bad. I hate going home because I know something else would have happened to make my mum sad. Lately my cousins are so rude to me and my younger brother because they know that they can get away with hitting me or shouting at me for no reason.'

'Do you think about the home situation when you are at school?'

'Not really but as soon as I get on the bus, I feel heavy right here,' he said pointing to his chest. 'Ma'am, the situation is becoming so bad that even my mum and dad argue in the bedroom every night. She is always telling him what happened but he doesn't want to know. But he will have to listen to her because how can he bear her crying every night? I can't stand it any-more. I stay awake to listen and always hear her quiet sobs. My poor, poor mother. My chachima is bullying her and she can't fight back because in our tradition, we respect our elders.'

If what he was saying was true, it was indeed a helpless position for his mother. The infrastructure in joint families is so orthodox in terms of eti-quette that it has been following the same pattern for generations. It's not easy for a woman married to a younger male member of the family to stand up for herself because the rest of the family will then look down on her as a trouble-maker and strictly instruct the husband to keep a tight check on her. However, in spite of the hierarchy, the older members do have a responsibility to respect differences of opinion and should amicably sort them out – as wasn't the case in Bhargav's household.

'I can't study properly ma'am. I feel so unhappy. What has happened to us? We were so happy! I hate my chachima! I HATE HER!!' He shouted it out so loudly as if he was venting the anger through the words. It was under-standable that any child would hate the person who was causing the person they loved the most – their mother -- distress. But while I empathised with his situation, it was very difficult for me to intervene in this particular issue because it was a very personal family matter. Joint families are very con-tained and like to handle their own issues themselves. I was pretty much at a loss as to what to do. I asked Bhargav if I could call his parents.
'OH NO!!! Oh my goodness, if you do that I will be badly beaten for tell-ing you about my family problems! No, please don't phone them and tell them anything. Please ma'am…..'
He looked like a frightened lamb, petrified that I was going to call them up. There are times when I cannot interfere in a situation because the repercus-sions due to my intervention could be far more detrimental to the student. But to sit back and do absolutely nothing didn't feel right either. In this situation I realised that I could motivate Bhargav to try to make a change.
'Okay, okay, I won't – but there's something you need to understand….'
He looked at me questioningly.
'Look Bhargav, I know this is easy for me to say, but your job right now is to focus on what is best for you. I know it's difficult to cut off from the anguish you are facing, but at the end of the day, these are adult problems.

The issues that go on between the adult members of your family should be between them.'

'But I can't help feeling bad for my mother...' Instantly his eyes filled with tears and his face reddened. He used his sleeve to wipe his eyes.

'I know you can't, Bhargav. I know your heart breaks to hear her cry – but can you imagine what a lovely gift it would be for her if you did well in your studies? Don't you think that would make her very happy and proud?'

'Yes, it would. She would be thrilled because she is always telling me to study hard and become a successful businessman like my dad.'

'So then, tell me Bhargav, how can you achieve that if you are worrying all the time?'

He looked thoughtful. I knew I couldn't directly ease the situation but I could change his focus to a bigger picture.

'I agree ma'am. I'll try to focus on the exams and do well as a present to my parents....'

'Yes, but one more thing – there is something else you can try to help your situation. I want you to do it today, this evening itself.'

'What is it, ma'am?'

'I need you to tell your father all that you have told me. I want you to confess to hearing your mother cry, the incident you saw in the kitchen with your chachima scolding your mother, the distress you are facing, the fact that you no longer want to come home from school ... and all the other things you have told me. Will you do that for me, Bhargav? *Please?*'

He swallowed as if he was ingesting what I'd just said.

'Yes, ma'am, I will. I'll tell him tonight.'

'Please do it tonight Bhargav. Don't delay it. And come to me next week to tell me what happened, okay?'

He nodded vigourously. There was a smile on his face now. The outward anguish had magically melted away. He seemed happier. He got up to leave.

The following week Bhargav confirmed that he told his father and he seemed less perturbed than the previous week but as the exams were imminent, he stopped coming. In fact, quite a few months passed after that. The next time I saw him he had already passed his annual exams and was now a student of Class 9. Amazingly in the space of those months, he had grown so much. He looked like a young man now with a soft downy moustache and was at least three inches taller than the last time he had come to my room.

'Long time, no see Bhargav! How have you been?'

'Fine ma'am!'

'How is the family situation?'

'Family situation?'

'The issues you had last year … have you forgotten?'

'Oh yes!' His eyes lit up and it looked as though he was trying to recall the problems of last year. 'Well ma'am, we all live in our own units now but within the ancestral home. We made the shift about six months ago but the house has been renovated over the past year. Now we three families live in our own quarters. It's been great after that. No more fights. Mum is happy now. And we often go over to each others' houses for dinner and parties!'

'Oh, all's well that ends well then!' I smiled, happy that there was a peaceful end to the persistent feuding.

'And ma'am, I studied so hard for the annuals of Class 8 that I was fifth in class!'

'That's great. Well done Bhargav! Keep it up!'

'But now I have another problem … there a girl I like …..'

I rolled my eyes upward. Adolescents never cease to amaze me!

Checklist

Whenever parents are fighting, the biggest threat to any child, whether a teen or pre-teen, is *insecurity* being dragged into their lives. This is because their happiness stems from routine, having a home, two parents, friends, school activities to be involved in – and being able to count on those things being constant day in and day out. Anything that threatens to take these things away will induce a negative reaction. Many do not like talking about it.

Red flags to watch out for

The symptoms are many and varied, as individuals react differently:

- Dwindling academic performance at school
- Not wanting to go to school or truancy from school on the sly
- Difficulty sleeping
- Recurring ailments like stomach aches, generally feeling unwell without any obvious cause

- Easily distracted with reduced attention span (especially noticed in school)
- Impatience and irritability
- Inapproachability or even emotional withdrawal from parents
- Keeping unusually quiet during an altercation or discreetly watching you both intently
- Inability to express themselves; bottling up of emotions
- Sad and lonely, easily tearful
- Low self esteem
- Isolated from school friends
- Needlessly worrying too much
- Fears related to school, of being alone, afraid of the dark
- Resisting of family rules
- Acting aggressively towards others
- Acting impulsively, without thinking
- Attention Deficit Hyperactivity Disorder (ADHD)
- Difficulties in forming relationships, due to emotional insecurity
- Taking too much responsibility for household chores and siblings

What you can do

It's not that you must stop arguing or fighting. That would turn any relationship pretentious. But the intensity of any aggressive altercation must be reduced and new methods of mutual resolution should be sought.

- ✓ Don't openly criticize your spouse to/in front of your children.
- ✓ Make a pact with your spouse that even if you do fight, you will resolve it before the day is out.
- ✓ Reassure your teen that your fighting is never their fault.
- ✓ Remind them that you're human too and need to let off steam by shouting at each other sometimes.
- ✓ Never make your kid a referee to your fight.
- ✓ Minimize or eliminate your children's exposure to violent parental conflict.
- ✓ Build the child's self esteem by showing interest in your child and her/his activities, loving unconditionally and treating your child respectfully.
- ✓ Fighting behind closed doors is preferable to open conflict BUT *amicable and speedy resolution is key*; just because your teen may not have *seen* you two argue, they can still sense the vibes between you.

✓ Teach other family members to listen to each other and talk about feelings without shouting and screaming. Practiced regularly, it could become a new home rule.

✓ Ways to stop a fight going from bad to worse:
  - Use a funny code word like 'Eyeballs!' to bring each other down to earth. However, this has to be used early in the fight before it reaches serious levels; otherwise it will skim off the surface like a smooth pebble.
  - Learn to gauge the seriousness of a potential argument. Not all warrant a full-fledged showdown; some can be let go of or handled differently.
  - If you must, involve an objective third person for their opinion, who must be non-biased and preferably not someone you live with. Never your child.
  - If you can sense escalating tension, intercept and delay the argument to a time later in the day, if possible, when you are both calmer.
  - Don't let issues die a natural death, even though it's a less stressful option. They must be mutually dusted down before being put away, but in a way that relies on amicable resolution rather than heated brawls.
  - Tell a trusted family member to call your spouse on their mobile during an altercation to intercept the argument. You'll be surprised to see how a person can change from a dragon to a sweet talking person when answering the phone! Conversely, ask someone to call you on your phone. This too will give you an opportunity to 'break state' during an argument. You can continue your conversation at a time when it won't impact your teen so much.

Chapter 6: 'I'm in Love!'

Of all the teenage problems coming to me in the counselling room, 'love' issues are arguably the most common. Indeed puberty, amongst all its other manifestations, kick-starts the sexual attraction engines which are the cause of many acutely-felt upsets and ecstasies during this period. An unrefined raw emotion from within can dominate the adolescent psyche, making them go through powerful feelings of passion, infatuation and intimacy. Though many of you may say that all this is nothing new and that all generations have gone through and survived this phase, the predicament of the modern adolescent is totally different to that of earlier generations for so many different reasons.

Today, adolescents are being exposed to a highly sexualized culture through a plethora of mediums. There is indiscriminate exposure to adult themes through mass media be it via electronic, print or computer culture. It doesn't even matter whether they are rural country bumpkins or urban city slickers, whatever they look at or listen to, they will inevitably come across raunchy images and explicit lyrics in some form. Billboards, song lyrics, dance sequences, magazines, movies and TV serials all effortlessly tap into this sexualized world and inadvertently condition their minds. Those with easy access to the internet, where pornography is just a click away, literally have it on their fingertips. Internet predators have taken advantage of this medium to accost unsuspecting victims through social networking sites, asking for sexual favours in the form of web cam images or explicit chat.

Being exposed to this sexualized culture through so many forms, our children have grown up faster. The onset of puberty in girls is happening at around eleven years old on average, which is much earlier than in earlier generations. It comes as no surprise therefore that our adolescents have become so sexually aware so early.

The irony is that, whilst this sexually-charged environment has robbed our kids of their childhoods, propelling them rapidly into adulthood, the growth of our cultural mindset has been rather slow; teens are still not entirely comfortable sharing aspects of their love life with their parents. In many households, it's unheard of to openly discuss girl/boy friends. It's not that teens don't want to tell their parents, but they are afraid of belittling reactions. Some adults take adolescent love affairs lightly, regarding them as temporary and inconsequential. Others express their amusement at the shallow quality of teenager's affection. Some even view affairs with dismay and fear that their consequences might be premarital sexual precocity. However, the most cut-off variety are those parents who prefer to bury their heads in the sand altogether pretending that their beta or beti are beyond affairs of the heart whilst, in reality, their teen may actually be living a double life: behaving 'as expected' in front of their families whilst living the way they want when they're with their peer group.

Those adolescents playing the two-faced game toe a very fine line. They are not stupid. They know that living a double life is not easy. It's not easy to lie and cheat. They have to be very careful and clever to get away with it all the time. The fear of getting caught, or having their secrets found out, constantly lurks in the back of their minds. They are only too aware of the price they will pay: lack of trust and the breakdown of their relationship with their parents if they're found out. They end up leading two lives because that's the only way they can get the best of two worlds.

I don't want to alarm parents but from my perspective, naivety in parents is no longer excusable. Parents must come away from the traditional mindset and accept that it really is a very different world that today's teens are living in. Their moral boundaries have stretched. Many are indulging in activities that would make earlier generations cringe. Sexual awakening is on the rise with teens more open to experimenting and taking risks. Premarital sex is accepted. Living together before marriage is cool. Being gay is fine. Public displays of affection (PDA) with boy/girl friends, which hardly went beyond holding hands in earlier generations, have gone to new levels. Night clubs, bars, hotels, cinema or even cars are places where they will blatantly indulge in PDA or even sex. Condoms may be found in boys wallets, just in case they meet a 'hot chick' when cruising in the car in the evening. Couples 'in love' know that i-pills can be bought over the pharmacy counter to stop an unwanted pregnancy, if they get carried away. It's scary, I know, and whilst you may well think that your teen is not 'one of them', from my experience I can tell you that even the most unlikely students know about and indulge in a great deal more than you would like to think.

Over the years, as I have gained deeper insight to the varied factors that today's teens are exposed to, I have come to understand that if a parent wants open communication in terms of love issues with their child during the adolescent phase, the groundwork has to start early. Parents must no longer be blinkered and should try to initiate friendly discussions on boy/girl friends, thus unconsciously paving the way for open dialogue, when the time comes. And even then, parents mustn't expect to know all the details of their children's love lives. They must understand there's no point in forcing their teen to tell them everything because our culture doesn't wire them to do so. Simply respecting whatever they have chosen to divulge is a bigger parental victory than having your teen hide the truth totally. Accepting their right to privacy and their choice in discriminating between what they want or do not want to tell you, will save you countless hours of argument with a stubborn teen.

I feel that in today's world, it's the parents who must try to align their mindset with that of their teens, in the context of *their* environment, and not vice versa if they want them to be honest. Telling them how things were and should be, will get you nowhere, but listening to their point of view, discussing it and reaching some mutual compromise is a constructive way of making progress. The truths of the present scenario are ugly but it's time for parents to accept the changes in society and find a comfortable resonance *within themselves* so that they will be in synch with their teen. Because savvy parents know that there's no hiding away from it anymore.

There are so many case studies on this topic that I am spoilt for choice. However, I have selected a few just to show you the variety that come to me in the counselling room. They may seem exaggerated and extreme but I reproduce the details exactly as they happened, though there may be slight deviations in identity to protect the real students. Kaishori had studied in a convent up to Class 10 and then came to a coeducational school for Class 11 and 12. Extremely pretty, she caught the eye of many a boy and was quite overwhelmed with all the attention. Unable to handle it with a cool head, her behaviour became so bold that she ended up not only doing things that she regretted but leaving herself a rather unflattering legacy of having been a 'fast' girl. Lovebirds Rudra and Ishani were besotted with each other but, oblivious to her, Ishani's snooping mother stumbled across her diary and almost swooned in shock after reading the contents. In fact, as you will read, her parents needed more counselling than she did! Shibani's infatuation with an unmarried male teacher was heightened by his personalised attention towards her. All was smooth until she found out something about him that left her shattered. Finally, I recount the case of Arihant and Sadhika, who broke up after Arihant confessed he had found someone else. However, while he thought Sadhika would be happy with his honesty, he never anticipated the extreme step she would take.

Kaishori

It makes me laugh now when I think about the first time Kaishori came to my counselling room. She was sent by the class teacher who had noticed that the knee-length skirt she wore during Assembly, miraculously turned four finger widths shorter during the rest of the school day. The mystery was solved when the teacher inspected her school bag and found the 'Assembly Skirt' in it. Kaishori wore the longer skirt during Assembly and, after the uniform check was over, changed into a shorter skirt in the cloakroom! After the initial scolding from the class teacher, she was then sent to me to investigate the motive behind this double skirt antic. So that was how Kaishori and I met. She was a pretty girl with brown-streaked straight hair, green-hazel eyes and petite features but it was her curvaceous figure that attracted attention, especially in short skirts. And she knew it.
'I NEVER wear ugly knee-length skirts ma'am! My mum says I have a great pair of legs and I just want to show off my legs, that's all.' She shrugged her shoulders. As far as she was concerned, it was as simple as that.
'So you're quite comfortable wearing clothes that reveal your legs, right?' Her kajal-lined eyes scrutinized me. She wasn't sure if I was trying to intimidate her. I put her mind to rest. 'Oh no no, Kaishori. Don't get me wrong. I'm not judging you. I'm just asking, that's all. It's not a big deal.'
She smiled. Her lips were coated in lip gloss, and wafts of strawberry fragrance came my way.
'Actually ma'am, I was brought up wearing shorts, mini skirts, spaghetti strapped tops, even tube dresses. So, I'm just more comfortable in skimpier clothes. I'm not prudish like other Indian girls who pin their dupattas or hide their bare arms or cover their legs because my parents are really cool about these things.'
'So, they don't mind how you dress?'
'No, of course not. They've always been very open about showing their bodies too. After my dad has had his bath, he walks around the house in his underpants! See, he's just damn cool! And as for my mum, well we used to have our baths together for a long time, so I'm used to seeing her naked anyway. And I often walk into their room while either of them are changing and no one bats an eyelid!'
Instantly, the pieces of her behaviour began to fit into the jigsaw of her upbringing. Obviously her parents were very liberal minded -- much more

than the average Indian parents – especially when it came to displaying one's body. Suddenly I remembered she had attended a convent prior to coming to our school, so I asked her how she coped with the strict codes of uniform discipline there.

'Oh, I've not always wanted to show off my legs or my boobs! And anyway, it was an all-girls school! But here, there are so many good-looking guys! I just want to be admired by them.'

'Do you have a boyfriend, Kaishori?'

'Not yet, but there are many who want to date me. I haven't yet decided which one to pick yet.'

Kaishori seemed to be as excited as a kid in a sweet shop. She was indeed heady with the first flushes of sexual chemistry and fascinated by the magnetism she caused. Voluptuous, with a small waist and long legs, she was quite Barbie-like and blatantly flirted with the opposite sex. One could see it in the way she twirled her hair, fluttered her eyelids, swayed her hips as she walked, attracting the boys towards her like moths to a light bulb!

That first meeting in my room ended without any earth-shattering confessions on her part or puritanical lectures on mine. I couldn't admonish her much more than to tell that in future she should only wear one skirt the whole day, the longer Assembly skirt, that is! Since her parents had already set the moral yardstick of her lifestyle, it didn't seem appropriate for me to contradict them and anyway, my area of concern was what she wore during school hours.

That first meeting was in August, just when all the new students of Class 11 were settling down into their new streams and the new school environment. Kaishori didn't come to me after that and neither was she sent to me by any vigilant short-skirt-watching teacher. She had probably understood and accepted her silly behaviour. But unknown to me at the time, Kaishori was going through a turbulent time of her own. Not only had that skirt incident sparked off vicious name-calling from the other girls but boys started to disrespect her too because they thought that she was 'easy'. Things came to such a point that by December her reputation had hit rock bottom because a friend she'd trusted with a personal secret chose to tell it to the rest of the girls in her class, causing it to spread like wildfire. A very unhappy Kaishori came to see me on a cold December day, on her own accord, to tell me how her life had taken a severe downturn.

'Ma'am, the last time I met you I think I told you that I hadn't decided on which guy to choose as a boyfriend. Do you remember?'

'Ahhh, yes I remember, Kaishori.'

'Well I chose this really cute, good-looking guy and we got paired up soon after that.'

Intuitively, I could guess where this conversation was heading. From her open attitude to sexuality, along with choosing a physically attractive boyfriend, there was only one route this relationship was going: an intimate physical connection. Sure enough, I wasn't too surprised by what she eventually confessed.

'We started going round like any other boyfriend and girlfriend. After about a month I invited him home and introduced him to my parents. After that he would often come round and we would do our homework in my bedroom together....'

I smiled. She couldn't fool me. I knew what she meant. 'Oh come on Kaishori! Don't tell me you were studying all the time!' I joked.

'Well, that was always the intention.....'

I laughed now. There was a cheeky glint in my eye. 'I know what you're going to tell me, Kaishori...'

She smiled guiltily. I thought I saw her blush. She didn't say anything.

'Look, I'm not stupid. I know what happens when two teens in love get close to each other in a locked room. I just need you to be honest with me because there are other concerns that I have, which you may not be too aware about.'

'Well, we didn't *do* it, if that's what you're asking...' she said bluntly.

I breathed a sigh of quiet relief, but she hadn't finished the sentence.

'What I mean is that we didn't do it *that* time...'

I looked surprised. My eyebrows must've arched.

'Oh, so you did do it *another* time?'

She kept quiet. She didn't look at me and kept her eyes on the floor. I realised that she had had sex with him. I knew that her having sex before the age of eighteen, irrespective of mutual consent, constituted rape. I had a moral obligation to clarify the facts first.

'Are you eighteen yet, Kaishori?'

'Yes ma'am, I turned eighteen last month.'

I breathed another sigh of relief. Having underage sex has legal implications too, and I was grateful that we didn't need to contend with that.

'When did it happen, Kaishori?'

'Umm ... a week ago, when my parents went out for a party, I called him over. That's when it happened.'

'Do you have any regrets?'

'No I don't. And anyway, many girls my age are doing it nowadays,' she tried to justify herself.

My mind was ticking. A voice resounded in my mind. I remained silent.

Why didn't you have the foresight to tell her about the risks of unprotected sex when you got the vibe that she would most probably end up 'doing it'? I silently cursed myself. I suddenly felt a little guilty for not making her more aware.

I think it's worth mentioning here that parents need to put across their thoughts and views on sex to their adolescent early on, preferably during puberty when their bodies are physically maturing. The topic of sex is sub-jective in that it has flexible moral boundaries depending on your mindset. Some parents may have strong views against pre-marital sex whilst others may be of the opinion that it's okay to indulge in sexual relations with a boy/girl friend, *as long as you are above the age of consent* and you are aware of the risks, which need to be specifically emphasized upon.

Each student who sits across my table comes from a different background and I cannot advise him/her according to the moral culture of their envi-ronment; neither can I enforce my personal opinion on the psyche of a teen. Parents therefore must take the responsibility of enlightening their adolescents on their perspective on such a topic. However, bear in mind, that flexibility of opinion is always better than rigidity. Don't hide behind a staunch mindset thinking that's what your adolescent will do too. Whether they choose to follow your opinion or not is entirely their choice. The ques-tion is: even if you do not agree with sexual relationship before marriage, are you broad-minded enough to accept that, if your child chooses to have sex before marriage, you will respect their choice? In Kaishori's case, taking into account her parents' hippy free-love attitude, her mother may have accepted her daughter having a sexual relationship as a natural outcome of her newfound sexuality anyway.

It took me a few seconds but I reconciled within myself that there was no need to feel guilty on my part. It was her mother's responsibility to have had a heart-to-heart chat with her about the consequences of sex with her boyfriend. The voice in my head subsided as I felt a sense of peace. I was not her mother and my take on this had to be objective, not personal. I had to look out for her well being *now*, not harp on something that had already happened. Kaishori picked up on my silence. 'Are you angry at me, ma'am? I knew I shouldn't have told you,' her voiced tapered off.

'No, no, I'm not angry! Why would I be angry with you? It just came as a bit of a surprise, that's all. Had I known earlier, I would have enlightened you about the risks of unprotected sex, sexually transmitted diseases, con-traception ...' I tried to smile reassuringly. She stifled a giggle.

'We already know about all that. We never have sex unless he uses a condom,' she stated.

Her talk amused me and, for a moment, made me feel quite silly. Modern day teens know a lot more than we think! 'Well, you seem to be at peace within yourself regarding your decision to have sex.'

'Yes, we had talked about it and it felt right. It's no big deal ma'am. Honestly.'

'I'm not asking you to defend your decision to me, Kaishori. The fact that you were able to tell me the truth is good enough. I appreciate it and anyway, it's not about what I think. It's about how deeply you thought about the implications of losing your virginity and how you now feel within yourself.'

'I understand what you're saying. As I said ma'am, I'm fine with it.'

'Just one question, have you told your mother?'

'Not yet, but I think I will have to tell her before she hears from someone else and judging from the rumours that are spreading around the school, it won't be long before she knows....'

'What rumours?'

'Well, that's why I've come to you. You see after that night, I told my good friend the next day at school that we'd had sex. And though I told her to keep it a secret, we had a petty argument the other day and fell out. After that she went and told some other girls and within a few hours, the whole class knew! Now, it's just a matter of time till teachers or even my parents hear of it. Oh my God ma'am, what am I going to do! My reputation has gone *totally*!'

Her head was now on the table, resting on her arms. She started to cry. I had to think rationally.

'Kaishori, listen to me: you *have* to tell your mother today itself, before she finds out from others. You and your boyfriend must be responsible for your actions and you should tell her immediately especially since the rumours are rife.'

She looked up, with her hair was strewn all over her face and tears streaked across her cheeks. She nodded.

'And you are not obligated to tell anyone else about your personal life in the future, especially your friends. I hope you will think twice before telling anyone from now on.'

She seemed to understand. She sat up now, wiping her nose and nodding as I spoke.

'But what can I do about the rumours, ma'am?'

I shook my head. 'There is nothing you can do at the moment. The more you react, the more they will backfire. As hard as it sounds, you will have to try to ignore them. They will die down. Public memory is short. Soon they will find someone else to pick on. I'm sure you're not the only one who has had sex with her boyfriend.'

'I know I'm not! There are many others. It's common nowadays. Anyway, I'll try to do what you say ma'am.'

'Oh but there is just one more thing I would like to say. Try keeping a low profile from now on, Kaishori. Don't attract unnecessary attention to yourself. You have already done much damage to yourself by that skirt antic from which there has been a snowball effect. I am only saying this for your own benefit.'

I heard her take a big breath followed by a long sigh. 'I do understand what you're saying and I think you are right. Thank you'

She got up to leave.

'And ….and *please* be careful, if you know what I mean. No sex without preotection!'

'Oh puhleez ma'am!'

We laughed together.

'Don't worry about me, ma'am. I'll be fine.'

Kaishori made a concerted effort to keep out of the limelight and the focus of attention left her. She went steady with her boyfriend through the rest of Class 12 and it did indeed seem that they were still committed to one another even after the initial attraction had had time to wear off.

As for me, though I already knew that developing romantic feelings and sexual attraction to others was a natural part of growing up, I wasn't aware that many adolescents of the modern generation have much more relaxed views on premarital sex. While I feel that the majority are still bound by moral conscience, there are some who instinctively seek to push the moral boundaries further, something which was less forthcoming in earlier generations.

Ishani

My phone rang. The school secretary informed me that the parents of a student in Class 11 had wanted to meet me urgently. They came in and sat down. They were simple Indian parents, the mother, a housewife – dressed in a sari, her hair in a bun and the father in a simple collared half-shirt and well-ironed trousers. They both had a worried look in their eyes and as soon as the introductions were over, the father started talking slowly in rather broken English. 'Madam, we have two children. One boy and one girl. Ishani is the elder. She very intelligent girl. She did goodly in her matric but we very worried about her behaviour now.' He paused momentarily and spoke the next sentence in a lower tone, as if letting on a secret: 'It seems, madam, that she is in love with a *boy* in her class, Rudra. They studied together since the Nursery class. He is good boy -- no doubt – but....'

At this point, the father looked at the mother who immediately sensed her cue and unzipped her handbag. She took out several photocopied sheets of paper neatly stapled together. The father pointed to the sheets and continued talking. 'You see, these are photocopies of some pages of her diary. You will not believe the things she has written. We are totally shocked that she has become like this!'

My eyes scanned through the pages briefly. It seemed she had neatly documented her relationship with Rudra on a day-to-day basis of what they had done together. The 'First Kiss' was a chapter in itself! She had started writing about it right from the morning bus ride up to 'the moment':

...and then during the short break, the classroom was empty and we sat together on the last bench holding hands under the table. All of a sudden, Rudra's face came really close to mine. It was tilted slightly and, before I knew it, he had kissed me on the lips! It happened so fast that I didn't know what to do. It lasted for about two seconds and all I could feel was that his lips were very soft and warm and a little moist but it made me feel really good. Our first lip kiss! I couldn't believe it! He told me that he loved me. I started to cry. Oh I was so happy! He wiped away my tears. After the bell rang, the students came back into the classroom and our next class (English) started. But I couldn't concentrate on anything! All I could remember was the tenderness with which we shared our first kiss. It was magical!

The other pages were sub-headed with the respective dates and spoke of their progressing relationship. Ishani wrote well and this diary writing was probably a good exercise in expressing herself! But the father didn't seem to be taking it so lightly. 'Can you believe it madam? How could it happen to our daughter?' he asked me, his eyes wide open. He sounded as if she'd been afflicted with a deadly disease.

Honestly speaking, for a moment, I thought he was joking but when I looked at the mother, she looked as if she was about to cry. I realised that they were extremely upset. I looked through more pages. The style was much the same – just details of every moment they spent together, her rambling thoughts and her dreams with Rudra for the future. I could see nothing that went beyond the excitement of falling in love for the first time and the intense new feelings of physical attraction that an adolescent goes through. Nevertheless, seeing their obvious distress, I decided to tackle this carefully because I understood that what their daughter was writing about shocked them to their cores. Obviously, they couldn't perceive that modern teens indulged in a lot more than just holding hands which, in their eyes, was bad enough.

'How did you get these photocopies of her diary? Does she know about it?'
They looked bashful. The father, as always, continued talking. 'No, no she doesn't know and *please* don't tell her. It would be very embarrassing for all of us.'
'So, how did you acquire them?' I asked.
The father fell silent and in the intermittent silence, the mother coughed slightly to clear her throat. She resumed the conversation, in Assamese.
'*Madam, jowa hopta moi jetiya taik good night kobo goisilu, tai kiba dungor kitaap ekhonot likhiasile. Moi janu je tai homework kora nai kintu moi janibo khujisilu tai nu ki likhiase? Tai osorolai jaote, tai kitaap khon bondho korile. Tuponi lagise buli kole. Moi tetiya gom palu je tai kiba lookaise mur prar.*'
(Last week when I went to say good night to her, I saw her writing in a big book. I knew she wasn't doing her homework but I was curious to know what she was doing. When I went close to her, she closed the book and said she was sleepy. At that moment I realised she was trying to hide something.)

She went on to say that the next day when Ishani was in school, she took the spare key of her cupboard and there she found the diary. Apparently Ishani wasn't aware of the spare key. Since she couldn't read English properly, she took it to her husband, who read it. The father started talking again, his voice sombre, as if in bereavement. 'We were totally totally shocked, madam. Immediately I photocopied some pages and put her diary back in the cupboard before she get home from school. But we were so upset that we couldn't eat our khana at night.'
'Do you think what you did was right?'
The father spoke up suddenly, seemingly agitated. He spoke very fast. It seemed I had hit a raw nerve. 'Madam, right or wrong, that is not the issue. Ishani is wasting time every night writing all this nonsense in her diary whilst she should be studying. She has gone bad! She is having *relationship*! What we can do to stop this, madam? They must break up or our daughter's life is gone.'
He wailed the last sentence. The mother had tears in her eyes. I tried to see things from their angle. They were living in an era where relationships between school-going students spelled nothing but disaster. I kept calm without showing any emotion.
'How were her first quarter exam results?'
'Fine. She is doing well.'
I took a deep breath. I needed to initiate a process of change. This was not going to be easy. 'Look, Mr and Mrs Das, you can't *stop* or break up her relationship with Rudra. Even if you did, do you think it would stop her feelings towards him? Do you think she'd stop writing her diary? NO! Adolescent

love is strong. The feelings are very real for them. Ishani will be devastated. And she'll hate both of you if you force her to break up and she may even continue the relationship by deceiving you. Is that what you want?'
He shook his head. 'But she is on the wrong path!'
'Yes, I understand what you are saying. I know it sounds hypocritical but if you had suspected she was taking drugs and you went to poke about in her room, I guess it would be justified. But this was just a diary! She is *not* going on the wrong path just because she's writing her feelings down in it! She is sensible. She has not declined academically. She has a happy and stable home life. There's no reason why she will step beyond any code of behaviour.'
'So what do we do? We are helpless.'
'There is nothing you should do. You have invaded her privacy. You need to let her be. You must stop snooping around. Can you imagine how upset and disappointed she would be if she found out that you read her diary?'
'How can we just do nothing?'
'From what I read in her diary, these are normal expressions of adolescents as they go through all these new emotions. She just wants to record it to keep the memories special, that's all. Since she's keeping check of other aspects of her life, you both need to trust her more, treat her like a young adult and give her some privacy. Just leave her. This is a phase, it will pass.'
'We cannot stand it when we know she is wasting her time writing when she should be studying.'
'Interfering into her life to the extent of wanting to know everything is not the answer here. Learn to step back and trust her. However, keep a general eye on her to make sure she's submitting her assessments and homework on time. She's not a stupid girl; she won't let anything distract her from her studies. But if it makes you feel better, from my end I will ask her subject teachers to keep an eye on her and I personally will have a word with her to tell her not to spend all her time with Rudra but to spend some time with her own friends too.'
I sensed some calm come between us but I wondered if they could refrain from snooping. I offered them a challenge. 'Do you both think you could just let her be, *unless* she gives you real reason to worry?'
They were silent. They had to reach a compromise within themselves first. 'It's going to very difficult madam because we know the truth....'
'I know, but remember, she doesn't know that you know. And if you tell her, she will never trust you both again. I don't think it's worth losing her trust. But you can speak to her about relationships with the opposite gender in general and how important it is to keep focused. She is bound to see that you two are softening on your staunch views'.

'Yes, I agree. We shouldn't tell her we know, we are aware of that, but we can tell her indirectly that, whatever else may be happening in her life, keeping her eyes on studies is most important,' he said quietly.

I nodded. We seemed to have reached some understanding.

'Look, trust me, if there were any warning signs, I would tell you. But I honestly think there is nothing to worry about. Give her space and privacy. These are normal phases. Just make sure that you have rules on mobile usage, computer timings, television viewing etc.'

'Yes, those areas, no problems! She is good girl. We love her so much.'

'I know you do but that "love" to protect her has suffocated you and her. She is growing up! You must accept that. Treat her more like a mini-adult!' I said smiling.

There was a knock on the door. The time for the next appointment had started. They got up.

'Well, here is my number,' he said scribbling a number on a chit of paper he took from his pocket. 'Please ring me na if you notice anything wrong.'

'Sure,' I said. 'Please don't worry.' They seemed lighter. The earlier worried looks had gone. 'I don't think Ishani will give us any problems, just as long as you two don't give her any problems!'

We all laughed and they left.

As I expected, Ishani didn't let her love for Rudra override her focus. She did well in her Class 12 board exams and also passed the medical entrance exams with flying colours. The apparent backwardness of Ishani's parents in today's world may be amusing but it is true that there are still many parents who are like them, who baulk at the idea of their teen being in a relationship. I still find that one of the most challenging aspects of counselling is breaking old mindsets to make way for a new wave of thinking. Not all parents are open-minded enough to make way for change, embrace new yardsticks and find acceptance within themselves. Those who can and do are the lucky ones for they have proven that they are one step ahead of those still stuck in a time warp. Unfortunately for those parents who cannot, they will always remain emotionally distant from understanding their adolescents, in spite of living in the modern world.

Shibani

Since class teachers get to interact with their students on a regular basis, they are in a unique position to spot unusual behaviour. Vigilance is a crucial first step in spotting downward-spiralling adolescents who are often prone to mood swings and melancholy and it is encouraging that many teachers do report deviances from normal behaviour in their students. This was how Shibani, a girl in Class 9, was sent to me. The teacher told me that she was depressed and had been inflicting self-destructive actions on herself. She had already called her mother who said that Shibani remained in her bedroom all the time when at home, only coming out when she was called for dinner, but even her food intake had diminished drastically. At school, she had stopped mingling with her friends, preferring to be isolated from everybody. Her class test results were declining rapidly and she seemed totally disorientated. The class teacher added another snippet of information: her friends said that her morose behaviour started ever since the geography teacher had taken leave to get married. With these snippets in hand, I needed to find out how much truth was really behind them.

Shibani was a bespectacled, plain-Jane who seemed to be rather mature, far more than her mere fifteen years. Unfortunately I didn't make any headway when she first came to me for she steadfastly refused to accept she was unhappy in any way. She simply shrugged her shoulders saying that everything was fine. She hadn't opened up in the slightest, leaving me completely in the dark. The only clues I had were what the class teacher told me. I decided to call two of her close friends to my room to ask them if they could tell me anything more.
'We don't know ma'am. She hasn't told us anything either!' they told me.
I knew that friends would rarely divulge their friend's secrets to a seemingly nosy adult, so I suspected that they knew the cause but were not willing to tell me. 'You know girls, I understand you wouldn't want to tell me but if you do know, please tell me, because I am very worried about Shibani's behaviour. She has been cutting her arms and she's not eating properly. If she does anything stupid and you knew about why she's so unhappy, you both will feel very guilty for not helping her. What you may think as being "just a teenager's habit" may actually be a sign of something much more serious.'

They nodded in unison but still they didn't say anything. Secrets are not easy to wrench out of a tight friends' circle. They got up to leave. I hoped they understood the implications of what I was saying. I was still unhappy that I couldn't get to the bottom of the problem but at least they knew how things stood. I had tried my best for the moment. Now I just needed to wait.

Luckily, I didn't need to wait long. By the end of the day, her two friends came to me again, this time on their own accord. They sat opposite me. 'We thought about what you said and decided that its better we tell you what we know. After all, we love Shibani and we must do what is best for her. Shibani didn't want us to tell you anything but we betrayed her by coming here. So please understand, we're only here because we want the best for her.'

'Why didn't she want you to come to me?'

'Because she wanted to protect Sir. She felt that if we told you anything, Sir would get into trouble. So, so please ma'am don't get Sir into trouble! Please don't tell any teacher!'

'Sshhh …. Sshhhh …. hang on girls, I'm confused! What do you mean by "Sir getting into trouble"?'

They looked briefly at each other and the more talkative of the two continued talking. 'Okay ma'am, this is how it all happened. Once in geo class, Shibani didn't understand something important Sir was saying so he told her he'd explain it to her after the class. She remained behind and he must've clarified it for her. But after that day, she began to talk about him a lot and she would always look forward to the geography class. During his class, she was so enthusiastic that Sir would ask her questions and praise her when she got them right.'

'Do you all like your geography teacher?'

'Yes, we do – but because he gave her personalised attention, she might have thought that he thought she was special.'

'Do *you* think he thought she was special?'

'No, Sir is good to us all, but because Shibani doesn't have many friends and has never had a boyfriend, maybe she took it in a different way – you know – as if he liked her in *that* way…'

'Do you know if he and Shibani were in contact outside school?'

'Well, they didn't meet but they did text each other regarding homework and such like. She showed us some of the messages. She always messaged him first and he always messaged back saying that he'd explain things to her in school.'

It was then that I realised that the geography teacher was partly responsible for not thinking about how his actions could affect a young adolescent girl student. Teachers are already in a position of great influence over young impressionable minds and giving her his personal contact number was possibly misinterpreted by her as a gesture of greater intimacy. Once he had personalised their contact outside school, it's possible that Shibani had greater difficulty identifying and coping with her feelings of infatuation and lust after which she began to equate them with love.

Adolescents' minds can be a breeding ground for steamy love affairs and tantalising seductions even though there may not exist anything even remotely like it in real life. They have great powers of imagination in which anything can happen and from what I could gather, Shibani had probably fallen in love with him and was creating scenarios in her mind in which they were having a relationship. This was her very private world, safe in the contours of her mind, and yet she couldn't dissociate the feelings towards him when it came to reality. So, when he left to get married, she took it personally, as if he was leaving her. The frustration of feeling so helpless and 'rejected' was the cause of self-cutting in this case.

I had got my answer now. Things were beginning to click. 'Thank you girls for being so open with me. You have been very helpful. Please ask Shibani to come and see me if ever she wants to talk. Is there anything else you want to say?'
'No ma'am, but please don't tell any teacher what we told you.'
'Trust me. I won't let you down. I promise.'
Both girls seemed relieved and left.

After some time thinking of how I was going to handle this, I realised that the answer to Shibani's problem lay in the source of the problem: the geography teacher. And though I promised her friends that I wouldn't tell any other teacher about the problem, I didn't promise them that I wouldn't tell the geography teacher himself! So once he returned from his leave, I asked him to come and see me. Speaking confidentially, I explained to him that it was essential that while he may continue to maintain a caring attitude towards Shibani, he must keep the student-teacher equation very clear-cut. There should be no personal contact with her outside of school whatsoever, as this was being taken in the wrong way, as if he had a soft corner for her. He seemed very surprised that she had taken his personalised attention in such a way. He said that he maintained such terms with many students but no one reacted like Shibani.
'Perhaps you need to be aware of how differently your actions can be interpreted by different students,' I cautioned him.
So now that he knew the effect he was having on her, we decided he was to slowly ease off the attention whilst still being pleasant.
It took a long time for Shibani to accept that he treated her in just the same way as other students. She slowly accepted that he was nice to her because he was simply a caring teacher. However, the firmest confirmation that Shibani was 'cured' of her infatuation with the geography teacher came from her class teacher who I met as we were passing each other in the corridor.
'Shibani's back to her normal self again!' she said cheerily.
'Oh that's good!'
'Yes, she even has her own special friend now!'

'Oh dear, not another teacher I hope?'

'Ha ha! No, not this time thankfully but a new boy who started school last week. I sat them next to each other and she's helping him settle in. They even share their tiffin!'

'That's good. At least she can divert her attention onto someone else now!' Our laughter resounded through the corridor because finally this meant that Shibani was free from the clutches of that infatuation that had once gripped her mind so tightly.

Arihant & Sadhika

In adolescence, boys tend to have a much more relaxed attitude towards relationships than girls. For them, physical attraction is very important and dating a 'hot-looking' girl can even be a status issue. Relationships are mostly about having fun, showing off how well they scored on the good-looking girl/boyfriend scale and having someone by their side to go places and do things with.

Arihant was in Class 12. He was a handsome boy and had had a string of relationships during the last two years. Sadhika was a dusky, curly-haired girl in the same year, who had had an eye on Arihant for a long time. Once he had got wind of her liking him, he coaxed himself into dating her because he knew she really wanted to go out with him and he wanted to have a 'good time' with her.

It was from Sadhika that I knew these details for she had been coming to see me for counselling ever since she started dating Arihant. She was an insecure girl with low self esteem and was ecstatic that Arihant had agreed to date her. It didn't matter that he said he wanted to have a 'good time', for she took it to mean just that – a good time in going places and having fun. She came to see me almost every week for no particular reason, just to chat about her life and share her thoughts. So I had quite a good idea of how this new relationship with him was progressing. She always spoke about him with great passion and an excited look in her eyes. But I became increasingly aware that their relationship was very much about physical appearances. Unfortunately for her, Sadhika wasn't the most beautiful of girls but she knew she had to keep looking her best if she wanted to keep Arihant. 'Every morning I spend over an hour washing, drying and straightening my hair,' she confessed as she tousled her gleaming crop of shoulder length straight hair with her fingers. 'Actually, it's naturally curly, but Ari likes it straight. Ever since Ari and I have been together, I have been taking extra care of myself. I do my eyebrows every two weeks, shave my legs and arms every morning. I've even stopped wearing glasses and wear contact lenses now,' she smiled.

Yes, Sadhika looked immaculate. She had a sheen of glistening clear lip gloss and her eyes were lined with a little eye liner. Her nails were short but perfectly filed and she had minty breath. As she got up to leave, I reminded her to dispose of the chewing gum she had in her mouth.

'Oh sorry ma'am, I forgot about that. It's just that I always like to keep my breath smelling fresh because he may want to kiss me suddenly! The other day during a free period, we ended up smooching in a lonely stairwell and since I'd just had dosa for lunch, he said that my breath smelled of onions and it made him feel sick. So now I chew gum, just in case it happens again.'

I was aware that this relationship was based on the wrong reasons. I also had an inkling that it could break off very suddenly.

Sadhika didn't turn up the following week. She was absent from school. I thought nothing of it but when I switched on my mobile on the Saturday morning, a disturbing text bleeped into my inbox. It was from Sadhika and was sent in the wee hours of the morning:

'Ari tld me lst nite dat he loved Annika and wntd 2 brk up wid me. I dont wanna live anymore. Wat's d point? Bt cudn't say gdbye widout thanking u for all u did 4 me.'

My temples throbbed. I tried to think straight. I read the sms again and again. It seemed that Sadhika, being so emotionally vulnerable, was possibly contemplating suicide. A sense of urgency gripped my mind. I couldn't take any chances, so I called her. Her phone was switched off. I started to panic slightly, my heart beating slightly faster. If Arihant *had* broken off the relationship, it was highly possible that her low self esteem and subsequent desperation to hang onto this relationship could have led her to have irrational thoughts. My mind recalled the words of a newspaper article I had once read: *one of the risk factors for suicide during adolescence is a broken romance.*

I forced myself to think clearly. And fast. Luckily it was the second Saturday of the month and school was open, though it was my day off. I called the secretary at school and asked her for Sadhika's home number. It rang over and over again. No one answered. I rang the school again and this time asked for Arihant's home number. I called him but as he was probably in school, he didn't answer either. Finally I tried the school once more and asked for either of her parent's mobile numbers. Luckily, I was able to get her mother's mobile number and wasted no time in calling her.

'Hello?'

'Oh hello, I am the School Counsellor and I got a disturbing text from your daughter Sadhika this morning. Could you see if she's alright?'
'She's still asleep. What sort of text message did you receive?'
'I'll tell you in a moment but could you please see if she's fine? It's important.'

Sensing the serious tone of my voice, the mother hurried towards Sadhika's room and then I heard a series of loud knocks on the door. There was a pause as she waited, but no answer came. She knocked again, a little harder this time. I could hear her turning the handle. It was obviously locked. She started banging. 'Sadhika!! Sadhika!! Open the door!' There was still no response. 'Hello? Are you there?' she said to me on the mobile.
'Yes, I am. Has she locked the door?'
'Errr, yes. I'm just going to my bedroom to get the spare key to her room …..'
She seemed short of breath. The mounting panic was obvious in her voice. A few moments later, I heard a jingle of keys. I assumed she was walking back to Sadhika's room. I heard the click of the key as it turned in the lock and the mild squeak of the door as it opened. There was a moment of silence. 'Oh my GOD!' shrieked the mother. 'SADHIKA!!!!' she screamed. I heard a loud thud and assumed the mobile must've dropped to the ground. Suddenly I could hear the mother calling out hysterically to the maid. 'DURGA!! Go and tell the driver to start the car. We have to get Sadhika to the hospital - FAST!'
The phone suddenly went dead. She'd obviously picked it up and terminated our call. From the cues I got from the sounds, I could tell Sadhika had indeed done something that needed hospital attention but I had no clue yet as to what it was. I assumed it was attempted suicide. I called the Principal of the school to inform her of the situation. I decided to call her mother again after an hour or so.

It was so difficult to wait around doing nothing. My mind flitted back to countless conversations I had shared with Sadhika. Yes, I knew that she was very emotionally dependent on this relationship but could she have really committed suicide? It takes courage to take one's life. The next hour or so were the longest I'd ever gone through. Worst-case scenarios were inevitably coming to my mind. I just prayed she was alive. Just then my phone rang. It was Arihant. He'd obviously seen my missed call and called me during the short break. Mobiles are incidentally not allowed in school, but most students have devious means of smuggling them in.
'Hello Arihant. I had called because I wanted to know when you last spoke to Sadhika?'

'Well, she called me last night.'

'Look, I'm sorry Arihant, I know you're not used to telling me about your private life but I have to know what happened during that call. Did she get upset?'

He hesitated. There was a moment's silence. 'Has something happened to her, ma'am?'

I answered with my question again. 'What happened during the conversation, Arihant? I have to know. Please tell me. I know about the two of you. She shares everything with me.'

'Yeah, I know.' He seemed reluctant.

'Please tell me Arihant!' I pleaded.

He waited for a few seconds. 'Well okay….' he said begrudgingly. 'I found someone else – I mean another girlfriend -- and so I told her that I had fallen in love with another girl and wanted to break up with her. It was the best thing I could do in the circumstances. I told the truth. It wasn't right to carry on with two girls at the same time, was it?'

'How did she react?'

'Shocked I guess. She didn't say anything. She just kept quiet.'

'Has she ever been upset during your relationship before?'

'Yes, once I told her I'd talked to my ex-girlfriend and she got really jealous. That night she rung me up and said that she was so worried that she'd lose me that she'd cut her arms. The next morning I saw that she'd cut the letters of my name on the underside of her arm with a razor blade.'

'Were there any other incidents she'd told you about?'

'She told me that once her father had slapped her when she was younger and she was so angry at him that she drank Harpic.'

'Okay…'

Suddenly I heard the bell ring in the background.

'Look Ma'am, I've got to go now. Classes are starting. Why are you asking me all these questions? What has happened to her? Is she alright? Has she done something?' Panic was starting up in his voice. He sounded scared.

'Well something serious has happened Arihant, but I don't actually know what it is yet, to be honest. But, I suggest that you don't call her UNDER ANY CIRCUMSTANCES for a little while. Any communication is to be made through me. Is this clear? We don't know what turns this incident will take and how you might be implicated. Call me whenever you want.'

'Yes ma'am. Thank you ma'am. Bye.' His voice was quiet.

I began to get a clearer picture of Sadhika's reactions. She had never told me her previous history of self-infliction before. Obviously she had often resorted to hurting herself when very upset. I tried her mother's number

again. She picked up after the first ring. The relief in her voice was palpable. 'Mrs Agarwala, thank goodness you called this morning to tell me to wake her up! If I had wasted another minute, she could have been dead! She had taken an overdose of sleeping pills late last night!'
'Is she okay?'
'By God's grace, we got her here just in time. She had to have her stomach pumped out. She is resting now but the doctor says she'll be okay.'
Suddenly my eyes were flooding with tears. The relief was immense. 'When will she be released?'
'They want to keep her under observation for a few days. She's still sleeping but wakes up briefly, screaming. The doctor says she's hallucinating.'
'Oh my goodness. I'll come down to see her soon.'
'Yes, she'd be happy to see you but Mrs Agarwala, I have a request. We do not wish to tell others that this was an overdose. It looks bad on her. We have told our family that it was a case of food poisoning, so I would appreciate it if you did the same. For Sadhika's sake.'
'Okay, I understand. I'll call again tomorrow before I come. Please tell her I called when she wakes.'

Sadhika recovered but it was a good two weeks before she returned to school. She looked better but still was very hurt by Arihant's rejection. He was her first boyfriend and his loss from her life was so crushing that she became bitter every time she saw him. Sadhika and I went through months of counselling during which she slowly picked herself up. Her self confidence grew once she saw how helpless she once was and how much power he held over her. The good thing was that as her self esteem increased, her self-destructive behaviour stopped, as she understood why she felt vulnerable and helpless. It was the only coping mechanism she knew. When we talked about the overdose, she said that she had never intended to kill herself but injure herself enough to bring attention to how unhappy she was. 'But maybe I went a bit too far,' she giggled.
Slowly her confidence enabled her to see that she didn't have to mould herself to fit into anyone's perceptions of how she should be; what was more important was whether she was happy with herself and thankfully, she began to have a growing sense of self-respect within her. Counselling worked wonders with her once I knew where her reactions were stemming from.

Today when I think back to Sadhika, I always get a little jolt in my system when I remember her reaction to what adults have proverbially termed 'puppy love'. Perhaps it's time we started to take the love teens feel in adolescence, and their reaction to rejection, a little more seriously.

Checklist

It's no secret that that there are more Indian adolescents who hide the truth about their feelings for another from their parents than those who openly tell them. Since teens are not always equipped to handle the emotional aspects of a relationship, parents must therefore remain vigilant without being overly intrusive.

Mild warning signs

Whilst there's no immediate need to get overly stressed and anxious, these mild warning signs are sure-fire clues that your teen may be getting too involved in a relationship, especially when you notice them on a regular basis:

- ✓ Detachment from daily family interactions, preferring to stay in their own room and locking the door
- ✓ Jumping up by instinct as soon as their mobile rings and taking the call in another room (even leaving their dinner half-eaten) and locking the door
- ✓ Hesitating for a moment when you ask them who called or who they're going out with tonight
- ✓ Preferring to stay at home than go out to a restaurant for a family dinner (or making an excuse to stay alone at home)
- ✓ Chatting/texting late into the night, even quietly under the bedclothes
- ✓ Excessive interest in themselves in terms of how they dress, style their hair, how they smell
- ✓ Losing track of the time they spend chatting or on social networking sites
- ✓ Grades going gradually down at school (though this may not always be so)
- ✓ Crying easily or becoming needlessly aggressive or argumentative
- ✓ Mood swings, monosyllabic answers when asked questions about their whereabouts
- ✓ Cringing with embarrassment or blushing as soon as a particular name of a boy or girl is mentioned.
- ✓ Wanting to go out more often than usual
- ✓ Being uncharacteristically over-friendly and affectionate with you after an outing (this may suggest a guilty conscience)

What you can do

- ✓ Insist that while you will allow them to take private calls in their bedroom, there must be a maximum time limit and no calls after a certain time at night.
- ✓ Adopt the 'I won't snoop, if you tell me the truth' attitude but if you find hard evidence they have lied, there will be consequences and you are then compelled to keep a closer eye on them. Consequences can include denying them a privilege they enjoy (such as confiscating their mobile) for a period of time, depending on the severity of the deceit but state beforehand how long you intend to keep the privilege from them. Under no circumstances should you re-instate it *before* the stipulated time, as this sends the message that you do not follow your own rules.
- ✓ Once the confiscation/denying privilege period is over, give them back their privilege and get back to normality immediately. Don't remind them of their misdeed and don't harbour any grudges towards them. What's done is done.
- ✓ Slowly re-introduce the trust-factor again by enforcing more flexible rules which are easier for them to adhere to. For example, insist they tell you what time they get back from a party or what time they will stop using the phone/internet at night. When they do as they say, praise them and say that you knew you could trust them. Don't ignore this obvious effort on their part. This way their confidence in you slowly begins to build up again. The point here is that begrudging compromise is always better than hostile defiance so being too strict (though tempting) is counterproductive. If they break this rule, you have no option but to introduce harsher rules the next time, like confiscating the privilege for a longer time. Only in extreme cases should you deny the privilege totally.
- ✓ Similarly, grounding them from going out with their friends will only bring on more bitterness towards you, so give them freedom to go out, but insist that they come home by a particular time. That way they will appreciate that you have come halfway too, and will be more likely to abide by their side of the deal.
- ✓ Remind them that as a parent you are enforcing consequences not because you enjoy seeing them suffer but because it is your duty to ensure that they remain on the right path. Make it clear that what is good for them may not be the same as what they want.

✓ As much as you can, try to avoid direct confrontation where they are then in a prime position to verbally abuse you or, in severe cases, even physically abuse you. Don't let arguments get to a peak where you are both screaming at the top of your voices. Sense the tone early and try to keep calm. If they continue to be aggressive, walk away from the scene and insist you won't talk or listen to them until they have calmed down.

✓ If your teen threatens to hurt him or herself as a way of getting to you, don't challenge them back by saying 'Go on, do it, as if I care!' Many adolescents will actually do it just to prove to you how capable and daring they are. So don't even go there. Instead, tell them with conviction that as your son/daughter you know they will not harm themselves. Positive reinforcement is the key to good behaviour. Stay on the same side as them.

✓ Insist that as a member of the family they have to balance family and friend time. If, for example, the phone rings while they are doing their homework or eating their dinner, your teen should tell the caller that either they will call back after they have finished, or ask the caller to call back at a certain time. Establish a sense of routine on school days where study/meal times are at fixed times.

✓ Insist that they must tell you where they are going and what time they will be home every time they go out.

✓ Accept that in hiding the truth from you, they may go to great lengths and tell elaborate stories. So keep your sixth sense antennae on and don't believe everything. For example, they may say they've lost their phone whilst it's just an excuse to keep you away from it. Similarly they may say that they are 'just friends' with a particular boy/girl when actually they are having a full-fledged relationship. So learn to spot the secondary reflex actions which often speak louder than words.

✓ Be extremely wary about sleepovers and make sure you are in touch with the parents of your teen's close friends.

Red flags to watch out for

- Severe sleep disturbances (either excessive sleeping or inability to sleep)
- Not eating/overeating
- Cutting themselves
- Suicidal talk

- Excessive use of over-the-counter medication (like paracetamol, sleeping pills, cough mixture) to ease minor symptoms
- Drastically deviant behaviour from the norm. For example, a normally bubbly teen may suddenly become morose or aggressive
- Attempted suicide (immediate help needed)
- Need for total isolation

What you can do

As primary caretakers, parents must not hesitate to resort to the expertise of counsellors, psychologists or even psychiatrists who have more specialized experience in handling teenage issues if these symptoms become frequent.

Don't try to solve the more serious issues on your own or wait for time to heal things. It may well be counter-productive and worsen the situation further. Many mental health professionals are trained to handle adolescent issues. Not only will they be able to take an objective view on the problem, but they can explain what is happening and give you certain tools and techniques that may have been overlooked, so the stress on you will be reduced markedly. Take time to find out who the professionals in your area are beforehand and don't hesitate to take your teen for a consultation. Some institutes/websites where you can get help are listed at the end of the book.

Chapter 7: 'I Know it's Wrong but I Can't Help it!'

It may surprise you when I say that not all the problems that come to me in the counselling room end up as success stories. Sometimes, things simply don't click into place and setbacks hamper a positive outcome. In my early days of counselling, I had the impression that I could solve every problem and whenever I was unable to see a problem through to a fruitful ending, an overpowering sense of failure used to come over me. I remember even seeking counselling myself to overcome my own mental blocks and accept that sometimes I may be unable to facilitate a positive change in the person I am counselling.

Soon I understood that even though my role as facilitator was important, what was equally important -- if not more -- was the effort and determination of the student. As soon as a student comes through my door, we begin a partnership to *work together* and if one of us fails, *we* fail. So, for the counselling process to work, there has to be a heartfelt desire for the person to *want* to change. Without that, counselling will always be a failure. Period. I have sat for many frustrated hours trying to help someone see an alternative perspective in order to come out of a negative situation, only to discover that nothing I had said made any difference to them.

It took me a long time to accept that I am not, and never will be, the 'eternal saviour' that I may have once thought I was. I have learnt to accept that teamwork is mandatory in counselling and a single weak link will set us back. There must be conviction and determination to initiate a change on the part of every person involved in the process, not only mine. What makes a person a weak link in the process is simply that they are imprisoned by factors which they find difficult to overcome. Most of these factors come in the form of emotions so overbearing that they cloud their judgment from doing what is best for themselves.

It can be frustrating for a third person to see how strong people become slaves to a situation. They may want to come out of a bad habit or an unhealthy relationship -- they know it's the right thing to do -- but a deep, almost instinctive, craving for it renders them helpless. They, in effect, become addicted and though it's not impossible, it demands great conviction to overcome it. It's the classic battle between the head and the heart but when the need is greater than the will to curb it, the head will always lose because it's the way the addiction *makes them feel* that causes them to be at its mercy.

Pushkal, who was only in Class 11, came for a relatively minor problem: girl issues. But his problems took a back seat when a casual comment changed the face of our conversation and took us on a dramatic detour towards the *real* problem: drug addiction, a secret habit that was slowly killing his aspirations and yet he was totally helpless to do anything about it. However, Harikesh's story had a more positive ending. He was worried that his failing grades had something to do with his masturbation habit. Even though it is a common habit amongst adolescent boys, it wasn't easy for him to talk about it. However, I applaud his courage in being so professional about it because we were able to put together a plan of action which ultimately helped him to control his habit. I have also decided to include one of the most pathetic cases I have come across in my career as a counsellor. Sasthi was born into a troubled home and found love in the arms of a so-called loving boyfriend. Unfortunately he became physically abusive towards her and, in spite of being a young school girl and having everything to look forward to, she couldn't muster the will to terminate the relationship. As much as I tried to give her the support to see otherwise, my words fell on deaf ears. For her, his love meant everything -- even if it meant putting up with the mental and physical torture he inflicted on her.

It takes a lot for someone to swallow their pride and admit that they are helpless. It demands courage to accept one's fallibility as a human being and a process of change cannot begin until someone can wave the white flag and accept they need help. So, for me, those who concede to their powerlessness are my silent heroes, for the very act of coming forward and accepting that they are struggling is a small victory in itself; the outcome is incidental. For this very reason, none of the students whose stories I have recounted can be deemed as being a failure because *real* failure is the failure to try.

Pushkal

Pushkal was only in Class 11 but already had all the trimmings of an upcoming rock star. To the girls, he was simply the 'coolest guy'. Everything about him – his swaggering walk, his rugged, unshaven looks, his laid-back attitude to life, the tiger-head tattoo on his bulging bicep, his prowess with the guitar, even his dabbling in smoking and drinking – upped his status as the proverbial 'bad boy'. And the girls loved him. He had the rugged smoothness of a John Abraham look-a-like. When he stood on stage at the annual Teacher's Day function, the screams were deafening enough, but when he strummed his guitar solo with the panache of Jimi Hendrix, the girls went positively wild.

So when Pushkal turned up to my counselling room one morning, I was quite surprised. He seemed to be having a gala time at school but his newly-acquired stardom, even on a schoolboy level, had its price to pay: girl troubles. With so many vying to date the school rock star, he was spoilt for choice and ended up dating two girls at the same time.

'So, you see ma'am, ever since that Teacher's Day function, I had so many girls asking for my mobile number, calling me up, asking to be friends with me on FB, it was unbelievable. I ended up two-timing but unfortunately wasn't smart enough to handle two chicks at the same time.'

'Why? What happened?'

He had a huge smirk on his face now. He shook his head in disbelief. 'The classic scene when you take one girl out on a date and bump into the other!' He laughed out loud now. He found it the biggest joke ever. I must admit, I was quite amused too. 'Well there's a lesson there, Pushkal. Perhaps it's not advisable to date many girls at the same time, eh?'

We laughed together. The conversation so far was casual and relaxed.

'And the best part is that they both started fighting like cats over me! Oh man!'

'Did that make you feel good?'

'Yeah, sure it did! But afterwards I decided that girls are just not worth the trouble. It's too much hard work and I just don't get any time to do my other stuff.'

'Can't you stick to just one girlfriend at a time?'

He thought for a moment, his forefinger twirling some arbitrary pattern on my table. 'I guess I could, even though it'd be half the fun, but then I could concentrate more on my music and other hobbies.'

'What hobbies do you have?'

'I play the guitar. I am a member of a band and we meet up whenever we can, usually at the weekends.'

'Anything else?'

'Nothing else as such. Only pastimes … like drinking or smoking.' That smirk returned. He looked at my face for to check for some reaction, but I didn't show any surprise. He put his elbow on the table and massaged his forehead with his fingers. Since I hadn't passed comment, the coast was clear for him to continue. 'In fact, last night I smoked too much and today my head feels so heavy.' He was starting to let his guard down and was talking to me quite candidly. I had a strange feeling that he didn't seem to be totally in his senses. He looked around the room. 'It feels like your voice is echoing all around this room, like it's booming out from the walls.' I looked into his eyes. The eyelids looked a little droopy and his eyes were slightly bloodshot. Perhaps he had a hangover. 'Did you drink last night as well?'

'No, not last night…'

I was confused. If he didn't drink, then why the red eyes?

He closed his eyes briefly and opened them, as if he was on the verge of drifting off. The earlier display of vitality and energetic talking was fading fast. He spoke as if he was sleepy. 'Oh …. I don't smoke cigarettes as in tobacco … I smoke ganja, you know, marijuana. Weed.'

The casual way he mentioned this took me a little by surprise. But I maintained the sense of calmness. 'Oh really? Hmm. So when did you start smoking marijuana?'

'Ever since Shivaratri last February. Some friends of mine were trying it and so, in the name of religion, I tried it too. It made me feel so good. So I smoke once in a while.' He smiled now as if he was pleased with his actions. He had his head up now as if suddenly woken up.

I did some mental maths. If he started smoking in February, it must have been just a couple of months before his Board exams. I clarified it with him. He nodded.

'So Pushkal, how did you do in your boards?'

'Not that good …. I secured third division and because I didn't score well in science or maths …. I was not good enough to study science or commerce…. only the arts stream would take me.'

He was now speaking in short snippets, as if he needed to summon energy before uttering the words.

'Do you think the drugs were the reason you didn't do well?'

'Well, not exactly … but c'mon yaar… who needs exams anyway?' He patted a closed fist onto his heart. 'It's what's here that matters.' I didn't say anything and allowed the silence to settle. He continued talking. 'But … I wanna be a musician anyway … You only need talent for that … I wanna make music … I wanna be the best guitarist in the world!' He pretended to strum an invisible guitar and started to make a twanging noise. His behaviour did indeed seem very odd.

'Do your parents know you take drugs?'

His mood changed abruptly. I saw a flash of anger in his eyes. His mood had shifted instantly from joyful imagery to aggression. A wave of fear suddenly came over me. This mood change suggested there was something wrong with him. I suspected he'd been taking some kind of intoxicant today, just before coming to my room. 'Nah! I hate them! They're always ganging up against me, making my life hell. Weed is my only friend! I don't care about anyone or anything else.' He held three fingers up to me and held my stare. 'Booze, ganja, glue – these are all my soul mates, not my f*cking parents!'

It was obvious that he held harnessed extreme anger within himself towards his parents. Under the influence of some intoxicant, he was venting it out. His sentences were brimming with fury. His uninhibited usage of the f-word surprised me because students rarely use bad language in front of me. Nevertheless, sensing that his behaviour was not quite normal, I didn't admonish him and anyway he didn't seem uncomfortable by it. 'My parents – I hate to call them my parents – have always been so uptight. They told me that they are ashamed of what I have become and that I'm nowhere near what they expected of me. So, now what do I care? I feel nothing towards them. Not a bit! Every evening I steal money from my mum's purse to buy my daily fix.' It didn't seem appropriate to dig too deeply into his family life just yet and anyway with his aggressive tendencies, I decided to wait for a later visit before delving into his family life and upbringing.
'How expensive is it to buy marijuana?'
He shrugged his shoulders. 'Depends on how much you need. Prices start from as low as 10 bucks a time. If I'm doing ganja, I take the chillim to the riverfront where I meet my friends and we sit on the banks and smoke. Ahh, what bliss! It's as if all my problems disappear.'
He seemed rejuvenated now, as if just thinking about it was energizing him. He spoke fast and with enthusiasm. He obviously was passionate about our topic of conversation. I tried to keep him talking so as to get an idea of the depth of his addiction. 'Yes, but Pushkal do you realise that this habit of yours is quietly destroying your life?'
That irritated glint was back. 'Please don't bother to lecture me into stopping cos I ain't gonna. I don't care if it's bad for me. I'm sorry but I won't listen to you or anyone. Anyway, I didn't come here to talk about my smoking habit. I came here to talk about the "girl problem." So what should I do then?'
He was in charge of the conversation. He was steering me to what he felt was the real issue. I went with the flow. 'Maybe you shouldn't be dating any girl, Pushkal. With your many habits and pastimes, how can you give even *one* girl your time?'
He clapped his hands and laughed out so loud, as if I had cracked a huge joke. 'Ha! You're funny ma'am! Yeah, maybe you're right, life is all about my guitar, my friends and my soul mates. That's it. Full stop,' he said with an exaggerated flourish of his hands. 'Yeah, no time for proper girlfriends. I'll just stick to one-night stands.'

I decided not to harp on the pitfalls of having one-night stands; we already had other serious issues to contend with. 'Pushkal, can you come again next week?'

'Yeah, I suppose I don't mind coming here but on one condition: that you don't lecture me to stop doing weed. I'm sick of doing what others want me to. I've spent all my life listening to the biggest f*cking morons in my life, my parents, and look where it's got me. Nowhere!'

'Okay, I won't lecture you Pushkal. I promise.' I said gently. 'We'll just talk.'

'Okay.' I heard him exhale. He seemed instantly relieved. I knew that if I wanted to progress, I had to keep contact with him and for that, he had to keep coming to me because *he wanted to*. Any hint of disapproval from my side, I knew I would lose him totally.

'Oh and another thing, please give me your mobile number because I want a friend of mine to talk to you. He was a big druggie -- much more than you -- and I think he'll be able to help you. He's a cool dude, just like you.'

'I don't need any help.'

'Okay, maybe you don't, but surely you could talk to him anyway? You'll gain another friend, at least.'

He smirked and nodded. 'That's okay with me. Hope he plays the guitar too! We can become ganja buddies!'

I rolled my eyes upwards. I couldn't believe how at ease he was with smoking marijuana. 'No, he's recovered, Pushkal. He doesn't take drugs anymore.'

'Poor guy doesn't know what he's missing out on!' He smirked.

There was no convincing Pushkal. He didn't see anything wrong in what he was doing.

'So, I'll see you next week.'

'Yes ma'am!' he saluted. His mannerisms were almost comical. He left with that same smirk in place.

I sat there thinking about what just happened. An extremely serious situation had disguised itself in a light conversation. Pushkal had totally overlooked the gravity of his predicament because he was so used to it. Within minutes I was on the phone to the founder of a drug rehabilitation centre who was a friend of mine, an ex-addict. He was hooked onto heroin and was on the brink of death… till he decided to make a choice. He chose life. Through months and months of gruelling therapy, he made a complete recovery and started up the centre to help drug addicts, like he once was. He also started a side career as a motivational speaker where he visited different schools lecturing young adolescents on the dangers of taking drugs using reflections of his own life story.

With Pushkal showing no interest in stopping, this was the only course of action I could follow for the moment along with general counselling every week. From his vehemence towards his parents, I could sense his anger lay deeply entrenched and was most definitely the cause of his addiction. His feelings of hate were so bitter and deeply ingrained that they had numbed any warmth towards them. He was indifferent to them. It was as if they existed simply to provide him with money for his habit.

Pushkal continued to come erratically till he left school but, on the whole, one-to-one counselling did little to deter him from his habit. Since I kept in touch with the friend from the centre, I could keep track of Pushkal's progress. Apparently, after Pushkal left school, he was still taking drugs. My friend told me that even though they had met a few times, Pushkal was totally addicted. He had to have his regular fix everyday and would go to extreme lengths to procure the money, sometimes through dishonest means. Unfortunately, my friend said that Pushkal was a mirror-image of himself and he would probably progress to bigger fixes and harder drugs to get the same kicks, as his system became more tolerant, before finally reaching rock bottom: this was the cycle he went through. Then, he said, there would probably come a time when he would want to change. I prayed the day would come soon when he would choose to turn his life around and, even though I never heard about him again, I still hope my prayers were answered.

Harikesh

Teenage boys who have their own bedroom, internet connection and a lock on their bedroom door have all the requisites to be a porn site viewer on the internet. Of course, many do not, but when the environment is conducive to doing something they know to be wrong but thrilling, many young teens will be lured by the opportunity. It's an easily accessible world that gives instant gratification and the more they view, the greater will be their thirst for a greater buzz. As with all addictions, the doses they need to get the same effects slowly increase. Those initial images from their early forays will dull with time and won't seem to create the same reaction anymore. Soon, they will venture from site to site or engage in sexually-explicit chats, or even worse, use their webcam to view their sex-acquaintances engaging in obscene acts.

For adolescent boys in particular, the whole mission of entering the sexual labyrinth is to climax through masturbation. On the whole, health professionals will agree that masturbation amongst adolescent males is healthy once in a while as it gives the body a chance to release pent-up sexual energy. However, when it becomes addictive to the point of incessant thinking of sexually explicit thoughts and seeking gratification several times a day, it will inevitably interfere in other areas of their lives.

This was what brought Harikesh to the counselling room. Tall, thin and dark, he had numerous pimples, one or two with pus-filled heads. Worried by his failing grades, he was initially quite reluctant to exactly tell me about his private habit. But as the conversation progressed, I was able to piece together what he was trying to say. 'I'm a bit worried ma'am because… well, when I am studying at home, something in my mind triggers a thought… and then I can't study after that until I turn on my computer… and go to some sites…'

I was getting the gist of it and, sensing his discomfort, tried to stifle a smile. He must've noticed. 'You know what I'm saying, right ma'am?'

I nodded.

'I can't help it ma'am. It's become a habit now and I don't get back into studies again for at least half an hour or so after that. And then after an hour of studying, I get bored and crave to do it again.'

'Do you do this every day?'

'Yes, at least two or three times a day.'

'Umm… do you climax every time?'

It was an uncomfortable question but it was necessary to know if he had reached climax, otherwise feelings of sexual frustration would manifest inside him.

'Err… yes… usually ma'am. I know it's not good, but if I don't do it then I keep thinking about it. So either way I can't win. It's affecting my studies and with my boards in a few months, it's distracting me completely. I'm surely going to fail!' Harikesh's eyebrows were furrowed together in worry. This was obviously something that was causing him much distress. He was caught in a vicious circle: the more he masturbated, the more it fuelled sexual desire, thus furthering his addiction. However, there was a sense of anxiety and guilt associated with it too. I needed to put his mind at rest.

'First of all Harikesh, let me tell you that masturbation is not "bad"; rather it's a healthy way of channelling your excess energies.' I smiled at him before continuing. 'However, it has dominated your thinking and in the long run, this will affect you in many ways.'

'Yes, but everyone does it, ma'am.'

'I know Hari, but when it becomes an ingrained habit, it will continue affecting you even when you have relationships.'

'How?' His eyes widened. He seemed shocked. 'What do you mean?'

'What I mean is that if you are viewing violent pornography, then this could change the way you view women. Many men lose respect for women because of this, even to the extent of not being able to have healthy relations with your life partner.'

I told him this to show him how far-reaching the effects actually can be.

'Oh, I never thought about it so seriously. Anyway, I don't view that kind of violent stuff but why does it tire me out?'

'Actually the body replenishes what it loses quite quickly, but when you are doing it so regularly, it is not a normal rate for your body. Usually the body does it through nightly emissions, as you know, but your actions are causing the body to produce more than it would have otherwise.'

'Yeah, I know, so what can I do? Every one of my friends does it. A couple of them wanted to come with me today but backed out at the last minute. I wanted to come last week too but I also couldn't gather my courage. But during the last week, I did very badly in a class test and then I told myself that if I didn't seek help then I would just continue getting worse and worse. So ma'am, why is it so addictive? Why can't I stop myself from turning on the computer?'

'Well it's because you're a young adolescent male with surging testosterone levels! The thing is that the media world has fuelled the normal desire for such activity so when young men like you are exposed to these images or any suggestive talk, you immediately get aroused…'

'Yeah… I know what you mean. Last week in class something happened…'

He stopped, as if he'd suddenly registered I was an adult.

'Go on Harikesh.'

'I promise this is true but please don't tell anyone.'

I nodded, signifying him to go on.

'It was after lunch and our usual geography teacher was absent so we had a substitute teacher taking the class. It was such a boring class but soon us boys noticed that the cotton kameez she was wearing was a little see-through and we could see her bra clearly. Plus her dupatta was not covering her chest area and so some of the boys began to get a little you-know-what….'

'Turned on?'

'Yeah kind of… and slowly one by one, the boys excused themselves to go to the bathroom. Every time one of the boys came back, there would be a big grin on his face. We all smiled and laughed because we knew why he'd gone and what he'd just done….'

I was mildly shocked by this revelation but at the same time aware that adolescent boys didn't need much titillation to get them easily excited.

'But ma'am, why do I still get a high even if just I think about incidents or images?'

'That's because when your brain remembers the images associated with sexual arousal due to a hormone called epinephrine which imprints them on your mind. That's why you can masturbate even if you have nothing to look at. It's all in your mind.'

'So how can I stop? That's what I want to know.'

'Well, I don't think you should stop it suddenly, since you are used to it every day but you can reduce the frequency by distracting your mind. When the urge comes, try engaging yourself in an alternative activity like sports or playing a musical instrument. You may even want to go for a brisk walk or talk to a friend or just eat an ice cream! Whatever you do, you have to divert your thoughts. This way the urge will pass. Slowly its importance will diminish and the urge will reduce. Try it one day at a time and let me know next week if the tendency has decreased or not. '

'Okay. Thanks for your help, ma'am.'

'Before you go, I just want to say that I am greatly impressed by your ability to understand that your habit is affecting your life in a negative way. Many people cannot see the long-term effects of a habit or obsession.'

'Thanks, but I just felt that unless I told someone who could help me, I would be unable to get out of it.'

'Oh, there's another thing you can do and that is to move your computer to a more busy room – like a living room – where other members of the family are present. That way you physically won't be able to surf the net when your family are around!'

'That's a bit extreme, ma'am.'

'It's just a suggestion! But never mind, just try what I suggested for now. Remember, Harikesh, it's all in the mind!' I laughed as I tapped my head. 'Anyway, see you next week!'

After he left, I was left to ponder. I wished more students were as frank as Harikesh. It was easy to talk to him because of his unabashed approach. He was merely sixteen years old and yet he had the wisdom of knowing that this addiction was making him lose control of his focus. I'm happy to say that Harikesh did come back the next week and told me that he would go and do some other completely unrelated activity until the urge passed. Though he still masturbated occasionally, the habit had reduced dramatically. The final proof that he was now the one in control came when he got his board results: he was amongst the top 10 per cent in the school.

I am sure that most parents would find it difficult to talk to their children about sex in general, let alone the harmful effects of pornography. Of course we want to protect the innocence and purity of children's childhoods for as long as possible, but the dominating influences of so many factors are difficult to keep at bay. Keeping teens sufficiently busy and engaged in extracurricular activities will help to channel their excess energies so that their minds don't wallow in boredom, which is one of the biggest reasons for surfing unhealthy sites.

Sasthi

Girls rarely came as pretty as Sasthi. And, unfortunately, rarely as unhappy too. I would have to enlighten you on her background before you hear her story so that you will get an idea of why she behaved the way she did in the face of grave danger to her health.

It sounds incredible, almost beyond belief, but Sasthi's mother simply walked out of the marital home one night after a fierce fight with her husband whilst Sasthi and her younger sister were asleep. She was only about ten years old but can still remember the moment when she woke up to get ready for school but couldn't find her mother. She searched the house high and low, only to be told by her father that her mother had suddenly left in the night. On hearing this, she hid her own devastation, bottling up her own tears, and comforted her crying seven-year-old sister as she tried to find a reason to explain why their mother walked out on them without saying goodbye. Her mother returned a few days later whilst they were at school to pick up her clothes and leave her marital home and her daughters forever. It probably sounds inconceivable, but in actual fact her mother had been living a double life for a long time. She had been having an affair with a Mumbai-based businessman, ever since her husband started to abuse her on a regular basis. One fine day she decided she'd had enough and simply walked out of her old life to start a new life with her lover.

So Sasthi grew up with her paternal grandmother, father and younger sister but without a mother. However, a couple of years later, when Sasthi was about twelve years old, her grandmother arranged a second marriage for her father with a girl from their ancestral village. It was another turbulent and abusive marriage which wasn't destined to last either. Sasthi's father was a heavy drinker and was unable to emotionally bond with new wife or his daughters; however being a shrewd businessman, was able to support them extremely well financially.

By the time Sasthi was in Class 10 her home situation had forced her to rapidly grow up and start thinking like an adult. Her grandmother had long stopped running the house because she broke her hip and became bedridden; she was now somewhat of a liability and demanded constant attention.

The father's second marriage had broken down and his second wife had returned to the village when he beat her up badly after a particularly nasty argument. He was an alcoholic now and Sasthi hardly saw him as he was never around when she got home from school, returning only when she and her sister were already in bed. So, while Sasthi was the one who was running the home like a housewife, she was also the schoolgirl studying for her board exams. Her life was exhaustive and it showed in her delicate face.

This was the story of her life as she told me. I could hardly believe it. It seemed she had endured many emotional upheavals in her mere sixteen years. Though eyes were light brown and round, a deep sadness was palpable in them. Deprived of love, she was always searching for a special someone to love her, care for her, protect her, someone she could trust and depend on, someone who would love her totally. Her mother's sudden departure left her emotionally desolate, as if she had a gaping hole in her heart waiting to be filled by someone worthy of her love.

On one of our earlier meetings, when Sasthi talked about her childhood memories, she brought an old photo of herself as a baby with her mother: Sasthi was the spitting image of her mother, who was just as beautiful. Fair, with smooth skin and dark brown hair, she was like a youthful Sophia Loren. The photo was worn and crumpled at the edges as a result of taking it out every night to look at her mother before going to sleep. She kept it safely between the pages of her diary because it was the only tangible reminder of her mother that she had. She hadn't met or heard from her mother in five years and lately, she had stopped hoping that she would ever return. It seemed she loved her and hated her at the same time. Whenever Sasthi came to see me she didn't really tell me much about her present, but only her past.

One particular counselling day, even before the first period bell, Sasthi was waiting outside my room. A surge of empathy came over me when I saw her, as often happens when I meet students who are so strong in the face of personal trauma. Her pretty face was slightly bloated and her eyes were swollen, as if she'd been crying.
'What happened?' I asked, obvious concern in my voice.
Immediately she started crying. I put my arm around her and ushered her into my room. She sat down and I handed her a tissue from the ever-present box on my table. She wiped her eyes and sniffly nose. Her face was flushed pink from all that crying. 'Ma'am I don't think I've ever told you about Hardev, have I?'

'Err, no I don't think so. Who is he?'

'Oh, he's my boyfriend. We've been going around for a year or so. He's a year older than me, studying in Class 11. He joined our school last year. Anyway, we've been having problems lately. We've been having so many fights and silly misunderstandings…'

'What kind of silly misunderstandings?'

'Oh, like…' She looked upwards deep in thought as if it was written on the ceiling. 'Like, for example, the other day, I had gone out to meet him because we were going to watch a film and as soon as he saw me he started shouting at me just because I was wearing a mini skirt. Just imagine ma'am, there were so many people around that I felt really embarrassed. And then when a boy looked at me, he blamed me for it, saying that what I was wearing was encouraging the boy to ogle me. He said I should have dressed properly and not like a ….' She stopped, conscious that she shouldn't be using vulgar words in front of me.

'Like a what?' I urged.

'Well he used the word "whore".'

Without commenting, I asked her if he often found fault in her.

'Yeah he does, in almost everything about me! He thinks nothing of shouting at me for no reason: if it's not something I'm wearing, it's something I've said or done. There's nothing that I do that's right!'

'Oh dear.'

He was obviously dominating her to such an extent that it was becoming extreme; he was finding fault in her for no reason and, because she was already someone who desperately needed to feel valued, he was crushing her self esteem more and more.

'Last night, just before I messaged you, he shouted at me because my phone was engaged and he presumed I was talking to a boy. When I told him I wasn't, he just didn't believe me. Then he wrote: *if you were in front of me right now, I'd have given you one tight slap!*'

'Have you seen him this morning?'

'Yes I saw him in the corridor this morning and as soon as he saw me he slapped me real hard right across my face in front of all my friends!' She started to cry again, her delicate frame quivering as the sobs overcame her. I became concerned for her. This boy didn't have any respect for her.

'Are you scared of him?' She nodded. I wanted to understand whether she felt she deserved such disrespect. 'Do you think you deserve his rude behaviour?'

She shook her head. The sobs died down. 'I don't but I don't like to make him unhappy. If he feels bad about what I wear or say or do, then I'll try to change for him.'

'But can't you see that you've not actually *done* anything wrong?'

'Yes ma'am, I do see it but as I already said, I love him so much and it's because he loves me that he hits me. He gets jealous because he cares for me and is protective. That's what he tells me. He says that no one can ever love me like he does.'

A strand of hair had stuck to her damp cheeks and she'd raised her right hand to push it aside when I caught a glimpse of the underside of her arm. There was a scab – perfectly small and round and rust-brown in colour. It looked particularly conspicuous against the fair colour of her skin.

'What's that mark?' I asked her, pointing to her arm.

She looked down and immediately straightened her arm downwards so that it remained hidden from me.

'Oh, nothing. I got hurt, that's all.'

'How did you get hurt?' I was trying to think of how she could get such a small, perfectly round mark.

'Um … um … hot oil. It splashed on me as I was frying puris last night.' She seemed a little hesitant, as if she was lying but I didn't probe any further. I knew drops of oil caused blisters to come up, so scabs like this seemed unlikely. I decided not to question her further because she was obviously hiding the truth, so I played along.

'Oh ok, but that sure is a *big* drop of oil! Please be more careful, Sasthi.'

She nodded and immediately resumed the conversation, as if in a hurry to divert the topic. 'So, as I was saying… about Hardev. How can I stop his angry reactions? How can I be the perfect girlfriend to avoid upsetting him?'

'Honestly speaking Sasthi, I don't think you've done anything *so* wrong for him to publicly humiliate you like that. He doesn't actually have the right to hurt you.'

'I know but last night he told me that if I continue to upset him, he'd leave me.' Tears welled up fast again. 'I don't think I could take it if he left me, ma'am. I need his love.'

'But he has slapped you and humiliated you. Is that *real* love, Sasthi?' I asked gently.

Her tears were falling down her face. Her cheeks were flushed pink. I took her hand and turned it around to expose her arm. I spoke quietly.

'Tell me Sasthi, how did you *really* get this mark?'

She didn't say anything.

'It's alright Sasthi, it'll be our secret, I just need to know if Hardev inflicted it. Please tell me.' She didn't say anything except nod her head as another cascade of tears rolled down her face. My doubts were confirmed. He was not only verbally abusing but physically too. 'How did he do it, Sasthi?' She was silent. The perfectly round scab suggested she was burned with a pea-sized circular implement. I remained silent too and allowed the silence to envelope us. I knew she would speak when she was ready.

'With a lit cigarette. He wanted to do something to me that made me uncomfortable, so he got angry.'

'What did he want to do?'

'It's embarrassing ma'am.'

'I don't get shocked easily Sasthi, believe me.'

'Well, last Saturday we went to see a film and after it was over, he was driving me home but he pulled over on a lonely road and kissed me….' She was sniffing as she talked. I could tell she was allowing the barriers between us to fall. I needed to get to this level of honestly if I was to help her.

'Then what happened?'

'He tried to put his hand under my skirt and touch me. I didn't like it so I pushed him away.'

'Did he stop?'

'Yes, but he was not happy. He lit a cigarette and smoked it without saying a word but I could tell he was angry with me. He asked me why I turned him away, if I loved him. I didn't say anything. He took my reaction as an insult to him because he thought he had the right to do anything to me. He threatened me by saying that if I ever stopped him from doing what he wanted again, he would leave a mark on my body. And before I understood what he was saying, he took my right arm, turned it over and stubbed the cigarette out on my bare skin. I screamed in pain but he didn't show any emotion.'

She was sobbing now, openly crying. I swallowed, feeling disturbed by the graphic details she was giving me. I waited for her to continue.

'Oh my God, the pain was unbelievable. The skin was burned immediately and the ash stuck onto my skin leaving a grey circle. Immediately I used my saliva to wipe off the ash and saw a patch of blood underneath. It was horrible ma'am. I still can't believe he did that.'

'Did he apologise?'

'No, he said it served me right and that the mark was a reminder of how I refused him. It will teach me a lesson for me for the future, he said.'

'Then what happened?'

'I started crying and told him to take me home. I didn't speak to him all the way. Once we arrived at my house, I got out of the car and walked away. A little later that evening he called me to say sorry and explained he did it because he loved me so much.'

'And did you forgive him?'

'Yes, immediately. He said he was so protective of me that when he got angry he didn't realise what he did. By me accepting his apology, everything was instantly okay again.'

I was in a fix. His behaviour was characteristic of abusive husbands who mistreat their wives in this way. Her symptoms were typical of the battered-wife syndrome but she was a mere schoolgirl and she could walk out any time she wanted to. Or could she? Her mind was holding her captive.

'Do you know what I'm going to say, Sasthi?'

'You'll probably tell me that I should leave him, right?'

'Well, in a way, yes, but only because of the way he's treating you. I'm scared for you, Sasthi. I would never force anyone to leave someone they love but his dominating behaviour is worrying me. Now that he's physically hurting you, he's entered a cycle. It's just a matter of time till he does it again, Sasthi. Can't you see that?'

'He might not, ma'am. I believe in my heart that he'll stop soon. He can't help it. It's not his fault! He has promised me that he'll change his ways.'

'I wish I could believe him, but I can't. From my experience Sasthi, the usual pattern for this type of behaviour is for the abuse to continue and to become more severe. And you to become more and more incapable of leaving him. Just love is not enough. There has to be respect too.'

'But, whatever it is, I'd rather suffer the physical pain than have him leave me! I don't want to be lonely!' she wailed.

'Ssh … ssh … I know you don't. Why do you think you won't be happy without him? Look at you – you have everything – brains and beauty. If you have to have someone who'll love you, you will find someone else who would love you for who you are and not disrespect you like this. You must have the courage to be strong to let go, that's all.'

She shook her head. 'I can't,' she whispered. 'I'm not strong enough ma'am. It's easy for you to say so ma'am but I can't do it. I just can't.'

Sasthi was so scared of being alone and of not being loved that she was prepared to stay in this physically and emotionally abusive relationship at any cost, even to the extent of suffering more torture. When Hardev entered her life, he must've soon realised that she was emotionally dependent on him and lacked self esteem. Slowly, he was able to dominate her mentally, physically and possibly even sexually; ever since that threat after the cigarette burn incident, I was quite certain that he had started to get his way with her sexually too.

As an outsider, I could see where it was all heading. I knew that it was hardly likely to get better. Hardev wanted to possess her totally. I tried to relay my fears for her safety but she just didn't see them. Whatever I said to her, she was adamant that leaving him was not the answer. I knew this was going to take time and patience on my part if I wanted her to gain self confidence. I decided that the only option I had was to ask her to come to see me every week and inform me of what was going on in her life. That way I could keep a tab on her. I hoped that encouraging her to talk about the abuse would help her to come to terms with it and gather enough motivation to come out of it. The onus of emerging from the relationship lay with her and only her.

I looked at her. My heart sank. She was so perfect physically and yet no one could tell how broken she was inside.

'Sasthi look, don't worry. If you can't leave him, you don't have to just yet. The very fact that you came to me and told me about this today is a small victory. I just need you to keep me informed about what's going on, okay?'

'Okay, but ma'am, I don't want you to tell me to leave him, that's all,' she said quietly, wiping the last remnants of tears.

I tried to lighten the load. I didn't want her to think that I would always keep forcing her to do something she was not strong enough to do. 'Okay, I won't, but slowly as time moves on, you yourself will tell me that you will be leaving him! Mark my words!' I laughed. 'Sasthi, in time you will be strong enough to fly, I promise you that!'

She managed a weak smile. She got up to leave. 'See you next week ma'am.'

Sasthi returned to see me every week until it was time for the Class 10 study leave. We had progressed a little in that she had gained some confidence in herself but she was still with Hardev. Just as I had predicted, as was the usual pattern with abusive partners, his aggressive behaviour towards her became more frequent, but she was still ambivalent and couldn't muster the will to move away. Sasthi never came back to school to study in Class 11, so I don't know where she went. She changed her mobile number and we lost touch, even though she had my mobile number. Perhaps she chose not to contact me for whatever reason. Whatever the outcome, I hope she was able to finally walk away from him. When I think of Sasthi's story, what still saddens me beyond belief is that, in spite of her unbelievable life, the greatest tragedy is that because the people closest to her had let her down, she totally lost faith and confidence in herself too.

Checklist

Any urge that happens persistently, interferes with ones daily life or can be self-destructive in the long run may be termed 'addictive'. Many things fall into this bracket be it lying, swearing, risk-taking behaviours like drugs, gambling or sexual exploits.

Red flags to watch out for

- Being locked in their bedroom for hours
- Very low self esteem and easily influenced
- Constantly asking for money to feed a habit
- Stealing
- Lying
- Going out and not telling you their whereabouts
- Angry if not able to go out
- Obsessive behaviour

What you can do

It's difficult to give general advice on addictive behaviours without knowing exactly what the addiction is. However, parents must understand that for teens, bad habits are often coping strategies for situations involving stress, boredom, insecurity, fatigue and frustration and are calming and soothing to the adolescent.

- ✓ Parents must employ a softly-softly attitude when dealing with teens who are trying to break a bad habit. Reprimanding and punishing will only make them want to rebel and develop a feeling of animosity towards their parents.
- ✓ Be Calm, Clear and Firm: calmly, yet clearly and firmly, explain what could go wrong and how it can impact their life if they can't let go.
- ✓ Patience and Perseverance: Sometimes, all your motivation and firmness will bite the dust as your teen refuses to back off from his or her bad habits. Don't give up or turn impatient. Remember a bad habit took a while to develop so it won't go away quickly either.
- ✓ Diversionary Tactics: Breaking a bad habit may mean more than just giving something up; sometimes it means replacing it with a good habit. Try to involve your teen in some hobby in order to

divert attention. This can be difficult for teens who may be stuck in a bad habit but negative attitudes and actions can be reversed, and positive, beneficial habits can be formed.

✓ Many addictions revolve around indulging in the habit socially, usually in a group. These people have a huge influence on your teen's behaviour so make sure they stay away from them. This will help them cope better. Support and praise your teen every time he or she is able to resist the temptation to indulge in the addiction. They might slip every once in a while and engage in the behaviour they are trying to change, but those slips are normal.

✓ Work together at making the good behaviours happen more often than the bad ones. The more this happens, the weaker the bad habit will get over time. After all, your goal in the end is not to successfully fight your bad habit, but instead to create good habits so that you do not have to think about the behaviour any more at all.

✓ Get professional help immediately if the addiction is life-threatening or your teen becomes depressed or suicidal.

Chapter 8: 'Stop Treating Me Like a Kid!'

There is an old saying in Assamese that translates thus: *When your son reaches the height of your nose, it's time to start treating him like an adult.* In the absence of no clear line between childhood and adolescence, I suppose earlier generations likened the demarcation to a fixed height which tallied with those teenage years. While many old proverbs are regarded as being obsolete in the modern world, perhaps this one is still quite relevant because it emphasizes the fact that there comes a time in our children's lives when we need to start treating them in a more mature way.

However, with many students coming to the counselling room to voice their woes about their parents still treating them like children, it seems the wisdom of such age-old sayings have been overlooked. Many parents don't accord a growing child the space, privileges and respect they need as they enter adolescence and continue to treat them in exactly the same way as they always have. In my line of work, it seems to be particularly so in those adolescents who are either a single child, the youngest child, the first born, or the only male or female in a set of three siblings.

Most teenagers, as they embark into this new phase, seek to establish their own identity and may demand some privacy in the form of their own bedroom or more personal freedom which they were not given earlier. It is this desire to assert their new status that causes much friction and misunderstanding in the parent-teen partnership, often characterized by arguments, screaming matches and lots of banging of bedroom doors! The hormonal changes of adolescence may cause them to style their hair for hours on end, fret about the shape of their body, worry about a pimple on their face, crave for a boy/girlfriend or want to wear fashionable clothes. However, those teens who meekly continue to remain in an extended childhood phase, showing no inclination to change, will have a harder time adjusting in many other areas of their life. By remaining in a time warp, they remain emotionally immature and will lag behind in the milestones of their peer group in terms of responsibility and independence. This widening difference may cause them to be ridiculed and teased by their classmates which can lead to distress and even depression.

Research has shown that the frontal cortex of the brain, which is responsible for the brain's executive functions (such as reasoning ability, making well thought-out decisions, and controlling impulses) does not completely develop till one is in the twenties. Teen brains therefore are in a critical stage of development which means they don't have the processing capabilities of an adult. Regardless of children entering adolescence, they still need guidance when it comes to making adult decisions. As care-providers, we are responsible for them and should be in the driving seat. We still need to hold the reins of freedom, but there should be relaxations of earlier boundaries to suit the individual's level of mental maturity. In all fairness to parents, I agree that it is very difficult to ascertain when it's time to loosen those reins. What complicates matters further is that the boundaries are different for every child: some children mature as early as eleven years of age and can be accorded a certain degree of responsibility whilst some may still be behaving like a child at sixteen. I wish there were red warning lights that beeped when the child reached a certain level of mental maturity, informing us to start changing our attitude!

In the complex world of human relationships, it might be interesting to ponder on why there is a hiccup at this phase at all. Which link is the weaker as adolescence sets in? Is it the parents who continue treating their children as kids, thus stunting their natural mental growth? Or is it the children who do not display the signs of mature thinking, thus inhibiting themselves from being treated as an adult? It's almost like the classic chicken-or-the-egg dilemma where either could be the cause. Personally, I feel the roots lie even deeper – possibly going back to early childhood. I believe that if children were given age-appropriate chores and responsibilities of their own as they grew up, the transition to adolescence would be far less problematic, probably even go by unnoticed. Those children who had everything done for them as children and were not given any tasks or responsibilities suitable to their age may well turn out to be at loggerheads with their parents in adolescence. Experienced parents will tell you that the best way to avoid the 'potential hazards' of adolescence is to tread a middle line in childhood: don't baby them but don't force them to grow up too fast either.

In this chapter, we meet the parents whose inadvertent 'holding on' to their child's childhoods caused a host of problems, especially in social adjustment. As I have already mentioned, a child who is immature in nature will have problems in other areas of life too, such as friendships, peer group dynamics and opposite gender relationships.

This 'ripple effect' is particularly evident in school because students do not think twice about laughing at those who are different. Aryahi was in Class 9 but her mother was a classic example of a parent who still treated her like a little girl. So when a fellow classmate overheard her mother baby-talking to her, it was enough to set off a ruckus of hilarious gossip throughout the class. Poor Aryahi was mercilessly teased to the point where she broke down and sank into a depressive state.

Somnath's story, on the other hand, has a slightly more unusual twist. As an only child born to two highly-educated but very reclusive parents, I was given a peep into his dysfunctional family life when he confessed to having witnessed something he shouldn't have seen whilst he was sleeping between them one night. You may be startled by the bizarre circumstances of his life but it just goes to show that even educated parents have yet to broaden their horizons when it comes to being more aware of the changes associated with adolescence.

The final story will resonate with all fathers who have a soft corner for their daughters. It is not always easy for any doting dad to accept that little girls grow up into mature young ladies! Vamika's father had difficulty in accepting that once she reached adolescence he was not the only male in her life anymore, for she had become close to a male class friend too. Unable to let go of the image of the frilly-pink-frock-wearing toddler that she once was, he became increasingly frustrated until a kind word spoken by a relative helped him to change his attitude.

Aryahi

Though Aryahi was a student in Class 9, she still wore her hair in two neat pigtails as she had done throughout her school life and, whilst many of her friends were starting to style their hair with trendy fringes or dangly tendrils, she never had a hair out of place because her mother religiously oiled and tightly plaited her hair every day. For the teachers, this age was notoriously deviant because girls regularly flouted school rules and often wore eye liner, mascara, lip gloss or nail polish. However, Aryahi was quite removed from it all. Bespectacled and always perfectly dressed, she didn't seem to be fazed by the trivialities of appearance that her friends seemed to be so concerned about.

Aryahi's problem started when she and her parents came to school to collect her report card. Nobody could have predicted that such a seemingly insignificant catalyst could have caused such a ruckus. Aryahi's report card was handed over to her mother who let out a squeal of delight when she saw that Aryahi had scored well in all subjects. The parents' happiness was furthered when the teacher told them that Aryahi had come first in class too. Her mother was absolutely ecstatic and, in her obvious delight, leant over and gave her daughter a big slobbering kiss. Since there were other classmates and their parents in the classroom too, she was overcome with embarrassment and silently wiped her wet cheek. But if that was bad, it was to get worse. As they left the classroom and were walking down the corridor, Aryahi's mother was positively walking on air. Still unable to contain herself, she squeezed her daughter's cheeks together and said out loud in a baby voice: 'My leetil Arhu-baby, you shweet, shweet cutie-pie. Mummy is sho proud of you!'

And, at that precise moment, three of Aryahi's friends were walking down the corridor from the opposite direction and saw her mother's coochie-cooing endearment. They instantly giggled between themselves and committed the moment to memory, for this was going to be great classroom gossip. Though Aryahi saw them pass by, she never anticipated the havoc her mother's baby-talk would cause to her life.

By the time Aryahi came to school on Monday morning, the damage was already done. The word had got round that a 'baby' had joined their class by the name of 'Arhu-baby'. Before she knew it, at any opportunity, the whole class started to tease her regarding the corridor incident. She kept up the pretence of being able to cope with the persistent teasing, praying it would die down, but even after a week they were still at it. Unable to cope with it any longer, she was found by the class teacher in the classroom during the short break with her head down on the desk crying uncontrollably. Her whole body was vibrating with pent-up frustration. It had all got too much for her. It took a while for the teacher to calm and soothe her down and once she had, she was brought to me. Her nose was pink and running as she was still sniffing from her crying spell. She sat down and I thanked the class teacher who gave me some brief details about her before leaving the two of us together.

Aryahi was still besieged by involuntary jerks of breathing every now and again. Her mini breakdown had caused some of her hair to come out of her plaits too and so this was how I started our conversation. Humour is a wonderful balm to many stressful situations and helps to bring two people together and relax the atmosphere.

'Your hairstyle got damaged whilst you were crying,' I said, pointing to the straggly strands.

She managed a weak smile to my comment before resuming the unhappy look. 'Tell me how it all started, Aryahi,' I whispered quietly as I touched her arm.

So Aryahi started to talk, her speech interspersed with sharp intakes of breath and she tried to regain her composure. By the time she finished, she was calm, as if the act of telling me has considerably lightened her load. She spoke consistently without any further tears. After hearing her, I needed to get to the crux of many underlying issues, and since she seemed quite open to talking, I started asking her questions. 'So Aryahi, did you have any idea that your friends were going to tease you after the incident happened?'

'Yes, I thought they might but I didn't think it would get to be so bad.'

'What do they say to you?'

'The three main girls who were in the corridor poke the most fun at me. Everything they say to me is in a baby voice but lately more girls are doing it and even some of the boys have started too.'

'How do you react?'

'I just ignore it, but it's been getting worse and worse day by day.'

'Did you tell your mother?'

'Yes, I did but there's nothing she can do to help me. We can't turn back the clocks. Anyway it's not her fault. She was so happy with my results that she couldn't stop herself.'

'Does she often talk to you in a baby-voice at home?'

'Err … yes usually …. especially when she expresses her love for me. But I'm used to it so I don't really notice that much.'

She had given me an insight to where the problem lay: her mother. I needed to know more about her home atmosphere. She and her little sister, who was only a year younger to her, had grown up in a very protected environment. They always slept with their mother whilst their father slept in a separate bedroom, even though she was fifteen now.

'Don't you want your own room, Aryahi?'

'No, actually I don't. I don't want to be separated from my mum. I'd be just too scared to sleep alone.'

'Do you do have any household responsibilities? Like chores?'

'What kind of chores?'

'Laying the table for dinner, tidying the bedroom, bringing in the dry clothes from the washing line, folding them or even just making your own snacks?' She shook her head.

'No. I don't do anything like that. Anyway we have a maid and my mum is so organised that neither me nor my sister have to help around the house. My mum even helps us with our homework.'

'Who sorts out your uniform, polishes your shoes, gets your school bag together, gives you breakfast?'

'Mum does it all – but the servant polishes my shoes!'

'So, there's very little you need to do, right?'

She nodded. I began to get a picture of how it was. It seemed she had limited responsibilities, except to study and as long as she kept her grades up, her mother was happy to do everything for her. She was the central figure upon which the entire house pivoted. They were all dependent on her – physically and emotionally – so much so that Aryahi would have felt like a boat without an anchor if her mother loosened her grip. She even overshadowed Aryahi's natural tendencies for independence and greater privacy which show their inclinations in adolescence.

'What shall I do about the teasing, ma'am?'

'It's easy for me to call the girls and scold them, but if I did that, it wouldn't help your ability to stand up to them. On the contrary, they would think that you are a weakling and continue the treatment, though more subtly. I know you are a strong girl. Let's wait one more week. If it doesn't subside, come and see me next week and I will think up an alternative course of action. If I get involved too quickly, they may end up teasing you more and we don't want that.'

She nodded in agreement. 'Yes, that could be worse than this.'

'So don't worry about anything, Aryahi. Now that I'm involved, I will see that things don't get out of hand.' She left looking much more relieved.

I took a deep breath. I knew I had to talk to Aryahi's mother. She was the only person who could allow her to grow up if she loosened her clutches; after all this was beginning to affect her life quite adversely.

So Aryahi's mother came to see me the following week. Dressed in a zari-bordered cotton sari, she was a simple Bengali lady who believed that children should only have one concern in life: studies. Her ideology was that there should be no other concerns in a school-going child's life except to do well academically and that was why she did everything for her daughters. But she confessed that ever since that report-card day, there was a perceptible change in Aryahi's behaviour. 'She has changed a lot,' her mother opined. 'She cries at the slightest instance and is just generally miserable at home.'

'Yes, teasing like she has endured can be devastating.'

'She talks about wanting to die. She was never like this. She hates going to school. She pretends she has a headache or tummy ache every morning. So I have to bring her to school in the car every day.'

The teasing had indeed taken its toll on her daughter. Suicidal thoughts such as these often stem from an overbearing feeling of wanting to escape from the situation. She was obviously finding it very difficult to handle a problem in which she was alone. Usually she shared her problems with her mother but in this instance, Aryahi felt alone because her mother was the cause! She must've felt desolate, as if she was standing all alone on the battlefield.

'I just can't understand *why* showing affection towards my own daughter can be a reason to tease her. Why are these girls finding it so funny? Don't they have mothers too?'

I smiled. Her mother wasn't thinking in 'adolescent mode'. She didn't realise how cruel their world could be. 'Actually, it was because you were treating her like a baby that it caused amusement. It only takes a small incident like that, or even something minor like a short haircut for example, to cause teasing. That's how teenagers are. Anyone who doesn't conform will be ridiculed and from the way you baby-talked her, it seemed that they found that a great excuse to taunt her.'

'But I have always spoken to my daughters like that. They are my babies, always will be, and I really don't like it when anyone hurts them.' She was being defensive now and my words were rebounding off her.

'Yes, I know but your open affection spoke a lot more about how you still think of her -- like a baby, as you have just said. From what I could deduce from Aryahi, you don't give her much responsibility or privacy.'

'Why would she need *privacy?* We are very open to each other. I know all her secrets. I'm like her friend. If she wanted "privacy" she'd have told me, but she hasn't mentioned it. EVER.'

'That's because you have not let go. How can she want something she has never experienced? You haven't given her the space to grow. As teens enter adolescence, they are capable of taking on some more responsibilities towards themselves like looking after their own basic needs.'

'There's nothing wrong with that,' she said abruptly. Her glasses had slipped a fraction down her nose and she pushed them up. I decided it was time to be blunt.

'Tell me Mrs Banerjee, do you still wash her underwear?'

'Umm ... yes I do, but I wash everyone's underclothes. I put them all in the bucket and wash them together. There's nothing wrong with that, is there?'

I didn't comment and instead asked her another question.

'Do you still give her a bath?'

'Well, sort of....'

'Sort of?'

'I mean she has her own bath, but I just go in to check that she's washed off all the soap.' She chuckled before continuing: 'She always leaves traces of shampoo on her hair or soap under her arms.'

'Doesn't she mind you seeing her naked body?'

She stopped for a second to think. 'Well .... she does cover her breasts with her hands, but I tell her not to be stupid.'

'So, that very act of covering herself up – can't you see that she's *wanting privacy?*'

'Well, perhaps, but I'm her mother. I can see her body, I gave birth to it. She should not hide anything from me!'

'You see, Mrs Banerjee, forgive me but that's where I think you are wrong. We don't *own* our children just because we gave birth to them. They are little independent beings that we have to slowly set free ...'

She was not amused by my philosophy. On the contrary, she seemed a little irritated, but in the course of our conversation, I had got all my answers. She was indeed a very domineering woman and had sucked everyone into her vortex. I only had one course of action, to tell her outright what I thought.

'With respect, Mrs Banerjee, many mums are in your position too.'

'What do you mean?'

'Well, many of us feel we have to know everything about our daughters but the thing is we don't. Just because we are mothers, it doesn't mean we *have* to know everything and they *have* to tell us everything. We're mothers, for God's sakes, not their "bosom buddies"!' The mother was listening but remained silent. I continued. My voice was quieter now. 'I think you are afraid of losing her if she keeps secrets to herself or becomes more independent. Perhaps you will feel insecure, as if you have no purpose, right?'

She was thinking. I repeated my question. I think she was confused. I asked it in a different way. 'How would you feel if Aryahi didn't need you for all her needs anymore?'

'I would feel as if I failed as a mother.'

'That's it! That's *exactly* why you can't let go. You feel that once you loosen the grip on her, she will no longer need you. You will feel useless, as if you have failed in your role.' She nodded. I continued. 'Forgive me again but I feel it's *you* who needs to feel wanted.'

She was slowly nodding now, deep in thought. 'Perhaps,' she whispered. I felt a glimmer of hope that I was making progress. I continued my reasoning. 'Mrs Banerjee, the greatest victory of motherhood is bringing up children who can be independent, who can think rationally and in a mature way, who understand that they have responsibility towards themselves. But unless we give our children the chance to prove themselves, they will always remain totally dependent on us. And that's not good for them.'

'But if I let go, she will make mistakes.....'

'So what if she does? As long as they are not life-changing, let her make mistakes and learn from them.'

She was beginning to acknowledge what I was saying but the atmosphere had turned quite heavy. I needed to turn it lighter. I changed my tone and tried to sound cheery. 'I have a suggestion! For example, next time she has a bath, leave her totally alone. Let her have soap on her arms or shampoo in her hair after her bath, it won't kill her. Don't interfere in these small things. By getting involved you are taking away her natural coping mechanisms.'
'But I still need her to be open with me about other things.'
'Of course you do and she won't be distanced from you. It's the emotional connection that you must have with her but you don't need to know *every little detail*. I'm sure she'll tell you the important stuff anyway. Just because our daughters may not tell us everything, it doesn't mean that they love us any less. As long as you know the main gist of their problems, we can safely give them more space and independence without feeling we're losing them.'
'I can't let her be like a wild horse.'
'No no! Of course not, but be more flexible. Start to inculcate responsibility and show her you can trust her.'
'So do you mean she should start doing her own chores?'
'Well, not all initially, but definitely some, especially those that concern her. Also, I think she should have her own bedroom. Even if she doesn't sleep in it straight away, at least let her study there and spend time there during the day. Let her arrange her things and decorate the room in her own personalised way. Later she will naturally want to sleep there one day. Also, Mrs Banerjee, don't go into the bathroom when she's bathing *and* PLEASE make sure she washes her own underclothes. And slowly when your younger daughter sees Aryahi being given more responsibility, she too will easily be able to slip into this phase without any hiccups!'
'Oh, I am beginning to see what you are saying.' It seemed she was beginning to realise that she was perhaps partly to be blamed for Aryahi's predicament.
'But don't make the change too drastically. Slowly and gradually start giving her more responsibilities and, while doing so, start giving your younger daughter more too.'
'Hmmm, I think you're right. I think it will be nice to be a bit easy on myself if I give them their own chores to do!'
'But as hard as it will be, keep your nose out of it! They won't do things perfectly at first but you will have to overlook it.'
'Okay, I will talk to my husband about this too.'
'Yes, please make him see my perspective on this. You have two lovely girls who love you so much. Now, if you really do want the best for them, set them free – but slowly! The freedom must be measured to suit their capabilities but let them fly on their own.'

'Yes, I will. But just one thing – what about the *real* problem? I mean the teasing that Aryahi's facing in the class?'

I had almost forgotten! We had detoured from the teasing by addressing the root cause, but at least I now knew that Aryahi was finally going to be given the chance to move out of this extended childhood phase in which she was stuck. 'Well funnily enough, Mrs Banerjee, the real problem was you! The teasing at school was just a symptom of the problem,' I laughed. She gave an embarrassed smile. 'It seems the teasing is dying down but I've already told Aryahi to come and see me next week if things haven't got better. Usually, classroom memory is short and soon they will find another issue and someone else to tease. However, if they are still upsetting her, I will then mediate and talk to the other girls directly.'

It is always preferable to allow a student to handle issues on their own by giving support than to intervene, because it strengthens their ability to handle their own life's problems. However, it's important to judge each situation on its own as some may have potential consequences which can be more severe. Fortunately, Aryahi's problem fizzled out on its own accord when the exams loomed ahead. Everyone went into hibernation as they prepared for them. Aryahi secured first position again and came to tell me.

'Congratulations!' I told her.

'Thanks ma'am,' she smiled. She looked very happy.

'How are things at home?'

'Oh, there have been some big changes! I'm being treated like a "mini-adult" now and have my own bedroom! Now I'm thinking about my new colour schemes!'

'Wow, that's wonderful! Oh, you once told me you didn't want your own room, if I remember rightly…' I said with a twinkle in my eye.

'That was then! Anyway, I think I'll choose yellow for the walls. It's such a happy colour and it will reflect how I feel. I feel so happy in my life now!'

'Me too, I feel so happy for you too, Aryahi!'

I think I had the bigger smile because finally, it seemed her mother was finally able to let go of those invisible apron strings and allow her daughter the chance to grow up and be an independent person.

Somnath

The only son of two extremely well-educated parents, Somnath was a very bright boy. The intellectual environment of his home was centered mostly around discussion on books and topics far from ordinary table talk. Though he was only in Class 8, the general knowledge he had acquired by reading so many books and encyclopedias was phenomenal and he was somewhat of a genius. Perhaps it would not be wrong to say that the family was generally a little eccentric too. They didn't own a television set and only listened to western or Indian classical music on their cassette player or the radio. Since their home was in a remote locality far off from any neighbours, Somnath had had a very lonely childhood. He often wandered around the large compound of his home where he intently watched the activities of the birds and insects. As a result he was very interested in nature. Even though Somnath had had a very sheltered upbringing, his parents had stressed proper etiquette. He was extremely articulate, well-read and his manners were impeccable. Always immaculately dressed, with gleaming shoes, oiled and side-parted hair and a perfectly triangular tie knot, Somnath was the pinnacle of a well-turned out student. He was chubby and looked particularly studious with his black-rimmed spectacles. Many students thought he was the proverbial school geek. He followed the procedure to make an appointment to see me and duly turned up at exactly the right time. His brow was furrowed and he looked quite worried. 'Good morning ma'am, may I come in?'

'Yes, of course, Somnath.'

'How are you, ma'am?'

'I'm fine, thank you. And you?'

'I'm not very fine today actually. My mind is a bit agitated and I have no one to discuss my thoughts with.'

'Well then you've come to the right place! Please tell me…'

He took a deep breath. I sensed he wanted to discuss a personal issue and that this wasn't easy for him. 'I love my parents a lot and we three are the best of friends. We do everything together. We eat breakfast together in the morning and in the evenings after I have done my homework, we sit together and read English poetry, or play Scrabble or sometimes we even sing old patriotic songs together. Then we have dinner together before going to sleep.'

'That's nice, Somnath. It's good for families to do things together.'

'The problem is that because I don't have any friends, I think of my parents as my friends. In fact my father refers to us as the three musketeers. So I don't really feel that I am missing brothers or sisters because I have my parents and lots of animals.'

'Oh really? What kind of animals?'

'We have a dog called Ketu, a little apso, who is my best friend. And there are lots of birds in our compound. In fact ma'am, I saw a koel's nest the other day and I keep an eye on it every day. There are about seven more days to go till the eggs hatch. There are lots of parrots that come too and pigeons and doves. So I'm not lonely.'

'But do you have any close *human* friends?'
He didn't smile. He was still quite serious. 'No, not human friends. Even at school, they keep a little distance. I don't have a mobile, so no one calls me. We only have a landline phone.'
'So what is your problem, Somnath?'
'Oh, yes – I digressed. Yes, the problem is that the other day I had a very unsettling experience.'
His English was so grammatically correct. I remembered the number of times I had told students to read books to improve their English; Somnath was the perfect example of how reading can help one's speaking skills. 'Go on. I'm listening…'
'You see ma'am, I have always slept between my parents for as long as I can remember. The other day I'd got up in the middle of the night to drink some water and saw that my mother was on my father's side of the bed and they seemed very engrossed in something. It was dark so I couldn't see her very clearly as I wasn't wearing my glasses but I remember asking her why she had changed sides. She suddenly seemed very shocked to hear my voice and immediately they both pushed away from each other. It was at that point that I realised that my father was actually lying face down on top of my mother. I think they were hugging each other but it was dark so I wasn't sure. So, without another word, my mother came back to my side and went to sleep. But I was left feeling very uncomfortable. Something just didn't feel right. I thought we three were the best of pals but it seems that my parents have their own secrets from me. The next morning when I asked her what she was doing, she said that it was simply "biology", but I can't stop thinking about it. We studied human reproduction in biology class and it's disturbed me to think my parents were doing *that*. I can't stop seeing that image in my mind over and over again.'

There is no doubt in my mind that to witness parents indulging in sexual activity is one of the most unnerving experiences of childhood. It can affect a child much more deeply than parents realise. I have heard many bizarre things in my career as a counsellor, but I was very alarmed to hear that a fourteen-year-old boy should still be sleeping between his parents. As for parents indulging in sexual relations in the presence of a sleeping teenage son, this was the height of sheer stupidity, utter naivety or simple irre-sponsibility. Not demarcating their roles as parents and insisting they were 'friends' was bewildering to Somnath. It was no surprise that he was now disturbed -- his vision of them being a team had turned upside down. But it's imperative to understand that they were an odd couple anyway and very different in their thinking. I had to tell them that they were unknowingly subjecting him to mental abuse by their tactless behaviour. Somnath was clearly shocked and distressed. Unless they understood the ramifications their behaviour was having on his psyche, Somnath could grow up having traumatic memories about this episode which could not only initiate a host of mental problems but even affect his own sexuality.

'Um Somnath, I can see you are very upset and quite rightly so. I need to speak to your parents. Can they come in to school tomorrow?'

'Not my father, because he's a professor and he has to go to college but my mother can. Can you ring her? I think that would be better.'

'Yes, I'll ring her tonight.'

'Ma'am I just feel so disgusted. How could they do that? I never thought they were like that.'

Until I knew more about the incident, it was premature of me to comment. It was possible that the parents were so out of touch with the present generation of teens that they didn't think that Somnath knew anything about sexual intimacy and so were totally unaffected by what he thought. It was not for me to justify their actions and tell him about the intimate part of their marriage. It would definitely be better if he heard the explanation from his parents. I merely said, 'What you saw was unfortunate but I need to clarify things with your mother first. There are things you will need to understand but only your parents will be able to settle your mind. For the moment, try to divert your mind whenever the thought disturbs you. Let me talk to her in the meantime. And come and see me next week and tell me if the baby fledglings have hatched or not, eh?'

The tone of my voice when I spoke to Somnath's mother on the phone was enough for her to realise that I wanted to see her urgently. She did turn up the next day dressed in a floral nylon sari. She looked like any other simple housewife but, as soon as she spoke, I could tell she was very well read. 'Actually I have done my doctorate in history, but because of Somnath I chose to stay at home. We want the best for our only son. We want him to excel in whatever he does.'

'Yes, he's a very well-behaved and intelligent boy. I'm sure he'll do well in life. How has his behaviour been recently?'

'Hmm ... for some reason he seems very morose lately, maybe even depressed as if he's in melancholy.'

I decided to broach the topic a little cautiously. 'Somnath told me that he still sleeps in the same bed as you and your husband.'

Her answers were matter-of-fact and straightforward. 'Yes, he has done so, ever since he was a baby.'

'But, now that he's so much older it's quite surprising.'

She paused momentarily as if she wanted to say something to me and then hesitated. I trusted silence to act as the prompter and sure enough she continued. 'We've always kept him between us.'

'Why?'

Her tone softened. She sank into a memory and her eyes glistened over. 'We lost a son before Somnath was born. He died in infancy from pneumonia. Two years later, Somnath was born and we didn't want to lose him like we lost the first one, so we kept an eye on him all the time.' She took out a handkerchief and dabbed her eyes. I felt my eyes fill with tears too. There can be no bigger sorrow than losing a child. 'I'm so sorry to hear that, I never knew,' I said in obvious regret.

'So that's why we were extra careful with Somnath. We don't let anything bad happen to him.'

Suddenly it made sense. I could see why they clung onto him, fearful of losing him too. I spoke really gently now, aware that she was upset. 'I know it's sad but you have to have your own space and he needs his own too.'

She sniffed. The tears were still flowing. 'I don't know if we can do that. We're so used to him sleeping with us. We're a close threesome.'

'But, with respect, when you two indulge in normal marital relations....'

'We don't.' She looked shocked.

'That's not what he saw....' I replied assertively.

'Well, not when he's awake anyway. Wait a minute, did you tell you he saw us?'

I nodded. 'He came to see me yesterday. He said he felt very uncomfortable. That's why I called you last night.'

'Oh my God! He remembered? Do you think he knew what we were doing?'

'Yes. He's knows all about sex – as most of his peer group do. He's a modern adolescent, you know. You made him feel very uneasy.'

'But I explained it all to him the following day.'

'I don't think a one-word answer is enough explanation for him. I think both of you need to talk to him about this in a gentle way, by explaining that his feelings are most important to you both, but the relationship you share with your husband is a part of your long-term happiness.'

'Yes, I don't want him to think of sex as a bad thing.'

'Well, unless you explain your actions as a natural thing that happens between two people who are married and care for each other, he will fall prey to misconceptions. It may even traumatise him to the extent that he has mental problems like depression, suicidal thoughts, eating disorders or even sexual confusion later on in life.'

'Oh my goodness! I never knew something like this could have so many ramifications. I feel so guilty now. It's unfortunate he saw...'

'Unfortunate yes, but there's still a chance you can salvage this, depending on how you handle it and promise to yourselves that this is the last time he'll ever be witness to it again.'

'I never thought he would still be affected this much.'

'Yes, this is why he is so depressed. He still seemed very upset about it when he came to see me yesterday. Just tell him matter-of-factly and don't bring it up again. The more you harp on it, the worse it will become.'

'Oh dear, I will discuss it with my husband and we'll talk to him.'

'And I think that even if you don't give him his own room immediately, at least give him his own bed.'

'Okay, I will.' She looked at her watch, obviously feeling a little embarrassed by the nature of our conversation. She stood up, poised to leave. I hoped she now understood why her son was so miserable. 'I've asked Somnath to come to me next week. I hope you will do whatever you can to clarify things to him. I'll ask him next week. I hope he will be happier. And slowly, please try to detach him from this idea that you are the three musketeers. You three are not peers, you two are the parents and he is the son. You all have your separate roles but that doesn't mean you can't be friends, because after all you are family. Just because he moves into his own room and does things independently it shouldn't compromise on your closeness; rather it will reinforce it.'

'Yes, I understand what you are saying. Thank you for your time.'

Somnath was much happier when he came to see me the following week.

'My mother explained that my father was hugging her because they love each other so much. I understood what she meant by "hugging her" and didn't ask any more questions. I guess that what they were *actually* doing is just normal animal behaviour!' he said with a twinkle in his eye.

I'm glad he could find it funny. Thank goodness he loved animals enough to understand that sexual behaviour was absolutely normal. I also suppose that because he'd commonly seen such behaviour amongst animals that he was more accepting about it as a way of life instead of falling prey to the negative connotations that society attaches to the sexual act.

Somnath skillfully changed the subject. 'Oh by the way ma'am the birds hatched! I can't see them but I can hear them!' he said ecstatically.

'Oh that's wonderful news!' I didn't dwell too much on the issue either as it could unsettle him again. His mother had obviously tried to make amends as much as she could under the circumstances. I was glad that she understood that she had a responsibility towards her actions and that she and her husband were the only ones who could ultimately salvage the situation.

Vamika

When Vamika was born, her parents felt that their prayers had finally been answered. To them it was as if the gods had sent her. After two boys and a fifteen-year gap, she was the little girl they had always dreamed about. Indeed, they were so ecstatic that they called her Lakhi, an affectionate Assamese term for girls, likening them to Lakshmi, the goddess of wealth.

Vamika grew up as the apple of her parents' eyes but especially her father's. She never had to lift a finger in the house to do her chores for they were all done for her by the servants. Her parents believed that since Indian girls stay with their parents for such a short time before they leave the family home to get married, they should not need to do any household work. As a result, they made sure that she was treated like a princess and her every whim and desire was granted. Her birthdays were always celebrated on such a grand scale that they were like little mini-weddings that needed days of preparation.

In spite of growing up in such a luxurious environment, Vamika was a loving and kind girl. In many ways because she was much younger than her brothers, she grew up like an only child. She loved her pet animals and her dolls and happily passed away many hours on her own. Her mother was more than forty years old by the time she was born and now that she was in Class 11, her mother was in her late fifties and their mental wavelengths didn't match at all. As for her father, well he was nearing seventy now and he was more like a grandfather than a father.

I had first come face-to-face with Vamika when she had once accompanied one of her friends to a counselling session in my room. That gave me a brief introduction to her, so I knew who she was when she came to see me. Tall and slim, she had very curly hair which she tied back into a tight ponytail. She was very fair and her hands were soft and dainty, as if they had never done any hard work. Already familiar with me, she wasted no time in getting to the heart of the matter. 'Ma'am, it's my dad. He's so possessive about me that he gets really angry if ever boys call me. I don't even know why they sent me to a co-educational school! The other day he saw some photos of my friend's party on my digital camera and he got really angry because in some of them I was with some male class friends. I think he got really upset. I don't know what's got into him.' She was shaking her head in disbelief.

'How is his behaviour with you usually?'

'Well, he's usually so nice to me. He always speaks to me with a lot of respect and never shouts at me. He's never even lifted a finger on me. But ever since he saw those photos he's been acting really weird. If I ask him something, either he'll give me a really irritated-sounding reply or he totally ignores me. If he answers the phone and if it's one of my male class friends, he tells them that I'm not in. His reactions are so peculiar.'
'So have you noticed this hostility ever since he saw the party photos?'
'Yes, it started from that day and has got worse and worse. Now he scrutinizes what I wear, makes sure I don't wear any make up and asks me a hundred questions if ever I go out to meet my friends. He no longer sends the driver to drop and bring me back but drives the car himself.'
'Hmm. It seems that he doesn't trust you, doesn't it?'
'Yes it does, but I've done nothing wrong, ma'am. Is it a crime if I have male friends?'
'No, of course it isn't, but for your father this is a much deeper issue. It's about how he sees you and has always seen you. Perhaps he still thinks of you as a little girl. How is your mother about this?'
'She's better than him but even she is a bit conservative.'
'They're very protective, aren't they?'
'I don't know if "protective" is the right word. They're control freaks and want me to wear stuff that I don't like or do things that I don't want to do or go where I don't want to go!'
'Someone needs to talk to them.'
'So what do you suggest we do, ma'am?'
I pondered for a few seconds. I felt it wasn't time for me to intervene just yet.
'Have you tried talking to your brothers?'
'They're both very busy. One's in Delhi and the other is in Pune. They're too tied up with their own lives.'
I thought of others she could turn to. 'Can you tell your mother about your father's change of behaviour? Maybe she will be able to make him understand how his reactions are spoiling his relationship between you and him.'
'I'll try.'
'Come and tell me what transpires next week.'
'Okay ma'am and thank you. Wish me luck!'

A week passed by till I saw Vamika again and I assumed that things were sorted after she talked to her mother. But I was quite shocked to see her transformation. She was looking haggard and weary, as if she hadn't been sleeping very well. It was like she was a different person. Her eyes had sunken into her sockets and she had dark circles around them.

'Oh my goodness Vamika! What happened?'

'I tried telling my mum last week but things got even worse. She just didn't understand and sided with my dad. They didn't think they were at fault at all. For the last week they've been keeping serious tabs on me – listening to my phone calls, forcing me to keep my bedroom door open, sending the maidservant to spy on me, sending the driver to walk me back from the bus stop – they even stopped me from going out with my friends!' Things seemed to be going downhill for her. Her voice was croaky. She was close to tears by now. 'And yesterday when I answered my mobile, dad asked me who it was and I had to lie otherwise he'd get angry. I said a girl's name when actually it was my boyfriend and I think he overheard that it was a male voice. So he slapped me right across my face so hard!'

'Then what?'

'They both started shouting at me saying that I had changed and had become boy-crazy.' She broke down as soon as she uttered the words. I was surprised because I was aware of how her father had always treated her like a china doll. I handed Vamika a tissue. 'They took away my mobile and banned me from speaking to any of my friends – even girls. I didn't eat last night and I couldn't sleep either. I think I cried all night. Even this morn-ing, I left for school without any breakfast.'

I was alarmed by this drastic metamorphosis of her once-loving home envi-ronment. There were many factors against her in this situation: her parents' age, her being the youngest, her being the only daughter, their old-school thinking. Their vehemence had turned them into people that she didn't even recognise.

'Would it help if I talked to them, Vamika?'

'No, I don't think it would. It would be worse if they knew that I had told you. If my dad has already slapped me, I hate to think of what else he could do. Now I'm scared of him. They're so different from my friend's parents...'

'Exactly. They are set in their ways of thinking. I'm hesitant to talk to them directly for fear of it backfiring. Is there anyone else who you think they might listen to?'

She looked upwards for a moment.

'Umm … um … yes there is! My uncle! He's my dad's youngest brother but he's cool. He's so nice to me. He'd understand. His daughter studies in Class 4 of our school.'

So that was my lead. This seemed the only route I could pursue in order to help her.

'Oh good. Let me try then. I'll speak to him. Let's see if it will yield some support for you in this. I will speak to him but I don't need you to get involved. You simply do what they say and maintain the peace at home just

for a few days more. I know what they're doing doesn't seem fair but if you react aggressively, it will get worse for you. So be smart for a while longer and once I speak to your uncle, I'm sure he'll try to speak to your father.'
'Hmmm….I think it might work, ma'am.'

And it did. Vamika messaged me his number and I spoke to him. He was very understanding of the situation and because he was family, he knew why his brother and sister-in-law were overreacting since he was well aware of the circumstances of Vamika's birth. He could see that their possessiveness stemmed from how much they loved and protected her but he could also understand Vamika's plight too, once I explained it to him. After that, I crossed my fingers and left it to him to try and make his older brother loosen his hold on his daughter and start believing that every boy with whom she was in touch with didn't intend to take her away from him!
The process was slow and it was a few months before I saw Vamika again. She saw me from a distance as I was walking across the school hall and waved briefly. I waved back and gestured with my hand as to what had transpired with her problem. She gestured back with a big thumbs up sign and an equally big smile! Finally it seemed there was peace and happiness in her life again!

Checklist

Actually, the entire crux of friction centres around disrespect. Anything in which teens feel degraded, belittled, humiliated, mocked or talked-down-to will catalyse feelings of anger towards you and their circumstances.

Red Flags to watch out for

- Tearfulness
- Argumentative nature
- Impulsive
- Angry
- Easily irritable

- Demanding
- Aggressive
- Isolated
- General melancholy for no reason
- Shouting at you

What you can do

✓ It's okay to be a buddy or friend, at times, but the bottom line is that you are responsible for their well being, so keep the parent-child demarcation very clear. You are in charge and it is YOUR responsibility to make sure they learn about choice and consequences in a safe way.

✓ Broaden boundaries together. Mutually discuss freedom levels in problem areas such as mobile phone usage, boy/girl friends, going out, study timings, pocket money, attire, even music sound-levels!

✓ Give your teen choices within limits. This gives them the confidence to feel they're in control of their lives. For example: 'What time will you be home, 6:30 or 7:30?'

✓ Listen and empathize. Focus on what they're saying, *not* on what you're going to say, and guard your response to them. Respect some of their requests but only the ones that are reasonable.

✓ Don't endeavour to know everything about them but keep vigilance on their behaviour. Warn them that as long as their secrets are small and non-life threatening, you'll give them their space.

✓ Give trust a chance. Don't bombard them with a hundred suspicious questions of where they've been and what they've been up to. Rather, maintain a happy and non-interrogative countenance and ask them 'Hey, how was your day, what have you been doing today?'

✓ Don't make everything a one-upmanship power-struggle. For example, you lose nothing if you allow your teen to listen to their favourite heavy metal song once in a while in the car. In fact, you are showing them that tolerance is love even though it might not be what you like.

✓ Steadfastly refuse to fight on petty issues. Learn to differentiate those from the more serious ones. Hold your tongue even though you might be upset. If you refuse to take the bait every time they throw out their hook, you'll save yourself and them from having to go through a lot of arguing about things that are irrelevant.

✓ Discipline yourself to not fume and get angry when they don't do what they were supposed to do. Follow the **As Soon As Rule.** For example, say to them: '*As soon as* your chores are done and your room is clean, you can go out with your friends.' Stick to this pattern. Using empathy and the As Soon As approach, you can effectively make it a win-win situation for both of you, thus, avoiding anyone having to be angry.

✓ Give them their own room and allow them the freedom to do the interiors, in terms of décor, colour schemes, posters, wall hangings etc. Have their friends round and be nice to them. This is a great one for building respect between you and your teen. Be pleasant but don't be too pally-pally. You don't have to be 'one of the boys/girls' too! If their friends behave in an unruly way, tell your teen in confidence and let *them* handle the situation.

✓ Be vigilant about what they do behind closed doors in terms of what films they're watching or what sites they're viewing on the net.

Chapter 9: 'You're Not Perfect Either!'

I remember once watching an Oprah Winfrey programme on television where a teenager was given the opportunity, via live satellite link, to talk to his father who was in prison. It was going to be the first time the son had seen his father ever since he was found guilty of robbing a bank. When the father committed the robbery, CCTV cameras caught footage of him threatening the staff under gunpoint and hurriedly leaving the bank with the money in a plastic bag. The police later aired it on the local news asking for people who recognised the robber to come forward so that he could be nabbed. The son happened to be watching the news whilst eating his dinner and almost choked on his food when he saw that the freeze-frame of the robber was his own father! After the initial shock, he was overcome with disbelief. This was the man who had raised him to never do anything wrong and yet here was his face splashed on the screen as a robber! His father was not at home at the time but the son was so agitated about what to do that he ended up calling the police to confirm that the photo-fit of the robber was indeed his own father. Immediately a police car was dispatched and by the time the father returned, the police were already waiting to arrest him.

I could tell that the boy was agitated as Oprah asked him if he was mentally prepared to talk to his father for the first time after his conviction. The boy nervously nodded as the cable link to the prison was switched on. He suddenly saw his father on the big overhead screen, dressed in orange overalls as a prison inmate. Oprah, in her own inimitable style, started up the conversation which went something like this: 'Your son is here with me. Would you like to say hello?'
'Yeah, sure! Howdy sonny, how yer doin?' the father said, with an affectionate grin.
The boy was obviously confused and surprised that his dad displayed no apparent anger towards him. 'Hi dad!' he said just as cheerily but the nervous edge was evident.
Oprah interjected and asked the father the question to which everyone wanted to know the answer: 'Aren't you angry at your son for turning you in?' And what the father said next is something I've never forgotten: 'Angry? No way! As a kid, I'd always told him to do the right thing. His conscience told him I was wrong and he acted on it. I'm not angry at all. On the contrary ma'am, I couldn't be more proud of him.'

'Do you regret what you did?' asked Oprah.

'Yeah sure I do, but I'm paying for it now. I feel sorry I couldn't be the role model I should have been. I've failed him. I've let him down. I regret that much, much more.'

The son had tears in his eyes knowing he was unconditionally forgiven by his father. It must've come as a tremendous relief, and any guilt he had would have vanished away. Indeed, he was so overcome that he couldn't speak anymore. Apart from the obvious message of the young boy being able to detach himself from the emotional connection to do what he felt was right, the programme highlighted one of the biggest paradoxes of many parents: *that while we acknowledge that we need to be good role models, sometimes we unwittingly demonstrate the very behaviour we want our children to avoid.*

Children are born with a nascent sense of right and wrong and as they grow older they will notice the increasing discrepancy between what we say and what we do and will question and ponder on our fallibilities. Before long, they will pick up their values more from our actions and not our words. 'Don't worry that your child is not listening to you but worry that he is watching you,' are the words of caution of one parent I spoke to.

None of us are perfect. We may indulge in habits like drinking, smoking or gambling and may not even want to stop for the sake of our children, in spite of knowing that we are setting examples that we don't want them to follow. However, though the risks of our children following suit are much higher, many parents overlook the dangers they pose. We have all seen toddlers using explicit language which they overheard from their parents or children of heavy drinkers or smokers who start doing the same thing in their early teens. However, if we were to differentiate between bad lifestyle habits and moral wrongs, I feel the latter poses to be even more damaging to a child's mindset. Being morally corrupt is like a poison that destroys value systems, the backbone of every good person. Deceptive parents will raise deceptive children. The quickest way for a child to think that it's okay for them to lie is to watch their parents do it. They will quickly adopt it as a normal part of their life without any pricks to their conscience. A child who learns how to lie must recognise the truth first, intellectually conceive of an alternate reality, and then be able to convincingly sell that new reality to someone else. Lying is not for simpletons. It requires advanced cognitive development and social skills that honesty simply doesn't require. So parents who set the example that lying is appropriate must understand that the chances of them one day losing their credibility and their child's faith in them are very high.

There is no doubt in my mind that those children who find out about their parent's infidelity take the biggest emotional blows. It can play havoc with their moral mindsets too, especially as teenagers, to the point where they become bewildered, confused and -- most of all -- scared. Take Jaya for example. She happened to stumble across an incoming message on her mother's mobile and was mortified to think that her mother could possibly be having an affair with an uncle she'd known since childhood. The shock was so overwhelming that she was paralysed as to how to react. She was convinced that telling her father would sort things out and came to confirm if she should. What I told her may not be what she was expecting but I still stand by my decision because I felt it was the least corrosive thing to do in an already fragile situation.

It's not a surprise that many children are so taken aback by the discovery of their 'imperfect' parents that their entire perception of their parent changes. However, this was not so with Trilokesh. His father confessed that he had once spent some time in prison for tax evasion but instead of hating his father, Trilokesh's respect for him grew. Finally, I reproduce Jatin's tryst with the gambling world when the innocent game of hand cricket he played with his friends on the bus, started taking a monetary twist. On closer investigation into his life, it was apparent that he grew up in an environment in which gambling was considered quite a normal activity and so, as you will read, his father took quite a bit of convincing to accept the deeper problems gambling could lead to.

Whatever the habits or vices may be – drinking, smoking, gambling, stealing, lying, cheating or infidelity – all parents know, deep in their heart, that they are setting the wrong examples. If they can accept that their actions play an instrumental role in their children's long term happiness, perhaps they may also accept that they owe it to them to change and be the best they can be.

Jaya

When a child discovers that one parent has been unfaithful to the other, it can shatter their stable world. For Jaya, the shocking discovery occurred when her mother had left her mobile on her dressing table when she went into the bathroom to shower. Jaya happened to be sitting at her mother's dressing table at that time, squeezing a pimple in the mirror. When the mobile beeped, Jaya instinctively picked it up and read the message: *Can't w8 2 c u tmrw. ILU. X.*

Jaya was not naïve. She was a mature Class 10 student and it instantly dawned on her that this message was from a man her mother knew quite intimately. When she saw that the message was from 'Veer', her mouth fell agape. She realised that it was from an old family friend - Uncle Veeresh. Within moments, her temples throbbed and her hand trembled as it dawned on her that he could be having an affair with her mother. However, as shaken as she was, she kept silent and put the mobile back down where it was and quietly left her mother's bedroom. With her mind in a daze, she went to her bedroom to absorb what she had just seen. She couldn't believe it. She was dumbfounded. After a sleepless night, she came to see me the next day. 'Ma'am, I can't tell you how I felt. To say I am shocked is an understatement. It was as if, in that moment, a ten-tonne-weight hit my head. So many thoughts went through my head all at the same time but my biggest sadness was for my dad. He is working so hard for us and my mum repays him like this!' her voice squealed at the end.

'What does he do?'

'He's a deputy commissioner and has been posted in another district, so he doesn't come home very much. Sometimes we go to stay with him but with my studies and tuitions, it's not always easy. My poor dad. He has no idea about this and it would kill him if he knew.....'

A pretty girl with hazel-coloured eyes and dark brown hair, Jaya was more concerned how this would affect her father's well-being, not paying heed to how destructive it already was to her own. She obviously loved him a lot. Her face grimaced as if she was in pain and then copious tears streamed down her cheeks. She was obviously devastated. What had this poor girl done to deserve such a jolt to her stable world? But she continued to talk, crying through her tears. 'When I read the message, I instantly felt guilty for looking into my mum's phone. I knew I shouldn't have looked into her messages without asking her but I couldn't help it.'

I patted her hand. 'It's okay. It wasn't your fault that you did. We're all tempted to read messages coming through on a family member's phone.'

'But the guilt is nothing compared to the impact of the message. I wish I hadn't seen it. It made me feel sick. How could she and Veeresh Uncle be having an affair? Ugh, they're in *love!*' She screwed up her eyes and her fists and cringed. 'I couldn't even eat my dinner after that. I felt nauseous. I told my mum I wasn't feeling well and went straight to sleep but I couldn't sleep a wink. All night I kept thinking of whether it was really true. It still hasn't sunk in yet but when I think back, I realise that there were actually lots of subtle signs in my mum's behaviour that I never noticed earlier.'

'Like what?'

'Like the way she started taking a big interest in herself and started going to the gym every day. She bought new clothes and shoes but, even more than that, I noticed that she became more secretive with her phone calls. In the evenings she would stay in her room and put the radio on so that I couldn't hear who she was talking to on her mobile. But once when I went to the bathroom at night, I heard whispering from her bedroom door as if she was talking to someone on the phone late at night…'

'And you say your father doesn't suspect anything?'

'I'm sure he doesn't know anything because she acts totally normally when he comes home. As soon as he leaves to go back, her behaviour changes again. I remember once when I was having a headache and didn't want to go to school, she forced me to go by giving me two paracetamols. At the time I thought it was because she was concerned that I shouldn't miss school but now I realise that it was because she wanted me out of the way. Her behaviour disgusts me!'

'How long do you think this has been going on?'

'Um … I'm not exactly sure, but I think it started after the New Year's Eve party at the club. I remember seeing them dancing together but then again even my father was dancing with other aunties.'

'How well do you get on with your mother usually?'

'We have a great relationship and I always trusted her. If she went out in the evening saying that she was going to the supermarket and came back late, I always believed her when she said there was so much traffic. I never had reason to doubt her. Now I can see that she must've lied to me. It makes me angry that she took advantage of my trust. I feel even worse for my dad.'

'Is your uncle a married man? What does he do?'

'He was married once but they divorced. His wife was a good friend of my mum's and we would often go over to their house. He's a businessman so he doesn't have fixed working hours. I guess that's why he can meet my mum at odd hours.'

'Does he have any children?'

'No, he doesn't. Thank goodness for that.'

'Why didn't you ask your mother about the message? Perhaps there could have been a logical explanation after all.'

'I hesitated because I was scared it could be true. I still hope to God that there is some big mistake but my gut tells me I am right. I also knew that my mum would divert the real issue and scold me for looking at her phone.'

Jaya's mature insight into the situation was admirable. It's easy to act on impulse in these circumstances but she was able enough to step back and think of how she was going to handle this. When children carry the heavy burden of knowledge that could potentially cause a break up of their parents' marriage, it affects their life in a big way. Ultimately though, since she had kept silent, it was suffocating her.

Now it was my turn to think logically. Based on one text message, was there still room for giving her mother the benefit of the doubt? I decided to buy time and wait for more conclusive information. 'Look Jaya, let's not do anything for a week and observe the situation. There could be a perfectly logical explanation for that message so we might be jumping to conclusions here.' She was listening and nodded slightly. Even though we both felt that her mother was guilty, it was wise to wait just a little longer. 'Let's keep observing for another week. Every time you come across something which suggests she is having an affair, send me a text message and keep me informed. This way I too can gauge the situation too. We'll be in this together, like detectives!'

I knew it to be a feeble joke in the face of a serious situation but I wanted to lighten her load and make her feel that I was with her and that she and I could confide in each other. She nodded and swallowed. She seemed calmer. 'I know what you are thinking but let's not think of the worst based on a single incident.'

'Okay,' she said quietly. 'Though the doubt and pain is still there, I feel better having told you.'

'I know Jaya. Sometimes, no action is the smartest thing to do for a while.'

So that was the first meeting with Jaya, who left looking more relaxed than when she entered.

During the following week, I received random text messages from her regarding her mother's behaviour:

Mum not at hme wen I got bck from skl.

Mum has locked hr bdrm door. I can hear her mbl beeping from time to time.

Mum got a new haircut.

Mum bought new stilettos.

It's 9 p.m. and she's gone out to the supermarket saying we need milk!

Jaya came to see me again the following week. She brought her mobile with her. It contained messages from Veer Uncle that she had forwarded to herself from her mum's mobile. 'Ma'am I have to show you these,' she said enthusiastically whilst frantically tapping onto the keypad . She passed me her phone. I read message after message:

U wr lukng damn sexy ystrdy … soooo hot!

Wear tht blck number whn u cum over

Gve me a mssd call once J leaves

Gt time fr a quck kiss? I'm outside. Cme out, baby!

Can't stay long 2day

A funny feeling came over me. It didn't feel right to be looking at the messages. It didn't matter that they confirmed the illicit relationship, they were still a personal exchange of feelings between two people. I felt I was snooping into their affair and it felt wrong. 'You know Jaya, you have to stop looking at your mum's mobile from now on. I feel a little guilty for looking at these, for snooping into your mum's life. Before long, it will become a habit.'

'I understand what you're saying ma'am. I always feel bad for prying into her mobile every time I look at it but I console myself saying that since she's indulging in something so wrong anyway, it kind of justifies me doing so…'

'It's not the same thing Jaya. *Whatever* she might be doing, it doesn't mean what you are doing is right. Prying, or snooping is an unethical practice. That's why you feel a twinge of guilt. And anyway, from what I can see from these, you won't need to look at her mobile anymore; these are pretty conclusive.'

'Yes ma'am, I agree. And anyway I always feel more unhappy after I've read them. I don't want to make myself sad anymore.'

'You know what they say about ignorance being bliss? Well, in a way, it applies here I guess. Not knowing the details is better than knowing them! '

We managed a little laugh between us but it was true, the messages left no room for doubt. This relationship was real and obviously very sexually charged, based on satisfying physical needs. In spite of the nature of the messages, Jaya was weirdly relieved that she now knew for sure that her mother *was* having an affair. 'Ma'am, the stress of not knowing was driving me crazy. There's a sense of calmness now that I know the truth.'

'Yes, I can understand that, Jaya. That's why I wanted to wait a little longer, so that one way or another we know how things stand.'

She nodded. 'Ma'am, there were more messages, some really explicit ones, but I deleted them. I was too embarrassed to show you. My mum's so stupid, she doesn't remember to delete them.' She managed a sad smile. 'What do I do now ma'am? She still thinks I'm not aware of anything and so makes a monkey out of me. Only now I can see through everything! If only I was more aware before!'

Perspectives change dramatically when children become aware of ugly truths. They will become easily agitated over the sudden inattentiveness of a parent as they become so swept up in their personal needs without realising the irreparable damage to their child.

'Have you heard from your father?'

'He calls every other evening. Mum talks to him so nicely, as if she's totally in love with him. I bet she feels guilty. I've begun to hate her for what she's doing. I deliberately talk back to her and scream at her. I can't help it. I get angry very quickly. I hate the way I have become. I want to tell my father everything now. Do you think I should?'

As much as it pained me to tell her, I felt that it wasn't wise for her to get involved. This problem was not hers. Her parents' relationship was their own private world, with its own secrets and emotions which even their own daughter could not fully know. The repercussions were too great. The damage it could potentially inflict on their family was phenomenal. 'No I don't, Jaya. I don't think you should say anything to your father. It's up to your mum to do that. I know it's hard because they're your parents, but ultimately they're both adults and what goes on in their marriage has nothing to do with you.'

Her beautiful eyes opened wide. She seemed shocked by what I was saying. 'How can I just do nothing? I am involved now! You've seen the messages. My mum's guilty as hell!' Her mouth remained agape, her eyes as big as saucers, even after finishing the sentence. It is perhaps the biggest thing to ask for a child who knows the truth to keep away from divulging the truth to either parent.

'Yes, you feel you're involved because you found out but you aren't actually *involved.* Knowing about something doesn't make you involved or responsible for the mess.'

'So, you're saying I do *absolutely* nothing?'

'Yes, I am. I still feel you shouldn't tell him. It *has* to be your mum who does that. Telling your mother or father about the other won't solve everything; in fact there's a lot more to be lost than gained. You may even end up feeling really guilty and regretting your action. You will instigate a huge argument and they may even separate – even if it's for a short time. Then you'll have to choose between the two people you love most and you might end up taking sides, which will affect your relationship with the other. The consequences are too many.'

Her forehead was creased in thought. She still wasn't convinced. 'But I have to do something, ma'am. I want to accuse my mother by showing her all the evidence!' Her eyes were bloodshot and angry. I spoke calmly.

'And then what will happen?' She was quiet so I answered the question for her. 'Initially, she will deny it. Once you show her the evidence, either she'll accept it and then convince you to keep the truth hidden from your father or she'll totally take a tangent and blame you for snooping into her mobile. She'll make *that* the real issue and try to make you feel responsible and guilty. Whichever way it turns, you'll be an extremely difficult position.'

'But if I at least tried?'

'Well you know what the consequences will be, so please think very, very carefully.' She was silent. She was thinking. 'I know how you are feeling, Jaya. I know you want to get it all out in the open, sort it out and get back to normality again, right?'

Tears filled her eyes now. She couldn't say anything and simply nodded. I didn't answer for a few seconds either and pin-drop silence entered the gap. Finally, she managed a whisper so quiet that I could hardly hear it. 'I would do anything to get things back to normal, ma'am.'

And there it was again. Children, however old they may be, depend on stability between the two people they love most in the world. If anything threatens that, they will go to any length, even if it seems irrational, to get back to a sense of equilibrium. Nevertheless, I had to get her to see my perspective. 'As passionate as you are feeling Jaya, I stand by what I say. It's not your business.'

'But ma'am you're saying that I have to keep quiet and carry around a burden of information that I will be unable to shake off.'

'Yes, I realise that. I know this secret is a heavy a burden on your shoulders but disclosing what you know could destroy the already-fragile situation. It's like an egg shell and your world stands to collapse. To ease the burden, perhaps you could confide in a family member. Is there anyone?'

She thought for a moment. 'Hmmm ... only my maternal grandmother. I'm close to her and I think I can confide in her. She's close to my mum too so perhaps she will be able to tell my mother.'

'Good idea, at least that's a start. You need to off-load your thoughts. I am here and you can phone or message me at any time but you also should confide in your grandmother too.'

'Okay ma'am. I'll do that. At least this way, things will remain stable for a while. I just don't want my little brother to be affected by all of this. His whole world will break apart. I think I am beginning to see what you are saying when I think of him. It will devastate him.'

'That's exactly what I'm thinking about you too.'

'Thank you ma'am,' she said quietly.

'I'm proud of you for understanding the impact of what you want to disclose. It's worth delaying, believe me, otherwise your life – and your brother's -- can turn upside down in a matter of seconds.'

She took a deep breath, as if she had been enlightened. 'I see it, ma'am.'

I smiled and touched her arm. 'I'm right here. Keep in touch with me, Jaya, and let me know what happens.'

It's rare for problems of this type to be resolved without some form of emotional pain and turbulence within the family. But surprisingly, Jaya's situation was sorted out relatively painlessly. It was her chat with her grandmother that proved to be the turning point. She went to stay with her one weekend and brought up the issue after dinner. She showed her the messages and told her about her mother's strange behaviour. Perhaps it was the consoling effect of having her mother's mother there to confide in that led her pent-up tensions and grief to explode like a geyser. She broke down as she tearfully told her everything. Apparently her grandmother was so numb with shock that she needed medication. As they both held onto each other and cried, her grandmother promised that she would speak to her mother.

Thereafter Jaya didn't know what transpired between them because she didn't meet her grandmother for a good few weeks but there were some palpable changes in her mother's behaviour. She noticed that her mother began to spend more time watching television in the sitting room, instead of being locked up in her bedroom. One night she even asked Jaya to join her in watching a Hindi movie on the DVD player. Her obsession with her phone ceased and she left it lying around in full view, and although she still continued to go to the gym, she often asked Jaya to accompany her. Saturdays were spent going to the shopping mall followed by lunch at a fast-food joint. Life indeed had become much happier for Jaya. Miraculously, it seemed that her mother had cut off from her boyfriend and had most likely made a decision to end the relationship, possibly after the grandmother told her about Jaya's discovery and her subsequent personal turmoil.

Sometimes, after sensing the great and very real upheaval an affair can have on the life of their child, many mothers or fathers may end an extramarital affair. It seems that in Jaya's case, her mother was lucky in that she ended it before her husband ever came to know of her secret affair. It is also true that she otherwise had a loving relationship with her husband though they were living apart most of the time.

There are never any foolproof ways of handling infidelity problems but as a counsellor, it is in the nature of my job to protect the vulnerable -- namely the innocent children -- who should never be placed in the crossfire. These problems are entirely between the parents who must address their marital hitches directly with each other when the truth finally surfaces. I say 'when' because affairs cannot be kept under wraps indefinitely. It is a statistical fact that they will somehow be discovered. However, it's those adolescents who can accept their parent's affair as an error or a character flaw, as opposed to normal activity, that show the greatest signs of surviving the traumatic episode of parental infidelity.

Trilokesh

Trilokesh came to see me just after the summer holidays. An extremely intelligent boy, he had aspirations to be a doctor just like his father. He had fluffy straight hair that refused to sit flat and two dimples that showed through even when he didn't smile. However there was a look of empathy in his eyes, as if he had a higher level of understanding than his mere sixteen years. He had just joined Class 11 and had chosen the science stream. It was wonderful to see him shape up from the little thirteen-year-old I had first met.

He looked refreshed after his family holiday to Goa but a frown was evident on his face. He was troubled by a closely-guarded family secret which his father had disclosed to him during the week. He told me of the conversation as he and his father sat on the beach, the distant waves crashing on the shoreline. 'Ma'am, that conversation is imprinted on my mind. I can almost remember it sentence by sentence.' And he told me. He closed his eyes every now and again, dipping into the moments as he recalled them.

'Babu, do you know you were born almost ten years after your mother and me got married?'
'Hmmm … I didn't know it was so long Papa…'
'Yes it was and a lot had happened to us before you were born. We went through some good and bad times.'
'Like what, Papa?'
'For a time life was good, ya. I had newly qualified as an orthopaedic surgeon and was in much demand. So I landed a job in a government hospital and also started up my own clinic at our house.' Trilokesh nodded, eagerly listening to these never-heard-before snippets from his parents' early life together. 'Soon I was able to construct my own clinic in the space in front of our house and because I was doing well, we took foreign holidays and even bought an expensive car. By God's grace, we were very comfortably well off and then we started thinking about starting a family.'

To anyone, let alone Trilokesh, their life sounded quite idyllic – almost the perfect way to start up married life. But then his father told him about the dark secret.

'But Babu, I made a big, big mistake,' he whispered as he looked blankly into the horizon.
'What was that, Papa?' asked Trilokesh, quickly licking his dry lips with his tongue and looking directly into his father's face.

'You know that when someone earns money, they have to pay tax on it, right?'

Trilokesh nodded. 'Well, I didn't declare the full amount I was earning and deliberately paid less tax. And I … and I … started to hoard the extra money….'

Trilokesh was silent, his eyes opening wider in shock. He couldn't believe his law-abiding father could ever have done anything against the law. A seed of fear starting to grow in the pit of his stomach as his father continued talking. He now knew this conversation was taking a serious twist. 'My clinic was always full of people and soon I stopped depositing the money at the bank. I started to bundle it up and keep it in a secret vault which a builder constructed for me in the wall of the sitting room, behind the cabinet.' Trilokesh listened in utter silence, stunned at what he was hearing. 'You see son, I was greedy then. The more I made, the more I craved. That's what money does to you. So it was only a question of time till someone turned me in and early one morning, the police came and arrested me.'

Trilokesh let out a gasp. He couldn't believe his ears. Just imagining his father in handcuffs was enough for tears to fill his eyes. He waited with bated breath for his father to continue. 'In court, I pleaded guilty, beta, and I was convicted. But because I pleaded guilty, the judge decreased my sentence and made me serve a three-month-imprisonment term.'

'How was it in jail, Papa?'

'Not good son, not good. I'd rather not talk about it. It was a horrible period of my life, but your Mama stood by my side, visiting me every day.'

'An-an-and th-th-then, wh-wh-what happened?' Trilokesh stammered.

His father took a deep breath and exhaled. 'After I was released, it was too humiliating for us to stay in the same locality. So we moved to a different district and started up life afresh. Within a year, you were born.' he smiled now patting Trilokesh's head, 'You were like a ray of sunshine after what we'd been through …' His eyes drifted back to the past. 'It took some time to build up my practice again but things began to look up and soon we forgot about my jail sentence. Your Mama and I don't talk about it but I thought you should know about that black phase of my life.'

I listened throughout without saying anything. 'That's how my dad told me about it, ma'am.'

I nodded slowly. 'So how do you feel now?'

'That's why I've come here. In spite of knowing that he had once cheated the system, I don't hate him, though I know I should.'

'Why *should* you hate him?'

'Because what he did was deceitful. It was wrong.'

'So what *do* you feel towards him, then?'

'It's weird, but I feel nothing but an immense surge of love, forgiveness and respect. Why, ma'am?'

'There are lots of reasons Trilokesh, but mostly because he accepted what he did was wrong and was genuinely remorseful.'

'Yes, when he told me, for a moment I didn't see him as my dad but just like any one of us. We all can make a mistake.'

'Exactly, Trilokesh. Parents are not superhumans. They are simply human beings and all humans can have weaknesses.'

'But why did I accept what he said with *no* anger whatsoever?'

'Because the love for him was already there and he didn't make any excuses for his actions. He accepted responsibility. You need a lot of humility to be able to do that. It can't have been easy for him to tell you, especially because the incident happened so many years ago. In fact, he needn't have told you but he did. Perhaps he felt that, rather than you find out from someone else one day, it was better that he told you himself. He probably felt you would understand.'

'I could sense his regret and shame. He was speaking in whispers. I felt very sad for him.'

'Yes, I can understand that, Trilokesh. In a way, we all have a dark side to us that no one knows about, that we keep only to ourselves. Even the most unsuspecting person may do something totally out of character if the circumstances tempt them enough to prevent them from doing what is right. Many people will do it. That's how human nature is.'

'So I forgave him instantly and thanked him for telling me.'

'That's good, being able to forgive unconditionally is a great thing and remember, he hasn't repeated his offence has he?'

'NO! No way. I guess he learnt his lesson after the humiliation of being in jail. It must have been awful for my parents.'

'Listen to me,' I looked at him. 'This might sound confusing but try to understand: don't question why you don't feel how you think you should feel. Your head is in conflict with your heart. Don't fight it. Go with the flow. You know what your Papa did was wrong but inside your heart you know that it's the greater man who confesses, repents and never repeats the dishonest act.'

'That's right ma'am. I am proud of him.'

'And he should be proud of you. You have a lot of genuine love for him. I don't think there's any more to say. Do you feel a sense of peace?'

'Yes ma'am, I do. I guess I wasn't sure of why I wasn't reacting negatively. If it was someone else in jail, I would have thought he was a bad person. But it was my own father…'

'As I said, don't question what your heart says. You know your father. He isn't just any person. Society lives on the stereotype that everyone who has done something wrong is always a bad person. You have seen a living example of how that is not so in your own father. Let me tell you that reformation is one of the greatest traits of human beings.'

He listened carefully. He was a treat to counsel. 'Thank you, ma'am. You have eased my mind a lot!'

'Just chillax, Trilokesh!' I said with a laugh.

With the conversation coming to a natural close, he got up to leave. After he left, I contemplated for a while and realised a few truths of my own. Honesty, humility and remorse are the antidotes of committing a moral wrong, and as long as parents are willing to turn it around, children are remarkably forgiving by nature and will easily feel empathy towards them. I realised too, that hidden within his father's confession was an important parenting lesson: that when parents are able to let go of pretence and can openly admit to setting the wrong example, they earn greater respect from their adolescents. Those parents who hold the narcissistic idea that they know everything and continue to defend their actions will not only cause their children to harbour deep resentment towards them but also run the greatest risk of ensuring that they will end up doing the same thing as them one day.

Jatin

One morning the Principal called me to her office and informed me that she'd be sending a Class 10 student – Jatin -- to meet me. Apparently he'd already been suspended for gambling on the school bus, after an inquisitive teacher happened to glance over his shoulder as he was writing down a list of boys' names against the amount of money they had pledged. It turned out that he was adding up the total amount of money due to the winner once the game was over. That particular day there were four other boys' names written down, one as young as in Class 7. In fact, the other boys on the list had been suspended too, but only for three days each and were also scheduled to meet me. However, since it was Jatin who was the leader and had influenced the others to gamble, he had been given a week-long suspension and was advised to come for immediate counselling in an attempt to make him see the potential dangers of his habit and hopefully try to put a stop to it altogether.

As a counsellor, I always believe in the reformation of a once-erring student so that s/he can go back into the mainstream after counselling. Unfortunately many schools are quick to expel these students, without any counselling measures, believing there to be no hope for their recovery. Whatever the so-called misdemeanor may be, school authorities do not want that student to 'contaminate' others; nor do they have the time or the resources to put them 'straight'. Many believe that they are better off without such students and duly issue a transfer certificate, without even thinking about that particular student's future. Whilst I agree that schools have a duty to protect the well-being of many other students too, resorting to the quick expulsion of a student who has wronged belies the very purpose of an educational institution's objective. Surely schools serve a dual-purpose of teaching and disciplining every student – even if s/he is in a minority of one? Many adolescents have yet to learn the ways of right and wrong, are unsteady on the path of moral consciousness and may waver from ethical activities from time to time. Isn't it more morally correct and gratifying to see a once-erring student back on the path of righteousness than to kick him or her out of school, without a thought to their well-being? I strongly believe that expelling a student should be the absolute last resort in every school's discipline protocol and should only be implemented after all avenues for reformation have been exhausted.

Even though Jatin was in Class 10, he was already sixteen years old. He was fair-skinned, had blunt features, neat and well-oiled black hair swept over to the right side of his head. He had a soft moustache and, whilst many boys his age often resorted to cutting off these downy tufts of upper-lip hair, I could tell Jatin revelled in his because he'd trimmed around it, the way older men do, in order to accentuate it. He appeared older than other students his age and dressed immaculately, the creases on his shirt and trousers ironed in perfectly straight lines. His shoes were polished to a shine, the triangular knot of his tie sat against the first button of his shirt, unlike many students who had open shirts and wore their ties loosely, the knot lying somewhere between buttons two or three. I was especially interested in knowing how this all started and more importantly if he had a predisposition to gambling from his home environment. Many habits start from the home environment usually from parents who indulge in such activities which are easily imitated by their offspring. It is because certain activities happen in the security of the home that they do not appear to be so 'wrong' or because the habit has been indulged in over a long period of time that it seems almost a normal activity. I started by asking him if he knew the implications of his suspension.

'Okay ma'am, I know what I was doing was not actually right but surely they were being really hard on me? I mean, what about those students who are caught drinking or smooching or sniffing glue? Surely playing hand cricket on the bus is no big deal? I just don't understand these teachers!'

'When you say it like that Jatin, I agree it doesn't sound like such a bad crime to play hand cricket but remember, the two players were playing for money, weren't they?'

'It wasn't like that,' he said softly. 'You lot are making it seem like I've committed a murder or something!'

'So how was it, Jatin? Why don't you tell me? I'm listening. And, while you're at it, please explain this "hand cricket" game. I'm not so clear on it.'

He looked at me briefly, his eyes widening ever-so-slightly as if he was mildly surprised at my ignorance. 'It's just a game that everyone plays on the bus coming home from school, even students from the primary section. Do you know the game Rock, Paper Scissors, Go?'

I nodded, remembering my children playing it between themselves when they were young.

'Well it's like that except that the two players put out their fingers at the same time. The number of fingers signify the number of runs the batsman gets, but if the bowler and batsman put out the same number of fingers at the same time, then the batsman's out. That's the game.'

I was listening intently. The game fascinated me as a wonderful way of passing time on the long bus journey from school. 'Wait a minute Jatin, how do you show six runs?'

'In our version we show the thumb though some people show a closed fist.' It seemed that this game had very concise rules. 'So, if both the players show their thumbs at the same time, then the batsman is out, right?'

'Yes, the bowler has bowled the batsman out.'

Now that I understood the game, I couldn't quite understand how they played for money. I needed to ask him but I had to do it tactfully, by slipping it into the light mood of our conversation.

'So Jatin, if I win, will I win a prize of money?'

'Well, at the beginning we never played for money but one day I halved a ten-rupee chocolate bar – one half to the winning batsman and the other half to the person who had given the closest prediction to his score .'

I nodded enthusiastically. Playing for a chocolate bar didn't sound so unethical. I needed to know from what point the chocolate became money. 'That's no big deal, is it?'

'Yes, that's fine so far Jatin. Giving the winner a chocolate bar is fine.'

I was winning him over. He was melting effortlessly. I hoped he would tell me now how they started playing for money. 'One day I didn't get time to buy a chocolate bar, so I gave the winner the ten rupees instead, telling him to buy it himself. It's the same thing, isn't it?'

That was it. It wasn't the same thing. By giving money, the game had turned into gambling. It's a fine line, I know, but it's a very crucial turning point. Without showing any expression on my face, I nodded for him to continue.

'So the next time we played, we didn't bother with the chocolate bar anymore. Money was easier. Soon we all were pooling in ten rupees each per game.'

I was still mystified as to how they could play a game of hand cricket with money.

'How did you determine who is the winner?' I asked.

'Well everyone gave the same amount of money, usually ten rupees each. The total amount varied, depending on how many players were playing that day. I kept a record of all the players playing on a particular day on a piece of paper or in my diary.'

'So everyone must have looked forward to the bus ride home, right?'

'Yes, we played five times a week on the way back from school on the bus.'

'So did you exchange money at school?'

'No, we only *pledged* the amount we would pay. So, for example, say if I was the main batsman that day, then each player would predict my total score of runs by the time I reached the bus stoppage where I get off. Of course every time I got out during the journey, the bowler would take the bat but if I got him out, it would be my turn to bat again. So if I got a total of 92 runs, the person who placed a bet nearest to my total score would get half of the total money collected and I, being the batsman, would get the other half.'

'How many of you were there?'

'Usually five of us but sometimes up to eight of us played.'

'Were you all from different classes?'

'Yes, we ranged from Class 7 to Class 12.'

Quickly I mentally calculated that they would be playing for prize money of between fifty to eighty rupees per day depending on how many students were playing. That'd mean the winner and the batsman would get between twenty-five and forty rupees per game.

'How did you choose the batsman?'

'By lottery. We randomly picked who would bat beforehand.'

This was a very carefully thought-out game that required a sharp mind and meticulous preparation. I took a deep breath. This boy didn't see where he was wrong. I wanted to know how it was at home.

'Have you seen your parents play for money like this, Jatin?'

'Not my mum, but my dad yes, I have. My father's from Meghalaya and there they have a game called 'Teer'. Have you heard of it?'

I nodded. I remembered that it's an archery gambling game where people strike arrows towards a target. The winning numbers are determined by the numbers of arrows hitting the target after two rounds. It's legal to gamble in this way in Shillong, the capital of Meghalaya, as the origins of the game are age-old. The winning numbers were often predicted from dreams of people. 'Well my father used to play teer when he was in college and even now plays whenever we go to Shillong. He always asks me what dreams I had the night before as a way of predicting the numbers that will turn up. Once, he only gave one rupee as his stake and he got it spot on and we won lots of money! He plays all sorts of gambling games now and tries his luck at everything!'

'The thing is Jatin, when the greed for money overtakes the fun of the game, then it becomes a gambling habit. And sometimes when people start to get addicted to it, they can lose everything.'

'Aw c'mon ma'am, we're nowhere near that! I'm sorry ma'am, but I think you're making a mountain out of a molehill. In our home, it's a normal bit of fun that my parents have always engaged in… and we still haven't run out of money!'

He was starting to poke fun at what I was saying. I understood that by his logic, playing hand cricket on the bus was simply an extension of the gambling culture he'd grown up in. He'd seen his dad play for money and for him there was nothing wrong with this. I had to speak to his parents, especially his father, to explain to them why their son must understand that not only was indulging in gambling games at school unethical but encouraging others to participate and stake their money was wrong.

Jatin's father came into school the following day. Again, he too was a well-dressed man wearing a light blue open-collared shirt and navy blue formal trousers. His hair was oiled and slicked back.

'I've already spoken to the Principal regarding my son's suspension. I do think his so-called "crime" was not in proportion to the punishment!'

'Well, the thing is we have received a lot of complaints from unhappy parents regarding your son's activities, so perhaps it's a little more serious than you think. Of course as a school, we need to listen to all parents.'

'It's harmless fun! There are much worse things he could be doing! Everyone gambles in some form or another. This is preposterous! My son wasn't engaging in vast sums of money, just piddly amounts! What's more, it was on the bus, he wasn't even in school!'

I could sense he was getting agitated. 'With due respect, your son's welfare is the responsibility of the school whilst he is on the school bus too – right until he gets off. And also, for your information, whilst they didn't exchange money during school, they brought the money from home every morning, pooled it together before giving the previous day's winners their winnings. It was a very regular routine.'

'So what?'

'So what? Is that your answer Mr Dutta? Have you ever thought of what you are teaching your son by encouraging his gambling habit?'

'Gambling habit? It's hardly gambling….'

'Whenever money enters a game of chance, it becomes gambling.'

'Okay then, if it is *so* bad, tell me what could happen?' he asked, his eyes squinting in defiance.

'Look, Mr Dutta, I am not pointing my finger at your pastimes. It's up to you what you do in your life but where I am responsible is for the welfare of the students of this school and if your child is responsible for getting them involved in gambling during school hours or *whilst they are still on the bus*, then I am sure as hell going to defend them.' I was getting angry now. I could see tiny globules of saliva flying out from my mouth.

'So, what could happen?' he repeated calmly.

I exhaled and swallowed. 'Gambling is as addictive as alcohol or drugs and even harder to cure. Pathological gambling is certified as a mental disorder. Parents who indulge in it are spreading distorted examples of getting easy money for nothing. They are showing their children that earning money through hard work is not necessary when someone gambles. As a result, those children often grow up to cheat others, become embezzlers, forgers, pickpockets, burglars and dacoits. Children learn the ropes from parents like you who see nothing wrong in it whatsoever. So yes, Mr Dutta, I am pretty irritated that you can't see that. This is IRRESPONSIBLE PARENTING!'

He listened and slowly started nodding his head. 'I never saw it in such a wide context as that. I only thought for the moment, you know, the momentary feelings of exhilaration.'

'That's exactly the addictive part of it and since students do not always have the means to pay for their growing habit, they will inevitably end up stealing money to fund it.'

'Okay, okay I can see the long term effects of it. I guess I was being a little short-sighted.'

'Ideally Jatin needs to stop this habit altogether. For that he will need to undergo counselling along with your support. You must accept responsibility for introducing him a world where gaining money is based on total chance. It is not a way of life and can never be. We can talk about that later but for now, he will be under strict vigilance at school so that he never, ever indulges in this habit at school or on the bus. If the school authorities ever have reason to suspect him, then you will be contacted Mr Dutta, and very strict action will be taken against him especially since he has been given a stern warning.'

He shook his head from side to side as if astounded by what I had just told him. 'I never thought that such a little bit of fun could escalate into such a big tamasha,' he whispered under his breath.

'Well, unfortunately, when other students are involved and parents point the finger of blame at another student, it becomes our issue. We become mediators. After all, we have to nip the problem early before it becomes like a cancer.'

He stood up. 'Thank you,' he said quietly as if in contemplation of our conversation. I nodded and he left.

Jatin came for counselling and with closer vigilance from the teachers during school and on the bus, he never played hand cricket on the bus for money again. His parents were counselled too but I don't think his father ever stopped gambling. Nevertheless, after this episode, Jatin got quite a shock, realising that gambling was actually a dangerous habit, which if left uncontrolled, had the potential to destroy a person's life forever.

Checklist

Unchecked habits – amongst both adults and adolescents -- pose long term ramifications because they can lead to a host of personality disorders or social problems. An alarming aspect is that many parents do not recognise how affected their teen may be by their behaviour and obliviously continue with it. Moreover, many teens may not openly tell their parents that their habits are disturbing them. The most common disturbing parental habits are: smoking, drinking, taking drugs or selling drugs, lying, cheating, stealing, promiscuity, viewing pornographic material and gambling.

Red Flags to watch out for

- Unjustified bursts of anger
- Snapping at you without reason
- Finding any excuse to argue/fight with you
- Watching you suspiciously in silence

- Cheekily impersonating your behaviour
- Justifying their actions saying, 'Well, you do it'
- Provoking you to react through deliberate impertinence etc

What you can do

✓ Don't blame anyone else/anything else for your teen's delinquency but yourself. Parents must accept responsibility *first* before they can make a change.

✓ Accept too that parental behaviour is a major factor in the emotional stability and overall well-being of your teen.

✓ Be honest about your habits and show your teens that you are trying to make a change. You present a powerful role model when you show that what you say is consistent with how you behave. That way you will get more respect from them instead of contempt.

✓ Never for a moment think that your teen isn't aware or concerned about your negative habits. It does affect them at some level or other and gives them a golden ticket to do the same should they want to.

✓ If you have behaved in a way that was wrong, tell your teen: 'I was really angry the other day, and I regret what I did….' This way, you will demonstrate that it's appropriate for all of us to admit when we're off base and then try to make repairs. And your child will not think less of you for it.

Chapter 10: 'Why Did You Die So Suddenly?'

Research has shown that adolescents grieve differently from children and adults; younger adolescents even grieve differently from older adolescents. Unexpected death takes its toll on the adolescent psyche surprisingly much more intensely than we may think. For example, the sudden death of a close teenage friend or a much-loved family pet may evoke more grief than even the death of a grandparent. Adults may minimise the impact because they were not aware about the significance of the friendship.

With adolescence already being a time of heightened awareness, the sudden death of a parent, sibling or a classmate may bring confusion, shock and denial. It may take weeks or months before the full blow of the sadness surfaces and the impact on daily life becomes apparent. It may even be hard to tell whether a teenager's emotions or actions are the result of grief or are a part of normal development. Another less-discussed possibility that often misleads parents is when the teen displays no apparent adverse reaction at all. In fact, the teen may excel in school and immerse themselves in sports or hobbies, suggesting that they're coping well. What may really be at work here is a defence mechanism where the teen subconsciously attempts to channel the strong emotions to areas where they feel comfortable, as a way of regaining control over a world that has been jolted out of orbit.

There are many bereaved teens who venture to the counselling room seeking answers and comfort at the sudden demise of someone close. While the finality of death can be explained more easily when it comes to elderly folk like grandparents, it's quite a different story when it comes to someone dying before the end of their natural lifespan. Sudden death is like a short-circuit in the ageing process and regardless of whether it is due to illness, accident or even suicide, it may result in a prolonged and heightened sense of disorientation. I honestly have no answers to give them. I can only raise my hands in defeat to the invincibility of death which comes with no clear-cut explanations. When grief overwhelms everything and takes centre-stage, there is no fixed time span to its various stages -- denial and shock, bargaining, depression, anger and acceptance -- the biggest comfort is to be patient without being judgmental and to listen without haste, in order for healing to begin.

Though any death of a loved person evokes grief, the most significant is when a teen loses a parent. According to the Life Events Survey of Indian Children (LESIC), also mentioned in Chapter 5, the death of a parent is the single event in the life of a teen which causes the highest intensity of stress. This is one of the hardest deaths to accept because it creates a sense of being 'abandoned'. To someone who is already trying to cope with the numerous adjustments of adolescence, it complicates their struggle for identity and can leave them feeling vulnerable. On countless occasions, I have sat in the counselling chair watching the grief-stricken face of an adolescent who has suddenly lost his/her parent. I have seen how the overpowering sorrow almost literally weighs them down, rendering them helpless. I have heard their unabashed sobs of shock, of pain, of anger, as they recount the last hours of their parent's life. I have held their trembling hands, clammy and cold from the memory of those last few moments when death snatched their parent away from them. While it is heartbreaking, no one can truly understand the depth of the raw pain in the context of their lives and, just as every death is unique, everyone's reactions are entirely different. Teens may act moody and morose one moment and carefree and spontaneous the next. We may feel that they don't seem to care where, in actual fact, their pain may be so intense that their coping mechanisms seem askew and haphazard. As a result, counselling approaches differ enormously.

Though only in Class 11 and already suffering unimaginably from the death of her mother, Nitya took charge as the chief nurturer for the rest of her family. Stoically she contained her own grief, not letting anyone know that she was breaking down inside. Soon, depression set in but the only person who she knew could help her come out of it was someone her father had forbidden her to meet.

While Nitya's grief was a natural outcome of her mother's death, young Saadhvi from Class 7 had no idea that the death of her domestic help was the cause of her decline in academic performance in school. From an outsider's perspective, the two seemed apparently unrelated but, after an in-depth conversation in which she started to unravel extremely unsettling details of the suicide, I became aware that it was still impacting her quite intensely.

Four months after the death of his close friend and with his Class 12 boards at his door, Neelkanth's escapism into heavy drinking was showing no signs of diminishing. The ongoing grief was so overpowering that he ended up coming to the counselling room and confessing his fears to me. It was only after he unfolded the unbelievable and shocking sequence of events leading to the discovery of his friend's body, that I became aware of the intensity of his emotional state. The story made local newspaper headlines because of its sensational circumstances, but no one knew how pivotal Neelkanth was in the police search. Almost a decade after my encounter with him, I can still remember that particular counselling session with immense clarity. I can see the goosepimples rise up on his skin, the tears overflowing in his eyes, his parched, quivering lips as he stumbled through sentences and the heavy silences when he was unable to continue. But, most of all, I am reminded of his courage in facing the traumatic memory and ultimately conquering his fears.

Nitya

The death of Nitya's mother was condoled in the school assembly, after which the entire school observed a minute's silence. That was the first time I had come to hear of her untimely death. She was suddenly rushed to hospital with severe abdominal pain and, two days later, her condition had deteriorated to such an extent that she died from internal bleeding. Nitya and her younger sister didn't come to school for two weeks after that and, once they did, things were never the same again. In spite of them trying to carry on from where they left off, their eyes held a deep sadness as they tried hard to mingle once again with their peer group. Aside from both sisters being physically opposite in appearance – Nitya was tall and dusky whilst her younger sister was fair and plump -- their teachers noticed that though they both were distant and melancholy in class interactions, the younger sister, who was in Class 5, seemed to express her emotional state quite openly; she wouldn't hesitate to cry quietly when the memories came back. But it was seventeen-year-old Nitya, who was the first to pay me a visit exactly a month to the day after her mother died. It was the first month death anniversary and she was getting intense flashbacks of the events leading up to her mother's death.

'I can't help it but during every moment of today, my mind keeps flashing back to the events of last month. I keep recalling exactly what we were doing this time last month at such-and-such time. But most of all, I keep remembering that my mom was still alive then.' Nitya was a doe-eyed beauty with long slender hands which moved when she spoke. She didn't cry as she spoke as if used up all her tears during the last month.
'Yes, I know, Nitya. I'm sure the flashbacks must seem very real.'
'It's just that, ma'am, I keep thinking that if things had happened differently, say if we had taken her to another hospital or shown her to another doctor, maybe she would have lived...'

'Don't do that, Nitya. We may all believe that perhaps we could have changed the circumstances if we had done things differently but ultimately there is no point questioning what *could* have happened. We can't turn back time and what was destined to happen will happen, regardless of whatever we do.'

'Hmm … I guess you are right … it's just that I feel so alone now. After she died and all the rituals were over, there have been times when I just needed her to be there. And she isn't. Her presence gave me stability and now I feel that I'm expected to be the rock for everyone else to lean on.'

'Have you been comforting other members of your family?'

'Well, yes I have, in a way. My younger sister and my father are my main concern now.' She was already talking as if it was she who would fill her mother's shoes and provide the stability that everyone needed.

'You are not ever going to replace your mother's presence, you do know that don't you?'

'Yes, of course I do, but at least if I am strong, my father and sister will gain strength to cope with it.'

'And what about you? How are you coping with it?'

'Me? Well I'm just pushing myself physically so that I don't have time to think too much. I am always keeping myself busy so that I can distract my mind. At night I am usually so exhausted that I don't have time to mope and fall asleep immediately. But I dream of my mom comforting me whilst I am crying and the other night I woke up and found my pillow wet from my tears.'

It dawned on me that she too was grieving but it was internalised. She was keeping herself so distracted that she wasn't allowing herself time to dwell on how she was feeling. By repressing the memories, she could avoid becoming emotionally weakened so that she could remain strong enough to look after the family. 'Lately ma'am, I find I can't concentrate on anything, even my studies. At school, I watch the teacher's mouth opening and closing as she speaks but I don't understand a word she says. I don't feel like eating or talking much. At home when I watch tv, my mind doesn't even register the sequence of images.'

'What are your most overpowering thoughts?'

'I only keep thinking about how it was a month ago. I remember what my mum used to do or say. I feel her presence near me all the time and so I can't help getting huge bursts of sadness that overwhelm me.'

'What do you do then?'

'I go straight to the bathroom to cry and afterwards I wash my face so that no one can see the tears. I have learnt to cry silently. No one knows how unhappy I am. I wish so much to be able to share my pain with someone in my family but we all are suffering in our own worlds. I certainly don't want to burden my father because he's already devastated.'

I could see that out of their concern for one another, neither Nitya nor her father were freely talking about the death, afraid of hurting the other by the memories.

'I just feel so alone.'

Because she was unable to express herself, Nitya felt detached, cut off and emotionally numb. The inhibited feelings were causing her to become even more depressed.

'Do you have any close friends?'

'Not any *really close* friends at school. And now that my mom has died, I feel different from them. It's weird actually, kind of "closed off". And anyway they wouldn't understand. But I did have a boyfriend.'

'Oh, so he's not in your life anymore?'

Instantly her eyes glistened and became dreamy. 'No, he's not. A couple of months ago, my parents found out about my boyfriend and they stopped me from seeing him because they thought I would be distracted from my studies. I loved him a lot and we were good friends but I broke it up after my parents told me to. I regret it now because at least I could have shared my thoughts with him…'

From her symptoms, I could see that Nitya was sinking into depression. She wanted to share her thoughts with someone close but there was no consistent person in her life with whom she could simply pick up the phone to express her grief. Of course, as her counsellor, I was available but I was bound by fixed timings; she needed someone who she could call whenever she felt a flood of emotion whatever the time of day, someone with whom she already shared a warm relationship, because only then would the person be able to give her unconditional support, whenever she needed it. I thought for a moment. Her last sentence gave me an idea. Even though I knew she was forbidden to contact him, her boyfriend seemed the only hope in being the comforter she was looking for. I could liaise with him on how to help her. But knowing my advice would go against what her father wanted, was I right to suggest it?

I thought of the consequences of letting things be. I was convinced that if they remained as they were, she was going to sink further; she was already suffering from short-term emotional damage and unless she could openly and honestly express her emotions, she would never be able to resolve her grief. Her emotional health at this stage of her life was paramount and whatever hope there was, it was worth taking the risk; I would deal with the consequences later. So, I made a decision. 'Nitya, would you want to contact your boyfriend again?'

'Of course I would want to ma'am but if my father ever found out, he'd never trust me again because he told me not to contact him. I can't go against his wishes.'

'Yes but *if* he allowed you to, would you?'

'Of course I would, but right now I can't.' She sighed, resigning herself to the situation.

I hesitated. My conscience pricked me. I asked myself if I was right to suggest talking to someone she was not allowed to contact. Nitya was looking out through the window. I was lucky to have a lovely view of a small lake surrounded by grassy hills from my counselling room and very often I have used this picturesque scene to calm a student's mind or even my own. She watched the wave of ripples through the water as a gust of wind blew and remained silent in her own world for a few seconds. I could see those tears coming back again as she took a deep breath and confessed: 'Sometimes I feel like dying too ma'am, just to be with my mom again…'

As soon as she uttered that sentence, my mind was made up. I knew that if there was a chance for her to heal from her predicament, I had to snatch at it. My loyalties had to lie with the welfare of the student, which may not always be what the parent may want. After all, he wasn't aware of her pent-up grief. He didn't know how she was suffering. The circumstances were totally different now and so what may have seemed appropriate then may not be so now. I rationalised that if I didn't act on my heart's instinct, I would regret it and I would fail her. But I decided that whilst I would tell her to reconnect with her former boyfriend, it would be me who would ring up her father and tell him of what I had done. This seemed the only right thing to do. Feeling somewhat relieved, I took a deep breath. 'Nitya, I know what I'm going to tell you is something you feel you shouldn't do, but for me your mental health is my main concern. I am concerned that if you don't express your inner grief to someone close to you every day, you may end up feeling worse. I have thought this over and over in my mind but the only way for you to find some relief is if you contact your old boyfriend again.'

'You do?' Her eyes were wide open. She seemed shocked. 'I told you ma'am, I can't. My dad will flip.'

'Not if I tell him that I suggested it.'

'You would?'

'Yes, I would, because I know you would be a responsible girl. I know you would be able to prove to your father that your studies won't get affected. Am I right?'

'Of course, ma'am. I know my priorities. When will you call him?' Her eyes twinkled.

'As soon as I can, but I want to tell him personally. In the meantime, are you hesitant to call your old boyfriend?'

'No I'm not! He'd told my friend that he's missing me so badly. He understands why I had to break up with him so he's kept his distance.'

'So he'd be happy if you contacted him?'

She smiled for the first time since she'd come into my room. 'Yes he would and so would I!'

'Then tonight, you contact him and renew your friendship. If you don't mind, could you ask him to call me too? I just want to tell him about your state of mind and how he can help you. And yes, I will call your father sometime today and ask him to come to school tomorrow, if he is free.'

'Should I tell my dad that I'm contacting my old boyfriend?'

'Umm … no, not yet. Let me speak to him first. I want him to see the logic behind my reasoning. Maybe he'll understand.'

'I hope so.'

'Look Nitya, you have a long way to go to heal. But at least this way we are making a start. If you want to, you may want to start keeping a diary and write down your sad thoughts as and when you feel them. Maybe you can even write to your mother telling her what you are feeling.'

'Hmmm … that sounds like a good idea.'

'Also, feel free to message me whenever you wish but you must come and see me every single week from now on and keep me informed of what is happening in your life, okay?'

She nodded. The instant lightness in her face was palpable. Since I said that I would be taking the responsibility of telling her to contact her boyfriend and justifying it all to her father as to why I suggested it, it was as if she was finally allowed to comfort herself without feeling guilty.

'Do you think my dad will agree?'

'He loves you, doesn't he?'

'Yes, he does.'

'Then he'll want what's best for you during this traumatic time of your life. I don't want you to feel so isolated in your grief. Though the pain will never totally go away, at least it will reduce in intensity, I can promise you that.'

She seemed to understand that we had taken a small step to cater for her needs. She needed comforting just as much as she comforted others. 'Thank you ma'am,' she said in a whisper, her eyes streaming with tears of relief.

She was a brave and strong girl. All this time, she had not become very tearful at all. She had learned to control herself to the extent that she simply

didn't cry in front of others. Perhaps the lightness she felt was allowing her to breathe a little more easily. I put an arm on her shoulder. 'Cry, Nitya, it will do you good. You are allowed to grieve openly, you know. Never be ashamed of your feelings. It's a natural expression for your love for your mother…'
Suddenly, a huge wave of sobs overcame her. I instinctively got out of my chair and put my arms around her. I felt her body convulse as her soul wept in raw pain. Being a mother myself, I felt a lump come to my throat. I could sense the void. It was like a gaping vacuum. I found I was getting teary too. Nitya could be anybody's daughter and death of a mother could happen to anyone. I waited for her to calm down. 'You will be fine, Nitya. Don't worry. You will be able to get through this, I know you will.'
She wiped the last remaining tears. 'I'll be back here next week. Please call my dad ASAP, ma'am,' she said before she left.

I didn't waste any time in contacting her father and two days later he came to school. He was obviously distraught by the death of his wife but I made him aware of his responsibilities towards his daughters and in particular of Nitya's silent suffering. I explained to him that in their home it seemed they had reached a stalemate where no one, except the younger daughter, was openly talking about his wife, their mother. So I urged him to talk about her in positive ways that brought pleasant thoughts or experiences they shared as a family. I also explained that in the absence of Nitya being able to share her inner thoughts with family members, she was more comfortable in expressing herself with her own peer group. So speaking to a close friend, like her old boyfriend, gave her an emotional outlet for her grief. His initial response was to get defensive but when I explained that Nitya was showing signs of depression and if she continued in the manner she was going she could break down, he softened. I told him that I felt she was trustworthy and would not let her academics decline. He shook his head and seemed a little skeptical but I asked him to give her a chance. I told him that I personally would be responsible. I simply asked him to allow her to have a simple half-hour private conversation with her old boyfriend every day. It would help her heal, I told him. He seemed convinced by my professional insight and placed his trust in my judgment.

The following week, the transformation in Nitya was astonishing. She had re-contacted her boyfriend who seemed happy to renew the relationship and she talked to him every night without feeling guilty. As I requested, he had given me a call too, during which I told him to have patience with her as she healed emotionally. I told him to bear with her if she called him at erratic hours and had mood swings. He needed to listen, reassure, and support her.

It must have been difficult for him too but since he cared for her, I knew he would be willing to be more understanding. At home, the father too had taken heed of my suggestions and the atmosphere had changed, with all three of them now openly talking about their mother and sharing happy memories as they ate their evening meal together. I was happy that he had initiated a change, even though they were going through a turbulent time.

It took a further six months of regular counselling for Nitya to be back to her old self again. She seemed happier and her grades improved. She had learned to cope by locating her mother within her life in a different way, so that she could keep memory alive forever without any bitterness, regret or sadness.

Saadhvi

You could never tell from her face that she was in emotional turmoil. The only signs to suggest there was something wrong was her sudden academic decline and a general disinterest in class -- unusual traits for a student like Saadhvi because she was otherwise very enthusiastic about school and did well in exams. So, that was why she came to my counselling room, sent by her class teacher. Many students are forwarded to me in this way by concerned teachers and Saadhvi was no exception. Usually I find that there is some upheaval in the home environment that causes some minor upsets and the problems are quickly sorted out, but with Saadhvi the conversation took a strange, almost sinister, twist.

Thirteen-year-old Saadhvi was that quintessential teen with pimples and braces. Her hair was tied back into two pigtails and her complexion was a dusky mocha. She smiled in familiarity as she entered my room because we often passed each other in the corridors.

'Saadhvi, your class teacher says that you don't concentrate in class and seem distracted and restless. Do you think she's right?'

'Well, I wasn't like that but lately I think I am. Yeah, perhaps she is right, but the reason I can't concentrate in class is because I get bored easily and then I feel sleepy.'

'Why do you feel sleepy? Don't you get a good night's sleep?'

'I used to sleep well -- and in my own room too -- but for the last few weeks I keep having scary nightmares and so I have to sleep with my mum now.'

'Nightmares? What kind of nightmares?'

She fell silent. Her countenance changed from chirpy to serious in a split second. Her smile was gone. 'I see Paatala didi again.'

I must've looked surprised. 'Who?' I asked.

'She was our domestic help and she was with us for many years – ever since I was five years old.'

I mentally calculated the number of years. 'So she's been with you for eight years, right?'

'Yes. She was like an older sister to me. We did so many things together.'

I realised we were talking in different tenses. I was talking in the present sense and she in the past tense. From her face, I got the instinctive feeling that this Paatala didi wasn't around anymore. Maybe she'd left to get married. 'Where is she now?'

She was silent. She looked down again, both hands held together and resting on her lap. 'She died, ma'am.'

'Oh I'm sorry. How did she die, Saadhvi?'

'She committed suicide.'

I raised my eyebrows. 'How? When?'

'It happened about three weeks ago. She died in our house. Do you want me to tell you what happened?'

'Can you? Do you feel okay enough?'

She nodded. 'Yes, I want to tell you, ma'am.'

I nodded, motioning her to continue but took a quiet deep breath to brace myself.

'Well it was a normal Sunday morning and I had a dance class at 10 a.m. Usually Paatala didi gets up before us and starts her housework, but this particular morning, it was silent. My parents were fast asleep too, because Sunday is the only day they get to have a lie-in since both work during the week. Thinking that didi had overslept, I got out of bed and started calling her name. Then I walked to the small room in which she sleeps. Her bed was made, so I knew she was up. Then I walked to the front door to see if she had opened the catch and undone the chain but I saw it was still securely fastened. So then I knew she must still be inside the apartment. As I was passing the main corridor, I saw her hawaii chappals neatly outside the drawing room and so I walked in, calling her name. It was still dark in there and I went to draw the curtains…' She paused momentarily to register the sequence of events in her mind. She swallowed, as if she was gearing up to tell me the finale. '…and just as I got near to the curtains, I saw her next to the grill facing outside in her pink salwar suit. Her chin was resting on her neck like this…'

Saadhvi physically put her chin as far down against her neck as she could to show me. I nodded, without saying a word. 'She was looking quite strange as if she was sleeping and because her back was turned to me, I thought she was playing a prank with me, so I laughed and pushed her to tell her to stop joking around but she didn't respond…'

I took a sharp intake of breath anticipating what she was going to say next. Simultaneously I literally saw the hairs on her arm stand up as she continued telling me the horrifying truth. 'That was when I saw that one end of her dupatta was tied around the grill and the other was around her neck. I looked down and saw that her feet were not touching the ground. She was actually hanging there. Oh my God ma'am…' She screeched but continued talking through a high-pitched voice. A cold shiver came over me. 'In that moment I realised that she was not joking with me. Her face was tilted forwards and slightly to the side and a big dribble of saliva was coming out of her mouth. I didn't know she was already dead, ma'am, I thought she was going to be okay but I was so shocked to see her like that that I screamed with all my strength.'

My breathing quickened. I tried to keep calm but I could feel my heart thudding faster. This was such a gruesome discovery that it could have a profound effect on the rest of her life. Saadhvi continued talking as if she was narrating a thriller movie she had just watched at the cinema. She was unbelievably in control now. 'My mom came running out. She gasped when she saw Paatala didi and immediately grabbed me and took me to their bedroom. She shook my dad to wake him up repeating over and over again *Paatalai atmo hoyta korile!* (Paatala has committed suicide!). My dad instantly got up and went to the drawing room but my mother didn't let me go there again.'

'What happened after that?'

'My mom told me to stay in the room and I think my dad called the police. She tried to distract me by putting the tv on but I just kept asking her if Paatala didi was going to be okay because I didn't realise that 'suicide' meant that the person was already dead.'

'Did she tell you that didi had died?'

'Not at that moment. She said that the police were on their way and they would be able to tell if didi had died or not. Of course, when the police did come they said that she was dead and took the body down. They had to cut the duppatta because didi had tied the knot on the grill so tightly. They took didi's dead body away but I don't know what happened after that.'

'Why didn't you ask your parents ?'

'I asked my mom later. She told me that Paatala didi's parents eventually came from the village and took her body home.' The last sentence petered out quietly, as if she had reached the end of the ordeal.

'Oh my goodness Saadhvi, I wasn't expecting that. It was quite a scary time for you, wasn't it?'

She nodded. 'I miss her so much. Why did she do it, ma'am?'

'Maybe she was having problems of her own.'

'My mom told me that no one knew why she committed suicide. We had to conduct a puja after that because she died in our house and no one talks about it now.'
'So, what exactly do you see in your nightmares?'
'I see her hanging there again, just as I saw her in real life. Actually it's like a flashback but it's scarier. Her eyes are slightly open and it looks like she's alive, but actually she is dead.'

This was proving to be a very serious incident, one that was leaving dramatic effects on her mind. I was aware that Saadhvi's parents had not told her much in detail about the death probably because they didn't want to distress her further, but in her young inquisitive mind, there were many unanswered questions that needed closure. It was essential that she knew enough age-appropriate details to be able to put them to rest, otherwise she would continue to have these manifestations. I really needed to talk to her parents but it seemed that Saadhavi was more comfortable with her mother since she was the one who had told her all the facts so far. She needed to tell Saadhvi certain details about the incident which were still vague in her adolescent mind. This was why Saadhvi was not finding mental peace. She needed to make judgments of her own and reach her own conclusions so that she could move on. Brushing the incident under the carpet was making matters worse because Saadhvi had reached a dead end in the healing process and, unless she could openly express her thoughts and feelings about the traumatic incident and discuss her own perceptions, the negative effects would continue to hamper her. I needed to act fast and speak to her mother immediately.

I was extremely happy to meet Saadhvi's mother who was a teacher, though she taught in another school. She and I were on exactly the same wavelength and it was easy for me to explain why she needed to be even more open in her approach to the details of the suicide.
'Really? But won't she get more disturbed if I tell her the details?'
'No, she won't. You'll be surprised by how much it will help to heal her. If you can explain it to her calmly and honestly, she will understand, I can assure you. But don't dramatise anything, just be matter-of-fact with your answers. Please reassure her that *none of you* had anything to do with Paatala's death and that none of you are responsible. Tell her that even though she lived and worked with your family, she still had her own personal life and was going through issues of her own which she couldn't share with anyone else. Tell her that it was those issues which ultimately made her so upset that she felt she had no other option, other than to take her own life.'

I was surprised to see that she was jotting things down in a little notepad as I was talking. She was obviously taking her role in this very seriously. I smiled as only a teacher can be so adept with writing things down.

'By the way, why exactly did she kill herself?'

'Oh, it's a complicated story,' she sighed. 'We only became aware of the details when the police went through her belongings and found the imprint of a letter that she had given to a particular driver in our apartment building. She had written the letter with a pen that caused a heavy imprint on the lower page of her diary. So that was how we knew. When the boy was questioned by the police, he revealed the actual letter. In it she said that she was aware that his marriage was being arranged by his parents with some other girl from his village but if she couldn't have him as her life partner she would rather die. It was the usual story of boy-meets-girl-but-can't-marry-due-to-parental-objection kind of thing but never did I think that Paatala would actually take her own life.

'It has been a really shocking ordeal for all of us. She planned her suicide carefully because all her clothes were folded neatly. She even placed her chappals neatly by the door. Even the stool from which she stepped off was pushed away neatly. She didn't kick it away and she could easily have saved herself if she wanted to. She wanted to die. She must have been very unhappy. Actually thinking back now, I did notice that she was particularly tearful the night before she died. I remember asking her what was wrong and she said that she was remembering her grandmother because it was her death anniversary. Now I realise she was lying. I feel bad for Saadhvi because it was her who discovered the hanging body but I didn't let her see it again after that and I didn't tell her anything more about Paatala's death, just in case it upset her more.'

'But, that's just it. By not knowing, she is more confused and is unable to close it off in her mind. If you don't tell her exactly what you have told me, she will sink into a mental condition which may need psychiatric help.'

'Oh, I thought I was protecting her by not telling her the details. I would never have thought that telling her more about it would actually help her to get through it.'

'It will, you'll see, but as long as you keep things open, candid and straight forward.'

As I expected, her mother did indeed tell her more details of the events. She rang me the same evening saying that as soon as she initiated the topic, Saadhvi had a barrage of questions to ask her: *Why did it happen? What was she going through? Am I to be blamed for it? Did we do something to upset her? How could we have avoided it? Is she haunting our house?* I was relieved because I knew that by being able to speak out, Saadhvi would slowly find some peace within her. Her mother rang me again the following night and said that for the first time in two weeks, Saadhvi had a calmer night with no nightmares. It was amazing how quickly things seemed to be settling down by just talking openly and letting off the pent-up confusions. Saadhvi was on the road to healing and closure.

The following week, Saadhvi seemed much calmer. It sounded as if her mind had accepted the death totally. However, teens have a strong desire to understand and make meaning of the suicidal act and she still had one question that still continued to irk her: 'Why do people commit suicide, ma'am?' I tried to talk in a language that a thirteen-year-old would understand: 'These things happen when a person's brain and thought processes are not working properly, just as liver disease happens when someone drinks too much alcohol, or heart disease when someone eats too much junk food. It's a bit like that when suicide happens. The diseased brain thinks that suicide is the only escape from sadness, which of course it isn't.'

'Yeah, you're right. She should have tried to sort it out. She should have talked to someone first.' She seemed to understand that expressing pain is the best way of find a solution to a problem.

It took many weeks of counselling and many more probing questions before Saadhvi's mind finally came to a slow rest. Luckily we were able to handle the trauma before it got out of hand and needed medical intervention. Left as it was, it could have developed into Post Traumatic Stress Disorder (PTSD), a severe anxiety disorder. Thankfully, her mother was aware of how easily her condition could have spiralled downhill and took her role seriously. She kept me informed of what was happening on the home front and after ten days or so told me that the nightmares had stopped completely and that Saadhvi wanted to move back into her own room. That was a good sign and confirmation that she was over the worst. Finally she was mentally strong enough to put the incident to the back of her mind so that it simply became a distant memory.

Neelkanth

One of the good things about counselling older adolescents is that many of them come forward on their own to seek help for a situation that is causing them distress. Neelkanth was in the arts stream of Class 12 but rarely attended classes. On the odd chance he did come to school, it was usually to hand in an assignment or sit an exam. It seemed he was doing the bare minimum he needed to be able to appear for the finals; otherwise he was totally disengaged from school life.

I first noticed his nonchalance when I took his class for a Total Personality Development session. He had come into school that day to hand in an assignment and wasn't aware that my class was scheduled. Dressed shabbily, his tie was loosely hanging from his shirt, his sleeves were rolled up and he wore the school trousers as low-waisted as one could get. He had a damn-all look about him and his stance was like a wrestler walking into a ring. As he sat in my class, it was obvious from his face that he didn't want to be there as he constantly fidgeted and kept shifting in his seat. His wandering eyes, which seemed to find more interest in the ceiling than my class, told me that he was probably wondering why he even bothered to come to school that day. But, ironically it was this laid-back attitude and total disinterest which irritated me and brought him to my attention.

Thus started our interaction on a one-to-one level which was, unbelievably, to last for the next nine years. I remember asking him his name and scolding him a couple of times to pay more attention to what I was saying. He didn't pay much heed to me and continued yawning away to glory. Finally, I told him that if he was finding it so boring, he could go and sit in the library. There was a tiny flash of rebellion in his eyes but he kept silent. Though he kept distracting me, I continued the class but I noticed that he watched me suspiciously, not really sure how to handle a cheerful-but-slightly-strict ma'am because I wasn't a regular teacher and he would have hardly seen me on a regular basis. During break time, whilst many of the others had left the class to get some fresh air, I noticed that he remained seated, doodling on a page of his diary. I walked over to him and decided to cheerfully start up a conversation. 'Hey Neelkanth, why are you so distracted and distant in class, huh?'

'Just,' was his reply, without even looking up from the page.

'Look, I really don't like to scold students but if someone finds more interest in other things than in what I'm saying during the class, it does annoy me.'

'Yeah, I guess, but you don't know a thing about me. You know, when you told me to go to the library I wanted to give you a sarcastic comment but I stopped myself,' he confessed.

Slightly amused, I asked him what stopped him. He stopped what he was drawing and looked up. 'I dunno, I guess it's because you seem like a nice person.'

When he looked up, I saw for the first time that he had slight buck teeth which gave a cute air to his rough and ruggedness. As gruff as he was and as uncouth as he seemed, I felt his reply was honest and genuine; I realised

that behind his tough exterior there was a soft heart somewhere. 'Is there a reason you were finding it difficult to concentrate on what I was saying?'
'Maybe.' He popped a piece of chewing gum into his mouth, right in front of me and started to chew on it.
'If you want to talk, I am willing to listen, okay? If you have something on your mind that is troubling you, maybe I can help. But you're the one who's got to seek help and come forward.'
'I'll think about it.'
'Good. Let me know.'
He thought for a moment as I walked back to my place by the whiteboard. Students were starting to filter back into the classroom once again though the bell had yet to ring.
'Hey ma'am!' he called out, trying to attract my attention. I looked his way. 'Can I come this Friday?'
I smiled. 'Maybe,' I replied with a twinkle in my eye, imitating his earlier reply to me. Instantly he understood the joke and flashed me a toothy grin. I gestured to my mouth and pretended to take something out. He understood I was referring to his chewing gum. He tore a page from his diary, took out his chewing gum and wrapped it up and came forward to put the chewing gum parcel into the waste paper bin. As he passed me, I said:
'Yes Neelkanth, do come on Friday. We'll have a chat.'
'Maybe,' he grinned, as he strolled back to take his seat.
We were being playful and the humour seemed to be breaking down preconceived notions, on both of our parts. The bell rang and I continued my class. I noticed that Neelkanth seemed less distracted now and was listening to what I was saying. Maybe, just maybe, something led him to think that he could trust me.

On Friday, as I sat in my counselling room, there was a loud knock and Neelkanth entered rather sheepishly. The tough-boy image he portrayed the other day in class wasn't evident at all. He was chewing the ever-present piece of gum as he surveyed my room before sitting down on the chair. Once seated, he read some of the inspirational quotes on my softboard. 'Nice room. Nice words,' he smiled pointing to the board.
'Thanks for noticing, Neelkanth. Many students don't bother.'
'Neel. Everyone calls me Neel.'
'Okay, Neel. I'm glad you came.'
He looked a little uncomfortable as if he was unsure of what he should do next. I tried to make him feel at ease. 'So Neel, tell me, you had mentioned the other day that I don't know a thing about you. So why don't you start by telling me something about you?'

He chewed quietly for a few moments to think about what he wanted to say.

'Well, there's nothing really much to say about me. I live at home with my mum and younger brother. My dad died when I was ten years old. We have a family grocery shop. That's our livelihood. I just want to get out of school as soon as possible and start working. That's my life and that's all there is to know about me.'

'What do you want to do after you leave school?'

'Dunno. Haven't decided yet. I just want to make money fast.'

I noticed the letters H – A – T – E tattooed on his knuckles. Being pricked by a tattoo needle over bony areas must definitely have been painful.

'Those must have hurt,' I said pointing to them.

'Nah! My friend did them when I was drunk. He said that I told him I hated the world so he tattooed HATE onto my knuckles. By the time I sobered up, it was too late to remove them.'

'Hmmm … you drink often Neel?'

'I booze. I smoke. Ever since my dad died, I grew up fast. I'm not a kid like the other students you know. I've seen a bit more of life. My mum's struggled to make ends meet. It hasn't been easy for us.'

'Yes, I understand Neel.' I softened when I heard how life had thrown him a few blows.

'Well, anyway, that's not why I came to see you. I've been having troubling sleeping at night for a few months now. Even if I have my regular drink, I still don't fall asleep. By the time I do, it's almost dawn.'

Sleep disturbances are the first sign that something may be wrong. I assumed that something could have happened just prior to him being unable to sleep.

'Was there something serious that happened in your life, say within the last six months?'

'Errr … yes actually there was. My childhood friend died four months ago.'

He looked at me directly as if he was astounded at my comment.

'It must've affected you a lot.'

'Yeah, it did. I was so sad that I couldn't eat or sleep but I found that I can fall asleep quicker if I drink enough alcohol to make me feel drowsy. I then drop off to sleep quite easily.'

'So it became a habit, right?'

'Yeah, kind of. It numbs the sadness, you know, lessens the grief.'

'So how did your friend die?'

'Well, it was a big incident and even got into the papers. I got involved in it and….'

'Wait, were you involved in his death?' I interjected.

'No, not directly in his death. I only became involved *after* he died. He fell into the river, so they say. No one really knows how exactly he died. Apparently he and his friends went to the riverbank for a picnic. And his friends say he fell into the water and got carried away by the current and drowned.'

'Oh my goodness!' My mouth fell open.

'But I know that he wouldn't have gone into the water on his own accord. He was petrified of water because he couldn't swim.'

He was in a daze. I saw his hand quivering ever so slightly as it rested on the table. It seemed that he was becoming overcome with emotion. He swallowed a few times, unable to continue.

'How long had you known him?'

'We grew up together and studied together till Class 10 but after that we went to different schools, so we lost touch. I sometimes used to meet him on the streets but he'd changed a lot. He fell into a bad crowd. He got involved in drugs and drink. Those friends of his were rough. They were *really* bad guys.'

'Do you think they caused his death?'

'Possibly, but all his friends are saying that he slipped into the water. And anyway, there are no other witnesses, so it was recorded as an "accidental death."'

Talking about his dead friend must have been very difficult for him, but he stoically continued. Outwardly, there were very few signs of the emotional playback of his memories but every now and again he stopped talking momentarily as his skin broke into hundreds of goosepimples.

'Did they find the body?'

'It's a bit of a long story.'

I kept quiet. I gathered that if he wanted to tell me he'd do it on his own accord and if he didn't there'd be a lull in our conversation. Thankfully he continued. 'At first, they couldn't find it. I had read about it in the newspaper and so I went to see his mum. I told her that I wanted to join the search to find his body. She was grateful and told the police. Since I'm an adult, they agreed and allowed me to accompany the River Police search party who were assigned the task. So for two days we searched along different parts of the Brahmaputra and even went to the picnic spot where he had last been seen.'

'Was there any evidence there?'

'There were some broken beer bottles on the ground. It's possible they'd been fighting. We took the boat down the entire two-kilometre stretch from that point but there was no sign of him. It got late and the sun was beginning to set so they stopped the search for that day. That was on the second day.' He paused for a few moments as the memories caught up with him. The heaviest silence came now. He tried to keep calm but the quiver of his lips and grimace of his mouth told me how he was reliving every moment of that ordeal again.

'On the third day, I joined them again. This time we went even further downstream. There was a stationary steamer on the water's edge and some dark tarpaulin material rumpled up underneath it. As we neared it, the detective started to prod it with a stick and we realised there was actually something solid within it.' He stopped talking and licked his parched lips. His eyes stared vacantly into nothing. 'Unbelievably we found him.' He caught a tear that had collected in the corner of his eye and flicked it away immediately. I remained transfixed to the story he was unfolding. It was quite extraordinary. 'He was so bloated that he was unidentifiable. The body had already started decomposing and smelled so bad. The police asked me if it was him and the only reason I could confirm it was him was because of the scar on his left leg which he had when he fell off his bicycle when he was a kid.'

His voice broke as he told me of how he immediately jumped into the waist-deep water. 'I got into the water and carried him to the riverbank. The police were talking to some forensic experts on the phone, who were asking if his fists were clenched or not. They said that if he had drowned, his fists would be clenched because when a body is drowning, it seeks to fight to stay alive and tries to grab at anything to help itself. But if the body was already unconscious or dead when it entered the water, the fists would not be clenched…'

It was an unbelievable story. It spoke of heroism and integrity. 'So, were his fists clenched?'

'No, they were open…'

'Which suggests that he had already died before he entered the water….'

'Yeah, right, but even so, my friend's family did not want to press any charges and turn it into a legal case and so the police dropped the case against the boys, who were all under eighteen anyway.'

'You acted with a lot of courage, Neel.'

'Who wouldn't? He was my friend. We grew up together, ate together, studied together, played together and even slept in the same bed. He was more than just a best friend. He was my soulmate.'

There was very little I could say. Here was a young teen, raw in his grief for his childhood friend. But the calming nature of the pauses between us told me that sometimes silence really is the better consoler, more than even the human voice. We had just emerged from an emotional journey. It was an incredible ordeal which would undoubtedly leave repercussions on his mind.

'After that, they conducted the post mortem and the body was taken home for the last rites. On the day of the cremation, I was overcome with so much grief that I couldn't even stand up. I was totally broken. Whenever I looked at his face it was as if he was saying "thank you" to me.

'So that's what brought me here. The thing is after all that was over, I thought everything would come back to normal but it hasn't. I began to see him in my dreams. Almost every night, I kept seeing him in different dreams. Sometimes they are like nightmares.'

'What do you see?'

'Sometimes I see his body as it came out from under the steamer, all fat and bloated. Other times I see that bloated body come alive – like the dead dancers in Michael Jackson's *Thriller* -- walking towards the river bank. Other times I see old memories of us as kids running along the grass dressed in our shorts and t-shirts. Sometimes I see him as he was when we were in Class 10, laughing and patting each other on the back as we share a joke. And you know, sometimes I even see him talking to me from the sky, dressed in a white kurta-pyjama....'

'What is he saying?'

'He's saying "thank you" over and over again. He keeps telling me that if it wasn't for me, they might never found his body.'

'Have the dreams subsided?'

'I dunno, I hardly sleep at night anymore. Nowadays I sleep in the afternoons. It's like I'm nocturnal now. I'm too scared to sleep when it is dark because, in spite of drinking enough, I still see him in some form as soon as I close my eyes.'

'How have you been able to come to school when you are having such difficulties?'

'I hardly come to school. I find all this a waste of time. I only come if I *have* to. I just want to appear for my twelfth boards and leave education altogether. I can't be bothered. School makes me angry. I am irritable when I come here and the teachers make me angry. Except you...'

I realised that he was aware that I might get upset and so he tailored what he was saying to exclude me. I was touched that he was able to reciprocate some warmth and he had an empathic heart under that hardened exterior.

'Do you think sleeping tablets would stop the nightmares?'

'No, I don't. I think the problem is much deeper than that and anyway you will become addicted to them, just as you are using alcohol to get you to sleep. We have to dig deeper than that. We have to find the cause of why you are unable to sleep normally. There's no point treating the symptoms without finding out the cause. Do you understand what I am saying?'

'Yeah, I guess that makes sense.'

'And you know, though I can help you through counselling, I am not qualified to prescribe you medication, which I think you will need…'

'So? Am I sick?'

'No, not sick, but you will need more help than just counselling on its own. A psychiatrist will be able to prescribe you the right medication to calm your nerves. Your problem is quite worrying and it's lucky that you were misbehaving that day in class otherwise I doubt you would ever be here in my room today!'

He smiled weakly but I could see that his mind was preoccupied. 'I don't want to go to a psychiatrist. What if I don't go?'

'There's nothing sinister about seeing a psychiatrist. They are competent mental health professionals and see patients who have a host of problems – not just the mad ones! The thing is that without medical intervention, the effects will continue to disturb you, eventually affecting your ability to function and the quality of your life. It's only natural to want to avoid painful memories and feelings but if you try to shut your memories away, it will only get worse. You can't escape your emotions completely -- they will emerge under stress, believe me. So you need a little more help, that's all.'

'Okay….'

'I'm just worried because usually, when someone experiences a traumatic incident as you have, the symptoms are short-lived and gradually lift. But you are still experiencing these scary dreams and hallucinations even after four months. That's why I think you need to see someone more experienced than me as well.'

'But I still want to talk to you.'

'Of course! You should come every week to see me and we can talk about how your symptoms are subsiding.'

'You think I'll get over this?'

'Of course I do. I don't think I've ever met an adolescent with as much courage as you. I am humbled by what you did for your friend.'

'Thanks but it was no big deal…'

He got up to leave.

'I'll be giving your mother a call tonight and I'll give her all the details. Trust me, you *will* get better and you'll get back to normal very soon. I will call the psychiatrist and make an appointment for you. I'll inform him of your case history too so he'll be aware. Please Neel, don't let me down. You must go and see the psychiatrist, okay?'

He turned to look at me just as he reached the door. 'Maybe…'

We laughed together, but I knew he would.

Neelkanth did go to the psychiatrist with his mother and began sessions with him. Along with medication to ease his symptoms, he continued to come to me once a week. It took many weeks for the frequency of the flashbacks to decrease but it took a good few months for his sleep cycle to return to normal.

In the meantime, whilst still under treatment and counselling, Neelkanth appeared for his boards though his mother wanted him take admission into Class 12 again and study for another year. Nevertheless, he secured a second division which was surprising considering he also was going through a process of mental recovery. He continued to live locally and joined a local college. We would have drifted apart totally had it not been for the Teacher's Day message he sent me once a year for the next few years.

However, one morning, I received a phone call from him unexpectedly.

'Hello ma'am? It's Neel.'

'Neelkanth?'

'Yup. You remember me?'

'Oh my goodness! Of course I do. Funny how you never called me ma'am at school and now you do!'

'Yeah, well I brushed up on my manners I guess.'

'What are you doing now?'

'I dropped out of college but did a distance learning course in business studies…'

'Wow!'

'And I passed….'

'Hey, that's just great news, Neel. Well done!'

'Yeah, just thought I'd tell you. Knew you'd be happy.'

'Well it's been so long. Everything well I hope?'

'Yup! No more bad dreams ever again. You changed my life ma'am.'

'Aw, c'mon Neel…'

'No, really ma'am. I owe you a lot.'

'No of course you don't. The fact that I could help you back to a normal life again is enough. I'm happy that you saw some hope in what I said.'

'Yeah well, whatever… it all turned out for the best.'

'Thank goodness for that. But I do ask one thing from you.'

'What's that?'

'That you keep in touch, okay?'

'Maybe….!'

The phone clicked. He continued to send me a Teacher's Day card every year but after a few years, I got an invitation to his wedding. He was about 26 years old now. Of course I could not miss his wedding. It meant so much to me, especially because I knew what he'd gone through in his life. When I walked into the marriage hall and saw him in the distance greeting the guests, his new bride standing by his side, I couldn't help a lump coming into my throat. The last time I had seen him was when he was still a school-boy, in his shabbily-worn school uniform. How he had grown. His face was angular now and he had slimmed down. He was dressed in a cream-coloured sherwani with his bride looking equally bedecked and resplendent next to him. I warmly greeted them both. He bent down to touch my feet.

'Oh, you don't need to do that, Neel!'

'I need your blessing, ma'am.'

'You'll always have my blessing, Neel – both of you!'

I turned around to walk away but a vision of him as that grief-stricken eighteen-year-old student suddenly came back to me. Unable to shake it off, I took a seat a little further away and watched him standing there on the raised platform with his bride. He looked so happy. It was radiating from within him. What a journey he had encountered. Today he was the victorious one, the one who had faced his fears head-on to emerge a winner. Now, as a newly-wed, he was about to enter a brand new stage of life along with his life partner. I knew he was equipped with all the emotional intelligence he would need to surpass any problems that lay ahead of him. What more could a school counsellor ask for than to see a student pass through emotional hurdles and ultimately be happy in life? As the hustle and bustle of the wedding guests swarmed around me, I suddenly felt the warm rush of tears come to my eyes as I recalled his words of needing my blessing. I shook my head silently at the irony of it. After all he had been through, he had shown me some important life's lessons about strength of mind and self-motivation, more than anyone else I knew. I dabbed my eyes with my handkerchief and smiled. Maybe, in my humble role as the counsellor, he felt he needed my blessing, but in all reality, it was *me* who was the truly blessed one.

Checklist

Grieving has no fixed symptoms or sequence. There are many manifestations and being aware about the spectrum of responses is probably the best way to be prepared. First of all, do away with assumptions! Some teens like to talk, some do not. Some engage in dangerous or self destructive activities to escape whilst some may be so shocked that they don't even acknowledge death and end up chatting and smiling at everyone. It is important for us to understand that just because someone doesn't conform to what we perceive to be 'normal', it doesn't make them 'abnormal'. On the contrary, it makes them true to themselves, because they are dealing with this complicated issue in the way *that feels right to them* and are not being obligated to follow expected behaviour. Whether or not it is good for them is where we, as their well-wishers, must guide them in the right direction if they need help. Also, we must be aware that even when a grieved teen goes back to school and resumes regular activities, the grieving process still continues, even though they may not talk about it.

Red Flags to watch out for

- Extreme pangs of anxiety, panic, sadness, and helplessness
- Being easily distracted, forgetful, moody, irritable or resentful
- Having difficulty concentrating at school
- Being unsettled in class, a change in class performance, not wanting to go to school
- Being overwhelmed by intense reactions, such as anger, guilt, fear
- Having difficulty expressing intensity of emotions, or conflict of emotions
- Blaming themselves for the death
- Anxiety such as increased fears about others' safety, and their own
- Having questions or concerns about death, dying, mortality
- Dreams about, or sensing the presence of, the person who has died
- Wanting to be near family or friends more
- Withdrawing to be alone
- Extreme anger towards the dead person, especially in the case of suicide
- Physical complaints, such as tummy aches, headaches,
- Being irritable, defiant, more antisocial or displaying aggressive behaviour
- Risk-taking behaviour to escape from and numb the emotional pain; for example, drinking, drugs, more sexual contact or reckless driving
- Changes in eating, sleeping habits
- 'Perfect' behaviour
- Bedwetting

- Cracking jokes or being humourous. This is because they are masking feelings
- Saying, or acting like, they don't care
- Wanting to take on more adult responsibilities
- Strained relationships with others – fear or awkwardness about being close to others
- Feeling embarrassment; feeling different from peers; may conceal their loss
- A sense of loneliness – isolation
- A change in self image, lower self esteem
- Possibly suicidal thoughts
- Possibly moving from sadness into depression

Get professional help when

- ✓ The grief is unrelenting, even after four months or more.
- ✓ Feeling totally depressed. In other words, the grief is so intense that they can't go on with their normal activities.
- ✓ The grief is affecting the ability to concentrate, sleep, eat, or socialise normally.
- ✓ They feel they can't go on living after the loss and contemplate suicide, or hurting themselves or have a death fixation.

What you can do

- ✓ Be honest and let them know what's happening. Talk to them about grief – what it is, that it's normal, that everyone's reactions are different.
- ✓ Be willing to listen and be available to talk about whatever they need to talk about.
- ✓ Acknowledge the emotions they may be feeling—fear, sadness, anger.
- ✓ It can be helpful for parents, or other adults, to share their own feelings regarding the loss.
- ✓ Frequently reassure them they are safe and which adults they can trust to ask for further support.
- ✓ Keep routines and normal activities going as much as possible.
- ✓ Inform the school principal of the teen's bereavement so that teachers are aware of the varied behaviour and don't get unduly angry.
- ✓ Ensure that they participate in normal activities without making them out to be a fragile ball of emotions.

✓ Class teachers can ensure that they can create an environment in which the bereaved teen can feel supported and listened to without anyone asking probing questions.

✓ Teenagers will often want to be more with friends than family so encourage your teen to spend time with friends of his or her own age.

✓ Avoid expectations of adult behaviour – allow them to be the age and stage they are.

✓ Encourage them to express their thoughts and feelings -- give them ideas of things they could try, such as doing physical activities, writing, singing, listening to music, talking with friends, reading etc.

✓ Allow questions and provide honest answers.

✓ Gauge their body language as an indicator of how they are, even if they say they're 'fine'.

✓ Many teens don't like to bother others, or be dependent on them with their problems, so you don't need to keep verbally expressing all that you are doing for them.

✓ Comfort them with hugs, cuddles, holding their hand, and by encouraging them. Do not, however, physically console them if they don't want it.

✓ Speak calmly and gently to them – and be calm around them.

✓ Validate how they feel.

✓ Talk about death together

✓ Let them help in planning the shraddha or something to remember the loss, for example, planting a tree, memorial tribute.

✓ Don't tell them 'to get over it'.

✓ Check that they are eating properly.

✓ Get them to engage in relaxation techniques such as taking slow, deep breaths from the diaphragm and visualizing a safe and calm place such as a sandy beach or pleasurable memory.

✓ Take a break from talking about the death all the time. Follow the teen's lead on when to talk about it and when to take a break. Allow time for mutual relaxation and engaging in ordinary tasks and activities.

✓ Don't treat a bereaved teen as incapable of making decisions that concern them. Allowing them to make decisions will help return control to them.

LIST OF USEFUL ORGANISATIONS

CHILD RIGHTS AND YOU

CRY works with marginalised children, their families and communities, and individuals who believe in the rights of children.

Mumbai/ Pune

189/A Anand Estate, Sane Guruji Marg,
Mumbai - 400 011
Tel - 91-22- 23063647 / 3651 / 1740
23098324 / 6472 / 6845
Fax - 91-22-2308 0726
e-mail : cryinfo.mum@crymail.org

New Delhi

632, 2nd floor, Lane No.3, Westend Marg
Saiyad-ul-Ajaib
New Delhi - 110 030
Tel - 91-11-30174700
Fax - 91-11-30174777
e-mail : cryinfo.del@crymail.org

Bengaluru

Madhavi Mansion, 12/3-1
Bachammal Road, Cox Town,
Bengaluru - 560 005
Tel - 91-80-2548 8574 / 4952 / 4065
Mobile : 0-99008 22828
Fax - 91-80-2548 7355
e-mail : cryinfo.blr@crymail.org

Kolkata

152, Kalikapur, Gitanjali Park
New No. 8, 2nd Street, Kolkata - 700 099
Tel - 91-033-2416 0007 / 8057 / 8069
Fax: 91-033- 2416 3322
e-mail : cryinfo.cal@crymail.org

Hyderabad

c/o Tata Business Support Services Ltd.
1st Floor, Gowra Trinity, Chiran Fort Lane
Begumpet, Hyderabad - 500 016
Mobile: 09948097127
e-mail : cryinfo.hyd@crymail.org

Chennai

No.11, 16th Avenue
Harrington Road, Chennai- 600 031
Tel - 91-44-2836 5545
Fax - 91-44-2836 5548
e-mail : cryinfo.mds@crymail.org

CHILDLINE India

*Foundation Childline1098 functions as a medium for children to connect to
the services and programmes offered by the state or society for their care and
protection. The Foundation plans to expand to over 597 districts.*

CHILDLINE India Foundation

Nana Chowk Muncipal School, 2nd Floor,
Frere Bridge - Low Level, Nana Chowk,
Near Grant Road Station,
Mumbai 400007
022 2388 1098/ 2384 1098

North Regional Resource Centre

F/F 252 K Sant Nagar
East of Kailash
New Delhi 110065
011-4608 8923

East Regional Resource Centre

AB 15, Sector - 1,
Salt Lake, Near PNB,
Kolkata 64, West Bengal
033-4065 6086

South Regional Resource Centre
Second Floor, No.2, Dr. Nair Road
T.Nagar,
Chennai- 600 017
044-2815 6098, 044-28158098

West Regional Resource Centre
Unit No. 204/A, Second Floor,
Parvati Industrial Estate Premises,
Senapati Bapat Marg
Lower Parel [W], Mumbai- 400013
022-2498 9630
dial1098@childlineindia.org.in

UNICEF India
UNICEF has been working in India since 1949 and is the largest UN organisation in the country.

India Country Office
73 Lodi Estate ,New Delhi 110 003, India
Tel: 91 11 2469-0401, 2469-1410
Fax: 011 2462-7521, 2469-1410
Email: newdelhi@unicef.org
UNICEF India Offices

Guwahati Field Office
UNICEF State Office for Assam, House no: 27, Basisthapur
Byelane No. 3, Adjacent to Regional Passport office , Beltola,
Guwahati – 781028
Tel: +91 11 0361 – 2235151/53
Fax: +91 11 0361 - 2235161
Email: guwahati@unicef.org

Raipur Field Office
UNICEF State Office for Chhattisgarh
503 Civil Lines, Raipur 492 001
Tel: +91 0771 424-5700, Fax: +91 0771 4245716

Ranchi Field Office
UNICEF State Office for Jharkhand
Vishwa Hostel Complex, Ground Floor, Near IIC Complex,
Jodapul, Kanke Road,
Ranchi 834 006,
Tel: +91 0651 3985100, Fax: +91 651 3985102

Bhopal Field Office
United Nations Children's Fund
UN House, Plot No:-41-42,
Polytechnic Colony,
Shyamla Hills, Bhopal 462013
Tel: +91 0755-2661555, 2661556, Fax: +91 0755-2661558
Email: bhopal@unicef.org

Bhubaneshwar Field Office
UNICEF State Office for Orissa
Plot No: 44, Surya Nagar
Bhubaneswar 751 003
Tel: +91 0674-2397977- 80, Fax: +91 0674-2397976
Email: bhubaneshwar@unicef.org

Chennai Field Office
United Nations Children's Fund
37/15, 2nd Main Road,
Kasturba Nagar Adiyar,
Chennai - 600020
Tel: +91 044 – 42891111 / 24410761 - 67
Fax: +91 044 – 24410760
Email: chennai@unicef.org

Gandhinagar Field Office
UNICEF State Office for Gujarat
Plot No. 70, Sector 19, Gandhi Nagar 382 019
Tel: +91 079 23230185/23230531/5366
Fax: +91 079 2322-5364
Email: gandhinagar@unicef.org

Hyderabad Field Office
UNICEF State Office for Andhra Pradesh & Karnataka
Plot No: 317 /A , Road No. 12, MLA Colony,
Banjara Hills, Hyderabad - 500034
Tel: +91 040 23540712 / 0722 / 0744 / 0239
Fax: +91 040 23555-156
Email: hyderabad@unicef.org

Jaipur Field Office
UNICEF State Office for Rajasthan
B-9 Bhawani Singh Lane, C-Scheme
Opp. Nehru Sahkar Bhawan, Jaipur 302 001
Tel: +91 0141 222-2694, 222-2636, 409-0500
Fax:+91 0141 222-1510
Email: jaipur@unicef.org

Kolkata Field Office
UNICEF Office for West Bengal
BIPL Building, Omega 18th Floor
Block EP & GP, Sector V,
Salt Lake, Kolkata 700091
Telephone: +91 033 40151600, Facsimile: +91 033 40151601
Email: kolkata@unicef.org

Lucknow Field Office
United Nations Children's Fund,
3/194 Vishal Khand, Gomti Nagar
Lucknow - 226 010
Tel: +91 0522 4093333, 4093151
Fax: +91 0522 4093322, 2304053
Email: lucknow@unicef.org

Mumbai Field Office
UNICEF State Office for Maharashtra
19 Parsi Panchayat Road, Andheri East,
Mumbai 400 069
Tel: +91 022 2826-9538, 2825-3663, 65740097
Fax: 022 2826-9539
Email: mumbai@unicef.org

Patna Field Office
UNICEF State Office for Bihar, No. 8,
Pataliputra Colony,
Patna 800 013
Tel: +91 0612 3984600
Fax:+91 0612 3984636
Email: patna@unicef.org

National Commission for Women
*The apex national level organization of India with the mandate of protecting
and promoting the interests of women*
4, Deen Dayal Upadhayaya Marg,
New Delhi-110 002.
91-11-23237166
91-11-23236988

Websites with more resource lists
http://india.gov.in/services/get-help-helpline
http://www.justdial.com/Mumbai/Women-Helpline/ct-297675
http://www.delhipolice.nic.in/parivartan/pcr.htm
http://www.tarshi.net/resources/other_helplines_list.
asp?cat=Emotional%20/%20Relationships%20Problems

ACKNOWLEDGEMENTS

There are a number of people who I would like to thank:

Banti Bhuyan, who believed in me enough to suggest I write this book.

Pradip Kumar Bhuyan, for his constant inspiration and positivity.

Amit, for being an unstinting, unconditional rock of support all the way.

Arnav and Akriti, for their endless supply of love which fuelled my vision every single day.

Loona, for a lifetime of love and encouragement.

Sarah, for her ever-present good wishes.

Junu Ma, for her prayers.

Achala, for the quiet confidence she has in me.

Nazneen, for being a good friend and well wisher.

Shalini Krishan, for being a sensitive and thoughtful editor.

Renuka Chatterjee, for her belief in this book.

And finally, to every student whose story I have reproduced.

A School Counsellor's Diary aims to bridge the gap in the modern Indian parent-adolescent relationship. Aimed at parents, and written in an easy-to-understand style, with numerous real-life examples, this book illustrates the genuine problems faced by modern adolescents in the classroom, family sphere, and wider world. Presented through thirty-four case studies spanning a wide range of problems faced by the new generation, the book includes seldom-spoken-about issues such as masturbation, homosexuality, sexual abuse, self-cutting and even attempted suicide.

A School Counsellor's Diary guides parents towards imparting the skills and confidence that adolescents need to protect themselves in the new world. Each chapter gently eases the reader into a new issue through anecdotes, stories, and even technical knowledge presented in an easy-to-understand way. Once the reader is familiar with the topic, several case studies are reproduced as if the author and the reader are sharing a chat over coffee. Written in the first person, the accounts are refreshingly compelling because they are presented as honest, easy-to-read conversational transcripts as they happened without the frills of text-bookish or technical language. They show the pain behind various problems, their manifestation, and ultimately, how the problem was solved/handled through weeks or months of counselling. Each chapter ends with a list of red flags to watch out for, and possible courses of action to follow in case of problems. Since there is no 'preaching' narrative or 'one-size-fits-all' recommendations, it is hoped that discerning parents will use the book to understand the pitfalls facing their adolescents and initiate a better connection.

www.ingramcontent.com/pod-product-compliance
Lightning Source LLC
Chambersburg PA
CBHW050504160726
48003CB00001B/163